1000
BABY ANIMALS

1000 BABY ANIMALS

NAUMANN & GÖBEL

© Naumann & Göbel Verlagsgesellschaft mbH, a subsidiary of
VEMAG Verlags- und Medien Aktiengesellschaft, Cologne
www.vemag-medien.de
Author: Ulrike Schöber, Dortmund, together with Simone Harland
Photographs: Okapia KG, Frankfurt/Main
English Translation: Michael Loughridge
Complete production: Naumann & Göbel Verlagsgesellschaft mbH, Cologne
Printed in China
All rights reserved
ISBN 10: 3-625-10775-9
ISBN 13: 978-3-625-10775-0

Foreword

The animal kingdom has an estimated 1,400,000 different species representing an amazing variety with huge differences in shape and size and behaviour. Some of the most fascinating things of all are to do with reproduction and the rearing of young – and here too there are enormous differences between different types of animal.

Take mammals, for example. Apart from a few special cases, their young are born as live baby animals and are suckled for a certain length of time with their mother's milk. In fact, that's what 'mammal' means – an animal that suckles. Birds produce young quite differently: they lay eggs and keep them warm ('incubate' them) until they hatch. Mammals and birds alike are divided into categories called precocial ('early leaver') and altricial ('stay-at-home'). The precocial 'early leavers' develop in the mother's womb, or inside the egg, fully enough to be ready very soon after birth to run with their mother – but the altricial 'stay-at-homes' need quite a long spell of being cared for and fed in the nest before they are ready to leave.

Tortoises and crocodiles lay eggs, but do not stay to incubate them – though crocodiles do look after their unhatched eggs. Amphibians such as frogs or salamanders, on the other hand, hatch from eggs in the same way but then undergo a complicated development process called 'metamorphosis'. These baby animals, known as tadpoles, look entirely different from the adults.

It is much the same with some insects, such as butterflies and moths. Who could imagine that a caterpillar is actually a baby butterfly or moth? At this stage it is called a 'larva', and it has to go through a process of 'pupating' before the adult butterfly or moth can emerge. But not all arthropods metamorphose completely. Many wingless species, such as spiders, hatch out out as so-called 'nymphs', looking very like the adults of their species except that they are smaller. Others again, locusts for example, look like adults from the start, but important parts of their body such as the wings have not yet developed.

These photos of a thousand baby animals show animal young at all ages and in all stages of development, from a just-hatched chick to a fully fledged young bird, from a newborn baby giraffe to a Common Wombat already several months old. There are baby animals familiar to everyone, like kittens and foals, and there are the babies of very rare species like the Southern Right Whale, a species that may soon become extinct. The photo collection is divided up according to the animals' principal habitats.

The accompanying text provides information about the various species of animal, explains their habits and describes how they rear their young. And it does not hesitate to speak out about the role human beings have played in their life – which in most cases has been a harmful one. It is true that species have always been dying out, for thousands of years past. All the same, for many of them it was Man that brought them to the brink of extinction, either through hunting or sometimes just through sheer thoughtlessness. Even today there are lots of animals being kept as pets, yet not having their real needs met. Animals are even being abandoned. It happens to young dogs most of all – just because their owners have not stopped to think before buying them. They have not realised pets may be sweet but are also quite a lot of work. A thousand baby animals are a thousand appeals to us humans to step in and do something for the world of animals, and help conserve it for the future.

The Publisher and the Editor.

Contents

Europe

In Field and Meadow

For a young animal, grass and earth offer very little cover, so in this habitat many leave the nest very early. The 'altricial' or nest-based animals are often born in burrows or in trees and bushes along field edges.

Skylark *(below)*

The skylark *(Alauda arvensis)* and its hungrily cheeping chicks in the nest are becoming a rarer and rarer sight, because intensive farming and urban development have drastically reduced its habitat. The skylark needs quiet grassland or meadows for its nest, which it builds at ground level. The eggs have dark flecks which camouflage them well on the ground.

Knot Grass *(right)*

This handsome moth develops into the inconspicuous knot grass moth *(Acronicta rumicis)*. The caterpillar is not picky about what plants it feeds on, so it can occur in large numbers, in late summer and autumn particularly. It over-winters as a pupa, from which the moth emerges in spring.

Cretan Spiny Mouse (above)

The Cretan spiny mouse *(Acomys minous)* inhabits barren, rocky areas on the Greek island of Crete. It gets its name from the long bristly hairs on its back. Unlike the young of many other mouse species, baby Cretan spiny mice can do things for themselves very soon after birth — they can see, they can run about and they even have incisor teeth.

(centre right)

It is at night that the Cretan spiny mouse is active, because many of their natural enemies are asleep. Spiny mice live in large colonies, very often foraging together for food. In fact they are so communal-minded that the females will suckle each others' young. A female will give birth to between one and five babies in each litter.

Summer Chafer (bottom right)

The larvae of the summer chafer *(Amphimallon solstitialis)* are also known as white grubs. They hatch from eggs laid in the soil by the female chafer, and they take two years to develop into adult beetles. Over that whole period, if there are a lot of them, they can do great harm to crops, because they gnaw plant roots.

Long-eared Owl (top left)

The Long-eared Owl (*Asia otus*) is not usually found in woodland, except sometimes at the forest edge, but more often in open country or in small copses. At three weeks old, the chicks are not yet ready to fly, but they leave the nest and clamber around on nearby branches.

(centre left)

As well as in Europe, the Long-eared Owl is found in America, Asia and North Africa. They prefer to breed in abandoned pigeon and crow nests or squirrel dreys, laying about five eggs. The female sits on them for four weeks, with the mate bringing her food, until the chicks hatch. The father brings food for them too, but gives it to the mother to distribute.

(below)

These Long-eared Owl chicks are just two weeks old. So it will be some weeks yet before they reach their full size of 35 cm long, with a wing-span of about 90 cm. Then they will be ready to go out hunting at night like their parents, for prey such as mice, other rodents — and sleeping birds.

Garden Tiger (top)

It's because of this extremely hairy brown caterpillar stage that the *Arctia caja* moth is known as the garden tiger. The caterpillar emerges from eggs laid by the moth on the underside of a suitable food plant such as thistle, nettle or willow. The caterpillar sheds its skin several times in the course of growing to about 6 cm in length. It overwinters in a cocoon near ground level, emerging in the spring.

Adalbert's Eagle (above left)

The three chicks in the photograph belong to an endangered subspecies of the imperial eagle — Adalbert's eagle (*Aquila heliaca adalberti*). A bird of the Iberian peninsula, Adalbert's eagle is associated especially with Extremadura in Spain, and so is often referred to as the Spanish imperial eagle. Fully grown, it can be up to 85 cm in body length, with a 2 m wing-span.

Green Toad (above right)

The female Green Toad (*Bufo viridis*), seen here sitting in the water with two tadpoles swimming by, produces spawn containing up to 12,000 eggs. The larval forms that emerge from the eggs need just under three months to complete their metamorphosis. They are unusual tadpoles in not being vegetarian like most other species but having a partly animal diet.

Spurge Hawkmoth *(left-hand page)*

The eye-catchingly garish caterpillar of the spurge hawk-moth *(Celerio euphorbiae* or *Hyles euphorbiae)* is probably much better known than the insect that emerges from the metamorphosis, because the moth form is active in twilight and in the dark. Also, it is obviously harder to observe, as it flies much faster than the caterpillar can crawl. The caterpillar's main food is cypress spurge.

Two-tailed Pasha *(top right)*

The photo shows a two-tailed pasha *(Charaxes jasius)* just emerging from its chrysalis. Once out, it will need time to unfold completely and to dry off. But then this decidedly large moth, with its distinctive glider-like flight style, will be ready to take off to the nearest arbutus fruit and start to feed. The two-tailed pasha moth is only found in association with this particular food plant.

Goldfinch *(centre right)*

The goldfinch *(Carduelis carduelis)* builds a neat bowl-like nest in bushes or isolated trees in open country and lays on average five light-coloured eggs. The female does all the incubating herself until the eggs hatch just under two weeks later, and then continues to sit over the chicks so that they have warmth and protection for a while longer. Meanwhile the cock bird feeds her.

Hen Harrier *(bottom left)*

The hen harrier *(Circus cyaneus)* is a raptor or bird of prey, fairly widely distributed in the British Isles, but the subject of some controversy. Its moorland breeding grounds unfortunately overlap with those of red grouse, which are seen by many humans as an important game bird, but by hen harriers as suitable prey.

(bottom right)

After hatching, usually around mid-June, young hen harriers stay in the nest for a further seven weeks or so. During all this time they have to be fed by their parents. The menu for the hen harrier chicks consists mostly of mice and smaller birds, but if the parents are bigger than average they may also prey on rabbits.

Corn Bunting (left)

The female corn bunting *(Emberiza calandra, Miliaria calandra)* makes its nest in a depression on the ground, lining the hollow with grass and small roots. She lays about four eggs in her nest and sits on them till they hatch, which happens within two weeks.

Yellowhammer (below)

Here five yellowhammer chicks *(Emberiza citrinella)* are impatiently awaiting the arrival of their parents bearing a beakful of food — which at this stage will consist mainly of protein-giving insects. Once the young birds have matured, they will also eat a variety of plant seeds. The nest is built from grass stalks and leaves, usually just above ground-level in a bush or actually on the ground at the field edge.

Common Tree Frog (top left)

The common tree frog (Hyla arborea) is well known for its emerald colouring and its loud croak. However, this young specimen has not yet reached that stage, though it will soon have completed its metamorphosis. It does already have the pale belly of the adult common tree frog, and the adhesive pads on its feet are clearly visible in the photograph. It is these pads that enable it to climb up branches.

Ocellated Lizard (top right)

The picture shows a young ocellated lizard (Lacerta lepida) in the moment of hatching. Fully grown, it will have a body length of 20 cm, but when measured full length including tail it will reach 90 cm. That makes it the largest European lizard. It feeds on insects and worms, but by no means exclusively, as it also takes birds' eggs, nestlings and mice.

Sand Lizard (centre right)

Sand lizards (Lacerta agilis) mate in late spring. After mating, the female digs a hole in moist earth with her hind legs and deposits from 4 to 15 eggs in it. Depending what the weather does, the young emerge about one month to two months later. On hatching, they are about 4–5 cm long, so they will need to eat a lot of insects to grow to the adult lizard's full length of 25 cm.

Colorado Beetle (bottom right)

Here we see the bane of every farmer and vegetable grower engaged in its favourite activity: this is the larva of the Colorado beetle (Leptinotorsa decemlineata) munching a potato leaf. Both the larvae and the adult beetles can wreak terrible havoc on potato crops, because they feed on the foliage. The Colorado beetle is so named because of its American origins.

Harvest Mouse (left)

The harvest mouse (Micromys minutus) is the only European rodent to have a prehensile (grasping) tail. It is also very much a miniature among rodents, weighing only about 7 grams. It conceals its nest as cunningly as it can in long grass or a hedge so that possible enemies will not see it. Inside the nest, the female will rear as many as twelve babies in each litter.

Swallowtail (centre left)

The swallowtail (Papilio machaon) is found not only on Europe's grasslands but in North Africa, Asia and North America as well. Once the female has laid her eggs in spring, the tiny butterfly caterpillars need only a week to hatch. From any distance they look like bird droppings, and this protects them from being eaten by birds. They don't get their black-and-green stripes until after they have cast their skin twice

Praying Mantis (bottom left)

Few insects make quite such an impression as a praying mantis, whose empty chrysalis can be seen in this picture, attached to a branch. They are green or brown in colour, well camouflaged against a background of leaf or branch, and looking for all the world as if they are praying, because of their angled raptorial legs. What they are really doing is lurking in wait for their next meal to arrive, when they will pounce like lightning. Mantises are found all over the world in the hotter climates. There are 1400 species.

Nightingale (bottom right)

The nightingale (Luscinia megarhynchos) is found in Asia and North Africa as well as Europe. The habitats it favours are copses, parkland and gardens. For its nest it uses leaves and grass, and it builds a little above ground level, mostly in bushes. There are usually about four eggs. It is from their father that the young nightingales learn to sing, and whether they will sing as beautifully as legend has always claimed will in fact depend on whether he does.

Great Bustard (above)

In a few months' time, this little chick of the great bustard (Otis tarda) will have grown into one of the world's largest flighted birds. Fully grown, the great bustard has a body length of 1 m and a wing-span of 2.1 to 2.4 m, and weighs 15 kg. Besides feeding on foliage, seed and buds, great bustards also help themselves to insects, mice and amphibians.

(left)

After reaching adulthood, this young great bustard will spend most of its time as a member of a group of the same sex as itself. These groups only split up during the mating season, when the males set about courting the hen bustards with a display that is like no other. They puff out their throat pouch, spread their long white 'moustache' bristles, and fold their wings back in a special way that makes the whole bird look like a big white fluffy ball.

Tree Sparrow (above)

While tree sparrows (Passer montanus) love open spaces, they also feel quite happy with humans around. But they are not at home in city centres in the way the house sparrow is. They nest three times a year, choosing cavities or nest boxes, and laying about five eggs each time. Two weeks incubation, and the chicks hatch — after which they remain in the nest for another two weeks. For a further ten days after that, their parents continue to feed them.

Large White butterfly (left)

The Large White butterfly (Pieris brassicae) is, just out of its chrysalis. It is one of the creatures that follows Man's cultivation, because cabbage crops help it to multiply. The black and gold caterpillars now feed mainly on cabbage leaves, whereas once upon a time their diet was limited to wild cruciferous plants.

Pheasant *(top right)*

The young of the pheasant *(Phasianus colchicus)* are 'early leavers', and soon after hatching they are following their mother around and beginning to peck at leaves, seeds and small insects of their own accord. After two weeks they begin to take to the air, and from then on mother and chicks will roost overnight on tree branches, where they are of course much safer.

(centre right)

The hen pheasant has to do all the work of incubating eggs and rearing young herself, as the cock will mate with several hens. She will lay ten or more dun-coloured eggs under a bush or in a thicket at the forest margin, in a little hollow in the ground. It will be about 25 days before the chicks hatch, using their so-called egg-tooth to break out of the eggshell.

(bottom left)

Pheasant chicks are covered in a brownish down all over which camouflages them well on the ground and in bushes. Females remain an inconspicuous dun colour even when adult, and are thus still well camouflaged. The cocks acquire a rich dark green sheen round their head, with red skin flaps, and grow long tail feathers.

(bottom right)

This pheasant chick is only a few hours old. As a precocial ('early leaver') bird, it already has a downy coat; it can also see from the moment of birth and so feed on small insects without need of help. These are rich in proteins and provide almost all the chick's nourishment in its first few weeks of life, but after that it switches to such things as seeds, berries, roots, earthworms and slugs.

Magpie (left-hand page, top)

With its black and white plumage, often showing off a metallic gloss, an adult magpie *(Pica pica)* is a handsome sight, but the juvenile bird in the photograph still has a scruffy look. As a chick it was naked, and was fed by both parent birds. After three weeks or a little more, it is big enough and feathery enough to attempt its first flight. But even then it will not be really independent for a further six weeks.

Brown Rat (left-hand page, centre)

The brown rat *(Rattus norvegicus)* lives close to humans, even though they do their best to eliminate it. That is because it can spread dangerous diseases. Given good conditions, the brown rat will multiply rapidly. Reproductive activity is the same at all times of year, and the gestation period between conception and birth is only 21 days.

Meadow Spittlebug (left-hand page, bottom)

The Meadow Spittlebug itself *(Philaenus spumarius)* is not so well known a sight as its emerald-green larvae or their surrounding foamy blob, the cuckoo-spit. Cuckoo-spit, seen on grass and twigs in springtime, is there to protect the larva both against drying out and against predators. It is a secretion produced from the abdomen of the larva, blown up into foam by the process of breathing.

Emperor Moth (right-hand page, top)

When this caterpillar turns into an emperor moth *(Saturnia pavonia emperor)*, the first thing to strike the observer about it will be the bold eye-shaped outlines on the wings. Their function is to frighten off enemies. The emperor moth is nocturnal. It can be encountered in the wild from May to the end of July.

(right-hand page, bottom)

One of Europe's largest moths, with a wing-span of up to eight centimetres, the emperor moth is most at home in heathlands or sometimes near the forest edge. So it is hardly surprising that the caterpillars like to eat heather — but blackberries and sloes are on the menu too.

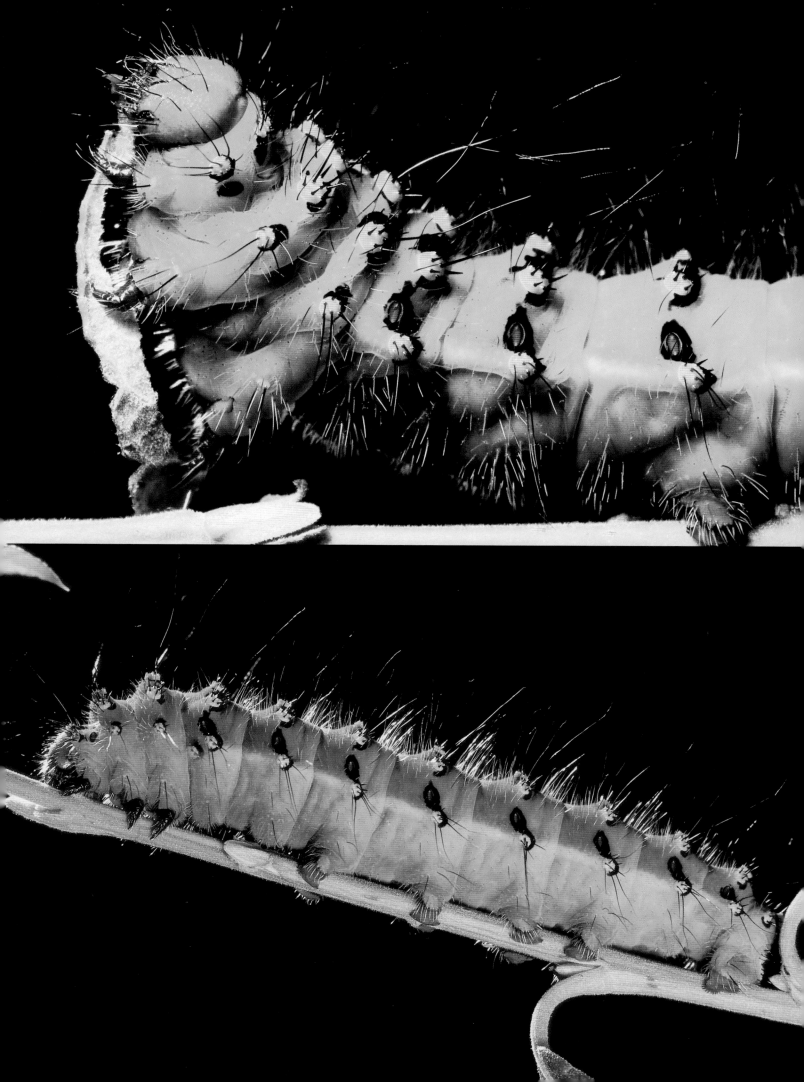

Common Starling *(above left)*

The Common Starling *(Sturnus vulgaris)* is widespread, in Asia and Africa as well as Europe. It is likely that bird conservationists have contributed to its abundance, as starlings find their nest boxes just right for breeding in. In the natural state they would nest in hollow trees. During the breeding season, starlings feed mainly on insects, and this is what they give their young as well.

(above right)

After a pair of starlings has mated, the female lays about six bluish eggs, from which the hatchlings emerge about two weeks later. Initially the mother enfolds the tiny creatures in her greyish-white underwing down to protect them from cold. The male starling helps with the feeding. After three weeks of their parents' care, the young are fledged and leave the nest.

Hermann's Tortoise *(right-hand page, top)*

Hermann's tortoise *(Testudo hermanni)* has a shell whose colours range from olive-green to a golden brown. Sometimes the shell may feature a darker patterning as well. Even a freshly hatched tortoise's shell is already like that of an adult. However, many of these tortoises do not even make it as far as hatching, as the nests are often raided by predators (martens, for instance).

Terrestrial Snail *(left-hand page, bottom left)*

Most terrestrial snails and slugs *(Stylommatophora)* are hermaphrodites and thus can mate without restriction according to the sex of individuals. Fertilisation is followed later by egg-laying, and later still by the hatching of baby snails from the eggs — as in this photo. The world total of land snails and slugs species is about 32,000, frequenting a wide range of habitats.

Mole *(left-hand page, bottom right)*

These baby moles *(Talpa europaea)* are still relatively safe in their nest. But once a young mole ventures into the outside world, it is exposed to a hast of dangers. It is a popular prey for hawks and other raptors and for cats, or it may even starve to death after straying on to a street and finding itself unable to climb the kerb. But if it survives all these hazards, it can then find a territory of its own.

Hermann's Tortoise *(bottom right)*

Traditionally associated with Greece, the Hermann's tortoise is in fact also at home in France, the Balkans, Italy and Spain, usually near the coasts. The female buries her three to five eggs in the soil in early summer. After hatching, the baby tortoises have to fend for themselves.

Pale Eggar (right)

This Pale Eggar caterpillar (Trichiura crataegi) eats the leaves of hawthorn (Crataegus), and of sloe, birch, poplar, hazel and alder. It pupates in summer in a hard bluish-green cocoon rather like a miniature egg, and metamorphoses into its moth form during August, and as it is attracted by light, it is sometimes an uninvited guest inside people's houses.

Death's Head Hawkmoth (below)

Caterpillars of the death's head hawkmoth (Acherontia atropos) are found on nightshade and hemp plants in high summer. They have hatched from eggs attached by the female moth to the underside of the food plants' leaves. The caterpillars pupate in the soil, and in autumn the moths emerge.

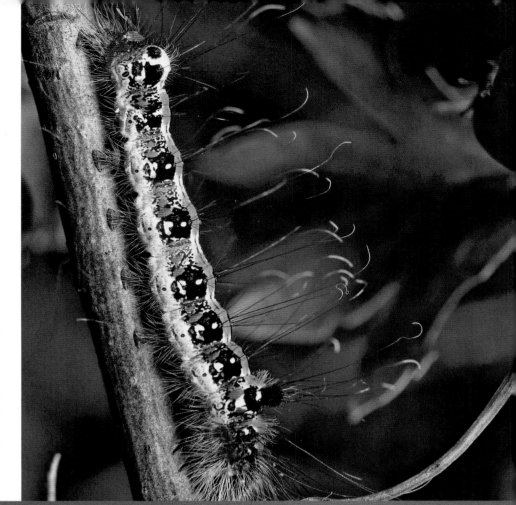

Lapwing, Peewit or Green Plover
(above)

This tiny lapwing chick *(Vanellus vanellus)* will one day be a 30 cm long bird with a wing-span easily reaching 70 cm. The relatively drab colouring of the chick's down coat serves as camouflage when the chicks cower to the ground in moments of danger. Later it will be replaced by the adult plumage with its striking contrast of black and white, and the cock birds will also have a dark, pointed feathery quiff on their head.

(centre left)

In spite of their down coats, lapwing chicks are very vulnerable to cold during the first two weeks of their life, so their mother keeps them warm at night under her wings. By day, if some danger threatens, the adult birds call to the young to warn them to take cover. It is a good five weeks before they are fully fledged.

(bottom left)

The lapwing (also sometimes called the peewit or green plover) often nests in shallow depressions in the soil of a field. The cock bird will scratch out a number of such little hollows, and the female chooses one, laying in most cases four eggs in it. After four weeks the lapwing babies, who are precocial or 'early leavers', will hatch. As protection against falling victim immediately to predators, the chicks have inconspicuous brown-coloured down, quite unlike the handsome plumage of the adults.

Little Owl (left-hand page, top)

It is getting increasingly rare to spot three young Little Owls *(Athene noctua)* like these at a time, as the species is now seriously endangered. Once the young birds have fully matured, it becomes easy to distinguish them from other owl species. They are no bigger than pigeons, and they lack the characteristic tufted ears of most other owls. Little Owls also have a particularly low forehead.

(left-hand page, bottom)

Little Owls nest for preference in hollow trees, masonry crevices or nest boxes. In April/May they lay three to five white eggs, which hatch after about a month. The young are altricial ('stay-at-homes'), remaining in the nest for five weeks after hatching, and requiring a further ten days to fledge. From then on, these now rare owls hunt mice, reptiles and insects.

European Hedgehog (top right)

The young of the European hedgehog *(Erinaceus europaeus)* are born with their bristles formed, but not yet protruding, so as not to injure their mother while she gives birth. But then only a few hours later the bristles emerge. Mating is another situation where the bristles get in the way, so the sow lays her spines flat, enabling the boar to copulate without risk of injury.

(centre right)

Hedgehogs almost always mate twice a year, the first time being in April. Litter size varies widely, and there can be anything from three to ten young at a time, born blind and pink-skinned with soft hair after a gestation of about five weeks. The mother rears them entirely by herself, suckling them for a period of six to eight weeks.

(bottom right)

This young hedgehog is now big enough to leave the nest — which will be hidden under stones or vegetation — and forage with its mother. Hedgehogs eat earthworms, insects, slugs and even young mice and carrion — augmenting this, as autumn approaches, with berries and windfall fruit. In winter they hibernate, which they do more successfully in the wild than in the keeping of humans.

Brown Hare *(top left)*

The brown hare doe *(Lepus europaeus)* suckles her babies just once a day. Newborn leverets are generally left alone for the rest of the day in their small hollow in the ground, their 'form'. They are not totally helpless, though. As typical precocial animals, they have their eyes open right after they are born, and can run for it if there is danger.

(left-hand page, centre left)
The hare's preferred habitat is open country, and it is hunted by many other animals (e.g birds of prey and foxes). So it is active mainly at night, when most of its predators are asleep. It goes out then to get food, preferably grass and other greenstuffs. The leverets get their first solid food when only ten days old.

(left-hand page, bottom left)
For hares, winter is a very lean season. There are hardly any fresh greens to be had, and seed too is scarce. So in winter the hare is often forced to keep itself alive by feeding on wood and bark. By now, the leverets are long since weaned, and they too have to forage for hard-to-find food.

Beech Marten (above)

The beech marten (Martes foina) is one of the animals that follow in the wake of human civilisation, and it likes living close to humans — but it will also be found in forests. Favourite places for the beech marten to make its den are lofts and barns. Often the human residents notice nothing at all until after young martens are born. As the cubs grow up, their wild mock fights make their presence well and truly heard.

Stoat *(top)*

The stoat *(Mustela erminea)* occurs over a huge area of the world stretching across Europe to North America, Asia and Australia. Depending on the time of year when a pair mate, gestation may last up to nine months (though in such cases the fertilised egg is dormant for most of the time), or may be as little as eight or nine weeks. When the time comes, the mother will produce four or five young.

(centre left)

Stoats are brilliant hunters. They can even prey successfully on animals bigger than themselves. Usually they kill their prey by a well-aimed bite to the back of the neck. But to be able to do this, they first have to gain some experience. The mother shows the young stoats how to hunt and kill.

Western Polecat *(bottom left)*

The Western polecat *(Mustela putorius)* has its summer habitat deep in the forests of Europe, but in winter the prospect of more plentiful food draws it nearer to villages and even towns. A predatory animal, up to 60 cm in length and classed as one of the martens, the Western polecat lives either in a burrow or in a barn or loft. As a rule it is in one of these hideaways that the young are born.

Aphid (left)

Aphids *(Aphidina aphid)* have unusual reproductive arrangements. In the course of a year, new generations will be brought forth by both sexual and asexual reproduction. In the latter, the females bear live young without any prior copulation having taken place. In the sexual mode, the male fertilises eggs.

Twentytwo-spot-Ladybird (below)

Like almost all ladybirds, the 22-spot variety *(Thea vigintid-uopunctata)* is extremely helpful as a biological means of pest control. This particular variety — not only the beetle, but the larva too — has become specialised in dealing with mildews, especially those affecting oak-trees. The larvae have to slough off their skin three times and pupate once before the beetle emerges.

Seven-spot Ladybird *(right)*

It is widely believed that the spots on the back of a lady-bird *(Coccinella septempunctata)* represent the number of years of its age. But this is not true. In fact the spots show what species of ladybird it is. The seven-spot ladybird selects aphid-affected plants to lay its eggs on, ensuring that its larvae will have enough to eat.

(below)

The red seven-spot ladybird is probably our commonest lady-bird species. But the future red beetle is not easily recognised at the larval stage, as the larvae are bluish-grey in colour, with yellow spots, and could be mistaken for Colorado beetle larvae.

Common Wasp (above left)

Although the common wasp (Paravespula vulgaris) and the German yellowjacket wasp can be a real nuisance at picnics or in pub gardens, both are in fact very useful — like all wasps. Their larvae need plenty of protein if they are to develop to their full potential. To supply this need — as shown in the photo — the worker wasps catch lots of insects to feed to them.

German Yellowjacket Wasp (above right)

The German yellowjacket wasp (Paravespula germanica) makes its nest out of chewed wood (paper), in a honeycomb of vertical cells which are open at the bottom. Inside the cells, the larvae are reared by the worker wasps. In Central Europe, the entire wasp colony dies in autumn. Only the fertilised queens, in well protected places, live through the winter and are there to start a new colony in the spring.

Sawfly (below)

In the world as a whole, there are more than 800 species of sawfly (Argidae), though only a small minority of them are found in Europe. Reproduction is on the same basis in all species: the females lay their eggs in the stems or leaf-ribs of the food plant. From this stage the caterpillars or larvae develop. The larvae live in social groups, feeding on foliage. They react to danger by adopting an S-shaped threat posture.

By River, Lake and Marsh

Many animals, including such different ones as dragonflies and frogs, spend their whole life there. Inland waters and their richly vegetated banks also provide the nutritional basis for a whole host of other animal species to be reared.

Southern Hawker Dragonfly *(top left)*

Over a period of less than two years, this southern hawker nymph *(Aeshna cyanea)* has developed in a small pond from one of the eggs that a female dragonfly laid there on plants below the surface. For the new dragonfly to emerge, the nymph or larva crawls up a reed stem or the like into the air above. Then the nymph's skin cracks open, and the dragonfly extricates itself, head down, and turns round.

(above left)

This southern hawker has just emerged from its larval casing. Its wings and body are still tightly folded. In order to fill out to its proper shape, the insect has to pump blood through its body and its wings. After that has been done, it has to spend about three hours drying off and hardening before it can fly. At 7 cm long, and with a wing-span of 11 cm, the southern hawker is one of the larger dragonflies.

Emperor Dragonfly *(above)*

The photo has caught the moment at which an emperor dragonfly *(Anax imperator)* breaks out of its larval casing. This is the final great effort the insect has to make over the course of its development from egg to nymph to adult dragonfly. While the nymph was only about 5.5 cm long, the dragonfly reaches a length of 7–8 cm and a wing-span of 10 cm.

Greylag Goose (below)

Most likely this little greylag gosling (Anser anser) will have hatched out in a clutch of ten or so eggs in a reedbed. It now needs to eat lots of grain, grasses and also 'meat' foods like worms so that it will be strong enough by autumn to tackle the migration to the Mediterranean area, along with all the other geese. Greylags are the wild original form from which modern domestic geese are descended.

Midwife Toad (bottom left)

The midwife toad (Alytes obstetricans) takes its name from a special 'service' rendered by the male. After the female has spawned, and working not in the water but on land, he winds the long strings of big fertilised eggs round his legs and takes them off to a hiding-place. Two to three months later, he looks for a suitable piece of water, and releases the eggs into it. Only a few minutes later, the tadpoles hatch.

Kingfisher (bottom right)

The kingfisher (Alcedo atthis) excavates a tunnel nest for its young in the steep banks of rivers and lakes. It burrows in for 0.5 to 1 metre, then scoops out a wider cavity and lines it with fishbones and its own down. When the kingfisher's white eggs — there can be as many as seven — hatch, the chicks will be born pink and naked. Yet they will develop into Europe's most richly coloured birds.

Grey Heron *(left-hand page, top left)*

Young common herons *(Ardea cinerea)* like this one suit their Latin name of 'ash-grey', as they have not yet acquired their plume or the characteristic black-and-white neck patterning. The young bird's plumage is plain grey. Herons grow as big as storks, and breed in colonies. They build large nests from twigs and line them with softer material.

Bittern *(left-hand page, top right)*

By the time the bittern chicks *(Botaurus stellaris)* hatch, the female will have been incubating them for nearly four weeks, well hidden among the reeds. Next she will spend a further two months rearing the young — without any help at all from the male bird. At two weeks old the chicks are capable of crawling away from the nest if there is danger.

(left-hand page, bottom)

Bitterns live among the reeds in marshland and at lake edges, and have a special way of camouflaging themselves. If it senses danger, a bittern will stretch body, head and beak upwards in a straight line. While it is holding this elongated 'alert' pose, its lengthwise striped plumage makes it almost invisible among the reed-stems. With the chicks' juvenile downy coat, this effect does not happen.

Great White Egret *(top right)*

The great white egret *(Casmerodius albus* or *Egretta alba)* was almost wiped out at the end of the 19th century, because the males have wonderful long ornamental plumes for courtship, which were much sought after in women's fashions. But now these elegant birds can be found all over the world again. They produce a clutch of three to four pale blue eggs each year.

(centre right)

It is rare for great egrets to nest in bushes or trees. Much more often, they will build their nest among reeds — generally as a single pair, but sometimes in small colonies of about ten nests. They break reed stems and use twigs and the broken reeds to build their nest. The young are altricial, remaining at the nest for about six weeks before fledging.

Beaver *(bottom right)*

Beavers *(Castor fiber)* live in small family groups. Male and female mate for life, monogamously, and produce about three young each year. The babies are allowed into the water when they are two weeks old. Young beavers have to go through a difficult phase when being weaned off their mother's milk to the adult plant diet, and many of them do not survive this critical stage.

Mute Swan (top)

The cygnets of the mute swan (Cygnus olor) are just about everyone's idea of the proverbial Ugly Duckling. Grey, duck-like and tiny, these babies do not remotely resemble their elegant white parents. Although cygnets will take to the water soon after hatching, they do still take rides on their mother's back during their first few days.

Mosquito (above left)

The female mosquito (Culex) needs only a tiny amount of standing water to lay its eggs in — even an old tin holds enough. The eggs develop into slender larvae with a breathing-tube at the rear end. After about twelve days (depending on temperature) the larvae will pupate, and three days after that the young mosquitoes emerge.

Club-tailed Dragonfly (above right)

The club-tailed dragonfly (Gomphus vulgatissimus) is a rare species of dragonfly. It lives in fresh water — but only where there is a beach with breaking waves. In Europe, places like that are not too common. The club-tailed is one of the few dragonflies able to break out of its larval casing from a horizontal position.

Black-winged Stilt (left)

Even as chicks, black-winged stilts (*Himantopus himantopus*) have extremely long red legs, and can be seen wading around on these 'stilts' in shallow water. They can also swim, however. Being migratory birds, they need to be fully grown by late summer so as to stand up to the rigours of the long journey south. This is a very widely distributed species, found also in Africa, America and South Asia.

Crane (below)

Destruction of its habitat has made the crane (*Grus grus*) now rarer in Europe than in Asia. Once a pair of cranes have mated — following the elaborate courtship ritual — they stay together as lifelong partners. The female lays two eggs, which she and the male take turns to incubate. After they hatch, the parents tend their chicks for ten weeks, to the point where they can fly and can fend for themselves.

Coot (bottom right)

A newly-hatched coot (*Fulica atra*) is black all over except for a bright orange-red neck and head. Once it gets older, its plumage will take on various tones of grey. Later, when fully adult, it will have all-black plumage with the coot's characteristic white forehead patch which is so reminiscent of a white blaze on a horse's head.

Otter (left)

Otters *(Lutra lutra)* are freshwater predators, which inhabit the banks of inland water systems in Europe, Asia and North Africa. They give birth after a gestation period of about 60 days, usually to a litter of three. Otters reach 1.5 m in length when fully grown. As they take sickly or less robust fish for preference, their effect on fish stocks is beneficial.

Broad-bodied Chaser Dragonfly (below)

One of the larger dragonflies, the broad-bodied chaser *(Libellula depressa)* is so called because the rear part of its body is noticeably flatter than on other dragonflies. After mating, the female drops its eggs into water. After four weeks or slightly longer, the dragonfly nymphs hatch. It will be another two years before they develop into adult dragonflies.

White Wagtail *(top left)*

The white wagtail *(Motacilla alba)* is a resident of Asia and parts of North Africa as well as of Europe, and can be found on fields and meadows or in woodland. It prefers to nest in crevices or cavities. When it brings food to the nest for its babies, the mother bird has no problem — even in the dim light of the hole — in locating the chicks' mouths, which are a particularly brilliant red.

Night Heron *(top right)*

The night heron *(Nycticorax nycticorax)* invariably nests in trees or bushes, usually laying two to four eggs. Once the chicks have hatched, three weeks later, the parents ensure they are kept warm, and feed them with regurgitated material which they have already almost fully digested. Later on they will get insects, tiny fish, and amphibians.

(centre left)

White wagtails breed twice or three times a year and nest near water if at all possible, as they live mainly on mosquitoes, small fish and freshwater shrimps. The chicks hatch after two weeks of incubation and are then fed by their parents for a further two weeks. In August these birds gather in great flocks.

Grass Snake *(bottom left)*

When they emerge from the egg, the young of the grass snake *(Natrix natrix)* are about 15–20 cm long. Fully grown, they will be about a metre in length, the females rather longer than the males. Grass snakes feed on frogs, toads and fish, and are completely harmless to man. Sadly, they are often killed because people mistake them for adders.

Parsley Frog *(left-hand page, top)*

Here a tadpole of the parsley frog *(Pelodytes punctatus)*, sometimes called the mud-diver, is consuming its prey. These frogs spawn twice a year — in fact, in hot regions they spawn all year round — and as a result the tadpole development varies according to spawning time. Autumn-hatched tadpoles will not develop into frogs until the winter is over.

(left-hand page, centre)

This young parsley frog has almost completed its metamorphosis. As a fully-grown frog it will still remain close to water, for the sake of the wet vegetation it needs to live in. It has an unusual technique for climbing, using adhesion between its belly and the surface to be climbed.

(left-hand page, bottom)

The parsley frog is a small frog, reaching only 5 cm in size, with a warty back flecked with greenish-brown. After mating, the female lowers its broad strings of eggs into the water. From these, the tadpoles later hatch. When they begin to metamorphose — which is happening in this picture — they will have reached 9 cm in length, distinctly longer than the frogs they will become.

Cormorant *(top right)*

The cormorant *(Phalacrocorax carbo)* is found in Europe, Africa and Asia, but always near water of some kind. Given the chance, it will nest in a tree, and it returns to the same nest each year. The young change their infant down for juvenile plumage after 35 days, but remain in the nest for two more weeks. It will be a further ten days before they are fledged.

(centre right)

A female cormorant lays three or four glossy bluish eggs, and for the next four weeks, till they hatch, will take turns with her mate in incubating them. The naked chicks open their eyes three days later, and their first food will be exclusively the well pre-digested mess regurgitated by their parents. Later they will reach into the parents' throat pouches, lifting out whole fish and drinking water — all brought by air.

Great Crested Grebe *(bottom right)*

The young of the great crested grebe *(Podiceps cristatus)* hatch in a floating nest, well disguised by reeds and other aquatic vegetation. As precocial or 'early leaver' birds, they leave the nest at once and thereafter spend most of their time on the water, with their parents. In their first three weeks of life they can take refuge when necessary in their parents' plumage.

Brown Trout (right)

When they hatch, brown trout *(Salmo trutta fario)* are only 1 cm long, and they will continue for some time yet to take their nourishment from the yolk sac — though in this young fish it has disappeared. Trout grow very quickly, reaching a length of 1 m at maturity. At spawning time in winter, they lay 1000 to 1500 eggs, from which, after about ten weeks, a new generation of young fish will emerge.

(below)

Here several brown trout are in the process of hatching. The one on the left is still completely inside the egg, all but its head; the one on the right is wriggling hard to free itself from its eggshell, while the middle one has succeeded. Comparison of this picture with our picture of the trout at a rather later stage shows how big the yolk sac is immediately after the fish hatches.

(bottom)

This photograph is of a brown trout *(Salmo trutta fario)* just hatching. The infant fish with its yolk sac has to free itself from the translucent eggshell, and for a tiny fish this takes quite some effort. The eyes give the impression of having already reached their full size, but that of course is an illusion.

Italian Crested Newt *(top left)*

The Italian crested newt *(Triturus cristatus carnifex)*, photographed here in its larval stage from directly in front, against a background of gravel, is a close relative of the northern crested newt. Biologists used to regard the Italian crested newt as a subspecies of the northern, but now say it is a species in its own right. The same applies to the southern and the Danube crested newts.

Common Frog *(top right)*

This tadpole of the common frog *(Rana temporaria)* is at quite an advanced stage of development: it has legs and can paddle with them, and the head and body of the frog form have already taken on their final form. But the metamorphosis is not complete until the tadpole tail has disappeared. Only when that happens can the frog make the move to dry land.

Great Crested Newt *(centre left)*

The great crested newt *(Triturus cristatus)* belongs to the broad group of newts and salamanders, and leads an amphibian life, spending part of the year on land and another period — for purposes of reproduction — in water. So that it can breathe and swim in water, the metamorphosis is actually reversed in part. When it is four months old, the 3-cm-long larva shown in the photograph will be twice the size it is now, and will move to the land.

Atlantic Salmon *(bottom left)*

This baby Atlantic salmon *(Salmo salar)* will go on feeding from its yolk sac for about six weeks. By then it will be ready to eat other things, initially worms and insect larvae, then tiny fish, and eventually also rather larger fish — the salmon is, of course, a predator. When it hatches, the infant salmon is minute, only 2 cm in length. But when fully grown it can reach a length of 1.5 m and weight of 35 kg.

Mallard (above)

No sooner is a mallard (*Anas platyrhynchos*) out of the egg than it can swim and feels at home in the water. And that is where the tiny ducklings seek out their food. They reach down with their head and neck under water to find plants and invertebrates, sticking their tail in the air. This technique for locating food is called 'dabbling'.

(below left)

Mallard are exceptionally adaptable and can find food in fields and meadows as well as in water, so it is not surprising that they are the most widely distributed European wild duck. From March onwards, they will incubate their eggs, sometimes 14 of them. The chicks are precocial, leaving the nest with their mother not long after they are hatched.

(below, centre)

The down on a mallard chick's face and underparts is of a bright golden-brown colour. The rest of its down coat is dark brown with a few brighter streaks. Adult females are an inconspicuous mottled brown, but the males — the drakes — have a glossy bottle-green head and neck, with a white patch above the dark brown of the breast feathers.

Domestic Duck (above, centre)

The young of the domestic duck (Anas platyrhynchos domesticus) generally swim close by their mother. This is the only means she has to warn them in good time of impending danger, and to protect them when necessary. They will not swim alone until they are fully independent. But sometimes inquisitive little ducklings will go off to investigate on their own — and then cheep pitifully for their mother when they miss her.

(above right)

When domestic ducklings are resting or settle down for the night, they cuddle up close to one another for warmth. However, they never retire to the nest where they hatched, but choose a place in the open, on a field or under bushes. The nest is used only for incubating eggs.

(below right)

The domestic duck is by no means only a European bird, being found all over the northern hemisphere. It loves to frequent ponds and lakes, but will also happily make do with a river. Pairs are formed in the winter; if they are migrants, the drake will fly off with the duck to her home territory, and the family will be reared there.

Pomeranian Duck (left-hand page, top)

These two Pomeranian ducklings (Anas platyrhynchos domesticus) belong to a breed of domestic duck that is kept mainly for the sake of the meat it gives. They are also easy to look after, being very hardy. When fully grown they will have a white breast and grey-blue or black plumage elsewhere.

Coypu (left-hand page, bottom)

The coypu or nutria (Myocastor coypus) is found near water or on marshy land in most of the continents. They are very prolific breeders, and their numbers increase fast. A female coypu gives birth about three times a year — not infrequently to a litter of ten. The young are exceptionally well adapted for life near water and in water, and can swim soon after they are born.

Mayfly (top)

The brownish larva of the mayfly (Ecolyonurus venosus) lives on the beds of lakes and rivers, though always near the bank. After passing through a developmental stage lasting anything from one to three years, it comes to the surface and casts its skin. What emerges is the mayfly, though it is not in fact ready just yet to take to the air. Another day passes, then the skin is cast again, and after that the insect is clear to fly.

Osprey (right)

Ospreys (Pandion haliaetus) always build their large nest near water, so that it is handily located for their food supply, and use it for years. Generally they lay three eggs, from which the chicks hatch five weeks later. The young leave the nest after another nine weeks or so, but the parents go on feeding them for another month — and it is during this time that they learn to catch fish for themselves.

In Woodland and Forest

The forest floor, the trunks of trees, even the leaves of deciduous trees and the needles of conifers — all of these provide food and/or shelter for the young of a whole range of animals, for instance squirrels, slugs and snails, and foxes. This is why woods and forests are among the world's richest habitats in terms of sheer diversity of species.

European Red Slug (above)

After rain, the European red slug (*Arion rufus*) is a common sight along the track, at field and forest edges and in gardens. It is out replenishing its body fluid, because it lacks any kind of retaining membrane. After mating in late summer — slugs are hermaphrodites and can self-fertilise — they lay up to 500 spherical eggs. They die shortly afterwards.

Elk (right)

When summer brings higher temperatures, the elk (*Alces alces*) prefers to be active only in the early morning or in the evening. To rest during the day it looks for a spot in marshy ground, where the dampness can help cool its body. The calves remain dependent on their mother for a full year and usually follow her wherever she goes.

Buzzard (above)

Its grey and white down coat protects the buzzard chick (*Buteo buteo*) fairly well, but when the wind blows cold it is still best to seek refuge inside the nest. In the first two weeks after the eggs hatch, the mother remains at the nest virtually continuously, while the father goes off to hunt for food for the whole family.

(top right)

The buzzard is not a purely European resident, being found also in large parts of Asia and Africa. It likes to nest in trees in open woodland, but will also sometimes build on the ground or on the faces of crags. Both parents are involved in incubating the three eggs, from which the chicks hatch after five weeks. The young need seven weeks before they are fledged, but even then are still dependent on the parents.

Eagle-owl (centre right)

The female eagle-owl (*Bubo bubo*) laid her two white eggs and incubated them for over a month on her own before these two chicks hatched. During this time, her mate will have brought her mice, birds and various animals to eat, but she never fed on these at the nest itself. The young are able to fend for themselves after about nine weeks.

(bottom right)

To look at this young eagle-owl, one would not imagine it, but once fully grown it will be capable of hunting and killing animals as big as hares or young fawns. It is in fact the biggest species of European owl, growing to a length of 70 cm. During the breeding season, eagle-owls use a special call to proclaim their territory — the 'whoo-whoo' which is echoed by their name in some countries.

Roe Deer *(left-hand page, top left)*

The coat of the roe deer *(Capreolus capreolus)* is normally reddish brown over the summer, but in winter it changes to a grey-brown shade. This ensures that the animal is well camouflaged whatever the time of year. The kid's white spots likewise help make it less easily seen by enemies as it lies in its hiding-place.

(left-hand page, top centre)

A roe kid spends the early weeks of its life in a hiding place chosen by the mother. She returns to suckle the kid, but not otherwise. It often happens that people out rambling will come across the young roe and imagine the mother has abandoned it. But it is wrong to approach the kid, because if there is human scent nearby the mother will smell it and then will not dare return to the hiding-place to suckle her kid.

(left-hand page, top right)

Roe deer mate in summer, but the young — like those of most European mammals — are not born until springtime. This is possible because the embryo does not start to develop immediately but has a period of dormancy. When the kid is born, the mother licks it clean. She stays with her kid for about a year — till her next calf arrives.

(left-hand page, main picture)

Gestation in roe deer is between nine and ten months, which is exceptionally long. There is a good reason, though. Following conception, the embryo remains dormant for about four months, and only then starts to grow. This pattern ensures that both mating and the birth of the young occur when food is at its most plentiful.

Red Deer *(top right)*

Red deer calves *(Cervus elaphus)* generally first see the light of day during May. Until October, when they shed their summer coat, they are speckled with white, which means they stand out less obviously from their environment. Then in winter they get a grey-brown pelt, and next summer it will change again to reddish brown.

Puss Moth *(bottom right)*

The puss moth *(Cerula vinula)* is a fairly nondescript-looking moth, but its caterpillar, seen here climbing a plant stalk, is a spectacular creature with its brilliant green body colouring and red-ringed head. The fork-like organ at the rear end is only extruded if something has alarmed the caterpillar.

Black Stork (top left)

Quite unlike the white stork, which likes to nest near human habitations, the black stork (Ciconia nigra) is a typical woodland species. It nests in old trees near water, where it will find fish and amphibians to feed on. Three to five white eggs will hatch after a month's incubation. The chicks when young have an orange-yellow beak and white down.

Cuckoo (centre left)

The young cuckoo (Cuculus canorus) never knows its biological parents, because it grows up as a parasite benefiting from parenting by other species. The female cuckoo lays her eggs singly in nests belonging to other birds. Often the male cuckoo helps her to get away with it by distracting the attention of the host birds. Once the cuckoo in the nest has hatched, it often pushes their eggs and chicks out of the nest and then enjoys their undivided attention.

Eurasian Reed Warbler (bottom left)

The Eurasian reed warbler (Acrocephalus scirpaceus) is one of the species most often singled out by the cuckoo to incubate and feed its progeny. It does not take long for the young cuckoo to outgrow its foster-parents and their tiny nest too, as the cuckoo reaches 30–35 cm in length and can weigh about 110 g, the reed warblers only 12 cm and 14 g.

Garden Dormouse (right-hand page, top)

Garden dormice (Eliomys quercinus) do indeed look like mice, but they actually belong to a quite different family, the dormice or Gliridae, of which the fat dormouse is a member too. They are rodents and nocturnal. They hibernate approximately from October to April, mating soon after hibernation is over. Any time from May onwards, about four young will be born in a hollow tree or a rocky crevice which the parents have lined with soft material to make a nest.

(right-hand page, bottom)

This little dormouse was probably born in spring or late summer along with three or four siblings. The principal habitat of these small rodents is unquestionably the forest, which provides hollow trees suitable for lining with nest material. However, they are also happy to move into outhouses and barns, because gardens ensure them an adequate supply of fruit and seed.

Chaffinch (right)

This baby chaffinch (*Fringilla coelebs*) will stay about two weeks more in the nest before its head and body have grown a covering of feathers. After that it will learn to fly and to forage for insects, seeds and berries. So that this can happen, the chaffinch family will stay together for about another month after the chicks have flown the nest.

European Wildcat (below)

Among the places still inhabited by the European wildcat (*Felix silvestris silvestris*) are some Scottish forests. But you would need a lot of luck to actually meet one, as the wildcat is a secretive animal and also rare. In one way they are just like domestic cats: in the mating season, the toms caterwaul loudly in competition for the females. If the mating has been successful, the female will give birth to two, three or four kittens, which she will keep well hidden for a while.

European Robin (top)

These three young robins *(Erithacus rubecula)* are probably at least a fortnight old, because that is the age at which they usually leave the ground-level nest which the parents had built for them. But they are not yet fledged. So the two adult birds have a hectic time stuffing food into hungry beaks. They cope mainly by catching insects.

(centre left)

This young bird is a robin during the moult. At this time, with its yellowish-brown breast colouring, the young robin is barely recognisable as a robin. It is not until they are adults that robins — both male and female — acquire the orangey-red throat and breast patch that gives them their popular name of redbreast. During the mating season in spring, cock birds will react very aggressively to the sight of it, defending their territory fiercely against other males.

(bottom left)

Once a young robin like this has grown up and reached sexual maturity, it will seek out a mate during the spring-time mating season and start a family. After fertilisation the female lays four to six yellowish or buff-coloured eggs and will incubate them by herself for two weeks until the new generation of robins hatches.

59

Jay *(above)*

A young jay *(Garrulus glandarius)* like this will be fledged in three weeks. But it will need a further three to six weeks before it is fully able to fend for itself. A brood of jays consists of between three and seven light-coloured eggs, incubated by the mother bird. While this continues, the male feeds her from his crop, but she also does some of her own hunting, for insects and other small live food.

(right)

Jays are found in Asia and North Africa as well as in Europe. They belong to the crow family and are considered to be very intelligent. They are often called the forest watchmen, because if anything unusual happens in the forest, or possible enemies approach, the jays call and the other forest-dwellers hear the warning.

Fat Dormouse *(top left)*

The paws of the fat dormouse *(Glis glis)* have a special roughened pad on the underside which helps it to climb. This is important to it, because much of its life is spent in a nest in the trees. This too is where the young are born, as can be guessed from the photograph.

(top right)

Fat dormice are happiest nesting in tree cavities, but will accept man-made nesting-boxes as a substitute. After a month's gestation, the female gives birth to about four babies. She looks after them entirely by herself, suckling them for about six weeks. From then on, the young ones will go out with her at night, foraging for seeds, insects or fruit.

(centre right)

The fat dormouse is one of the broader family of dormice. They are not related to mice, but their name may have something to do with sleeping (as in 'dormitory'), because they have a long period of hibernation. During this winter sleep, they do sometimes wake briefly to take a snack from the 'winter stores' that they have left ready. The babies are born in summer, when there is plenty of food for them and their parents.

(bottom right)

The fat dormouse is omnivorous — it has a very mixed diet. What it most likes are fruits, seeds and nuts, but it will not turn up its nose at insects or baby birds when it can catch them. Young dormice are suckled for a while, but very soon they are left no option but to switch to solid food.

Edible Snail *(top right)*

This edible snail *(Helix pomatia)* is laying its pea-sized eggs in a hole in the ground that it has excavated itself to about the size of a tennis ball. The baby snails hatch after about a month, but linger underground after hatching for about a week, climbing to the surface when the weather is wet. Tiny though they are, they instinctively take to branches or plant stems and climb up for greater safety.

(centre right)

Edible snails like these two are never found now in vineyards, because there they are regarded as a pest and are not tolerated. Nowadays they live in undergrowth and bushes along field and forest margins, or in hedges. Their shell can reach a diameter of 5 cm. It protects the snail from enemies, also from drying out, and it can even be sealed closed with mucus.

Common Garden Snail *(bottom left)*

The common (or brown) garden snail *(Helix aspersa)*, rather smaller than the Central European edible snail, is found everywhere in Europe where the Roman Empire once held sway. The reason is simply that the Romans took the snails along with them as part of their rations. This snail is still a delicacy today, and is farmed under glass or in open-air colonies.

(bottom right)

Here infant common garden snails can be seen in the process of hatching. Snails are hermaphrodites and deposit the clutch of about 50 pea-sized eggs in the soil. Since then the embryos will have been developing for about four weeks.

Gipsy Moth (above)
These gipsy moth caterpillars (Lymantria dispar) are beautiful to look at, but they can wreak havoc if they build up in large numbers. They are not at all choosy about their food, and so are capable of stripping whole woods. When the female gipsy moth has laid its eggs, it covers them with hairs from its abdomen.

Eurasian Lynx (left)
Europe's biggest cat, growing to a body length of up to 1.1 m, the lynx (Lynx lynx) is at home primarily in the far north and in Russia, but sometimes penetrates eastwards into Asia. It takes nearly a year before the young are ready to leave their mother, because they have to become skilled enough at hunting to be able to provide for themselves.

Pine Marten (above)

Just after birth, the young of the pine marten (*Martes martes*) are about 10 cm long. It will be several weeks before the cubs can first venture out of the nest their mother made for their birth. Later, the pine marten — once much hunted for the sake of its prized fur, and now a correspondingly rare animal — will live mostly in broad-leaved or mixed forest.

Beech Marten (right)

Grey-brown fur and a forked white patch on the throat — those are the visible signs by which we can identify the beech marten (*Martes foina*). As a predatory animal it feeds mainly on small mammals, birds and insects, but it will also eat berries and fruits. For this, the beech marten has a very useful skill: it is an excellent climber. Its cubs quickly learn to climb too.

Raccoon Dog (top left)

So called because its mask-like face resembles that of a raccoon, the raccoon dog *(Nyctereutes procyonoides)* is related to the canines (dogs). In its Asian homeland the raccoon dog has a host of enemies, and because of this the female produces from six to as many as 19 young in a single whelping — contributing to the conservation of the species.

Polecat (top right)

The female polecat *(Mustela putoris)* has mated in spring, and 42 days later gave birth to its litter. She suckles them for six weeks, and continues to support them until autumn — always on her own and without the male, as polecats are solitary.

Red Kite (centre left)

The red kite *(Milvus milvus)* was brought to the point of extinction at the beginning of the 20th century. But in our time, thanks to a comprehensive ban on hunting them, these elegant raptors are now back in quite large numbers. Two thirds of all breeding pairs — and thus two thirds of all young birds — live in Germany. One distinctive feature is the red kite's forked tail.

(bottom left)

A red kite nest is less likely to be found in deep, dense forest than in copses with grassland in between. For nest-building, the red kite uses natural materials and also any rags or paper scraps it finds. It lays three eggs, and four weeks later the chicks hatch at intervals. Often the youngest one is shouldered aside by its older siblings and will die.

Moufflon *(left-hand page, top)*

The moufflon *(Ovis ammon musimon,* also *Ovis orientalis musimon)* is the world's smallest wild sheep. An ancestor of the domestic sheep, it is now found in the wild only on the islands of Corsica and Sardinia. Mating takes place in autumn, and after about five months of gestation the females give birth usually to a single lamb, occasionally two. Young moufflon quickly learn to follow their mothers.

Golden Oriole *(left-hand page, bottom)*

The photo shows a male golden oriole *(Oriolus oriolus)* bringing prey to its ravenously cheeping chicks. The cock bird is easily recognised by its brilliant yellow body plumage, black wings and yellow-and-black tail. The female, by contrast, is yellowish-olive in colour, with pale underparts.

Blue Tit *(top left)*

The blue tit *(Parus caeruleus)*, characterised by its blue tail, blue wings and blue cap on its head, builds its nest in a hollow tree. And then, every day, it lays an egg — the clutch may have as many as 15 in it. If it leaves the tree cavity during the incubation period, it covers the eggs over with nest material. The young continue to be fed for two to three weeks and then gradually leave the nest.

(top right)

Blue tits — like this female, busy feeding her chicks — also readily accept nesting-boxes hung up by humans as a help in rearing their family. Blue tits occur in Asia and North Africa as well as Europe, and they feel at home in parks and gardens. The chicks hatch successively, in the same order as the laying of the eggs.

Coal Tit *(bottom right)*

The coal tit *(Parus ater)* lives and nests in coniferous forests. The female bird uses moss and animal hair to line a cavity and make it into a nest, then lays up to ten eggs in the nest and incubates them without help. The chicks hatch after about two weeks and both parents then co-operate in looking after them. Within three weeks the young birds will have fledged.

Great Tit *(left-hand page, main picture)*

These two great tit chicks *(Parus major)* have already left the nest, but are still expecting food to be provided by their parents. When fully grown, they will weigh about 20 g and their body length will be 14 cm. They can reach an age of 15 years, and usually breed twice a year. The second clutch in a given year will have fewer eggs than the first.

(left-hand page, top right)

Great tits like those in the picture readily accept nesting-boxes to breed in. The female lays up to twelve speckled eggs in the box, and is fed by her mate while incubating. Once the rearing of the chicks — a task which the parents share — has been completed, they will have a second family, which as a rule is distinctly less numerous than the first. The young in this photograph could well be a second brood.

(left-hand page, centre right)

In spring, great tits lay up to twelve light-coloured eggs with red spots, from which the chicks hatch about a fortnight later. The parents feed their chicks quite systematically with caterpillars, in other words soft, protein-rich food, while they themselves consume insects during the breeding period and otherwise seeds and fruit. The chicks fledge after about three weeks.

(left-hand page, bottom right)

Great tits are widely distributed in Asia and North Africa as well as Europe. Their preferred habitats, apart from open woodland, are copses, parks and gardens. Some even nest close to humans, for instance under roof tiles or in letter-boxes. The nests are soon full of grey downy chicks waiting hungrily for the parent birds to come and feed them.

Green Woodpecker *(right)*

A green woodpecker *(Picus viridis)* is seen here feeding its chick — which is old enough to scramble up to the access hole for its food. In its first week of life that would have been beyond it, and the parents climbed down into the cavity to feed it. After about three weeks the young woodpeckers leave the nest and clamber around nearby. They will not be fledged until a further week has passed.

Tawny Owl (left)

The tawny owl (Strix aluco) is not exclusively a forest bird, being found in parks and gardens as well. What it really needs is an old tree with hollows for it to nest in. But it will accept a nest box, or may even seek out someone's loft. The female lays three eggs in March/April and incubates them herself. She will remain with the chicks through the first ten days after they hatch.

Bullfinch (bottom left)

Parent bullfinches (Pyrrhula pyrrhula) share the task of rearing their young, and are quite often both at the nest at the same time. The male of the pair is easily recognised by his gleaming red underparts. It was the female who incubated the eggs throughout, over a period of a fortnight, and during this phase the male brought food to her.

(bottom right)

The bullfinch's favourite place to breed is in conifers, in which it builds a platform-like nest. The female lays about five bluish, brown-speckled eggs in it. After the chicks hatch out, the female takes them under her wings for about the first week. The brood remain in the nest for two to three weeks, and then are fed nearby for a further week.

Fire Salamander (top)

Fire salamanders (*Salamandra salamandra*) need more than the shade of the forest to live in: they also need running water, because that is where the females drop their juveniles. About three months later, the juveniles leave the water and become land-dwellers again. The young salamanders will not reach sexual maturity until they are three years old.

Red Squirrel (above left)

The young of the red squirrel (*Sciurus vulgaris*) spend nearly two months being cared for — by the mother only — before they achieve independence. Male and female squirrels do not bond as a pair. Adult specimens of this rodent lead solitary lives, and the males mate with a number of different individuals. The female squirrels have three litters a year, distributed across the warmer seasons.

(above right)

Individual squirrels are born in a litter with one to seven other brothers and sisters. Once adult, these rodents lead a solitary life. They are highly intelligent, and for instance stock up on food for the winter, squirrelling it away in a hiding place. At the same time, they know the food put out for birds is tasty, and they help themselves to it as needed.

Wild Boar (above)

Wild boar *(Sus scrofa scrofa)* avoid completely open country, as they want to have cover available in case of danger. But they choose to spend a lot of their time — as this young boar is doing — in clearings in deciduous and mixed forest. In times gone by, their preferred habitat was the woodland of river valleys, but such riverine forests have almost all been lost.

(bottom left)

Wild boar piglets in their first six months of life have a brown-and-white striped coat. From then on they acquire the blackish-brown coat of the adult animal. The mother sow and her young live together in what is called a 'pack', and if there is a threat of her offspring being attacked, the sow will defend them to the last.

(bottom right)

The wild boar does not have particularly good eyesight, but it hardly matters, as their sense of smell is highly developed. With their short snout they can detect delicacies buried in the forest floor, including such things as worms, insect larvae and seeds. They also use their snouts for digging through the soil.

(bottom left)

It is always easy to spot places in the forest where wild boar have been looking for acorns or beech-mast — there will be a sizeable patch of ground where the earth has been completely churned up. Rooting in the ground is just one of the habits young boar are born with: they also love to wallow in mud. But they don't wallow just for pleasure — it also helps them get rid of vermin.

Blackbird (above)

Blackbirds *(Turdus merula)* were originally pure forest birds, but they are one of the species that follows in the wake of human cultivation, and so are now often inhabitants of parks and gardens. They can vary their habitat because they are flexible about diet, taking what is available. Cock blackbirds are all black, with a brilliant orange beak, but chicks and the adult females have greyish-brown plumage.

Song Thrush (bottom right)

For these four chicks, hatched from greenish-blue eggs, the song thrush *(Turdus philomelos)* very carefully wove a nest together from twiglets and grass stalks. Then she 'papered the walls' by smoothing wet soil and rotted wood fibre round the inside of the nest. The young song thrushes are altricial ('stay-at-homes') and are fed in the nest by both parents over a period of two weeks, then for another two weeks nearby.

Red Fox *(left)*

At about ten months old, young red foxes *(Vulpes vulpes)* become sexually mature. The annual mating season for this species, when the vixens are on heat, is in January and February. This ensures that the cubs are born at a time of year when food is abundant.

(bottom left)

Unlike other predators, this young red fox does not have claws. So it has to learn to seize prey with its teeth and also to kill quickly, because it has no other means of holding its quarry fast. These limitations mean that the fox's menu consists mostly of relatively small animals, from mice up to hare. However, occasionally a fully-grown fox will take a roe deer kid.

(top left)

Red fox cubs do not open their eyes until about two weeks old. Until then they are blind. Later on they will need their eyes to hunt in darkness, foxes being nocturnal animals. Their eyes accordingly have a similar structure to the domestic cat's eyes, ideally adapted for good night vision.

(centre left)

The fox cubs' father helps in rearing them, at least for a while. So long as the vixen is confined to the drey, tending the newborn cubs, the dog fox will bring food in for her. But as soon as she can go out to forage for herself again, the room service stops abruptly.

(below)

At about one year old the young fox will leave its mother and seek out a hunting territory of its own, where it will also mate. However, it will live most of its life alone, as foxes are solitary by nature. It will only seek the company of other foxes when the mating season comes round.

Yellow-necked Mouse (left)

The yellow-necked mouse (*Apodemus flavicollis*) usually nests in burrows it has dug out for itself, but also sometimes under roots or in hollow trees. The young are born after three weeks of gestation, weighing less than 3 g. When fully grown, they reach a weight of 20 to 45 g and can be as much as 13 cm long. But after this there is an even longer tail, up to 13.5 cm in length.

(below)

The natural territory of the yellow-necked mouse is broad-leaved or mixed forest. It is an excellent climber, often searching out food (seeds, insects etc) in the crowns of the very tallest trees. The young mice need only eight weeks from birth to sexual maturity. A single litter may have as many as eight baby mice.

Processionary Caterpillar *(top left)*

The processionary caterpillar *(Thaumetopoea proces-sionea)*, which eventually turns into a rather inconspicuous moth, is so called because of its unusual lifestyle. It lives high up in oak trees, in huge cocoon-like nests. By night the caterpillars crawl up the oak trunk, one after the other – as in a procession – to the crown of the tree, and gorge themselves. By day they remain in their nest.

Elk *(top right)*

The elk *(Alces alces)* is at home in northerly latitudes, and suffers if the temperature rises above 14 °C. Accordingly it is found mainly in Scandinavia, where it has few natural foes to fear. Given ideal conditions, 90% of elk cows will calve annually, and about a third of them will have twin calves.

European Bison *(centre left)*

The continent's heaviest land animal, the European bison *(Bison bonasus)*, was almost extinct by the beginning of the 19th century, but has survived into our own time thanks to strenuous efforts to keep it breeding. Even a newly born bison is a colossus: the 40 kg that an average calf weighs in at are a pointer to its size at maturity, when it may weigh a full 1000 kg – a ton.

(bottom left)

European bison, which are a form of wild cattle, are in fact seldom encountered in the wild within Europe. Only in Poland and Russia are there a few herds living free. But in reserves and animal parks there are now plenty of bison to be seen. They live in herds, which have one 'lead animal' as the natural leader. Bison calves have to accept the hierarchy which the herd imposes.

Barn Owl (top left)

Apart from the polar regions, the barn owl (Tyto alba) is found in every continent; it is not choosy about its habitat except that it must not be too dry. Often they nest close to humans — for instance, this photograph was taken in a stable. At this stage the chicks in their downy coat still look very different from the adults, but they do already have the adult owl's distinctive heart-shaped face.

European Brown Bear (top right)

This little bear cub is only two weeks old, and is still being fed solely on his mother's milk. Only when the cub is seen alongside his mother can it be appreciated that the European brown bear (Ursus arctos arctos) is the continent's heaviest predatory animal. It is a good climber and a good swimmer, and so is just as much at home in marshland and mountain as in forests with rivers.

Tengmalm's Owl (centre left)

Tengmalm's owl (Aegolius funereus) is found in the forests of northern Asia as well as in Europe. The young birds can easily be identified by this owl's characteristic X-shaped face markings. About a month after hatching, they leave the nest cavity, which in most cases is an old woodpecker hole taken over by the owl pair. Outside the nest, the parents go on feeding their offspring for quite a bit longer.

Ant (bottom left)

Ants (Formicidae), like bees, are social insects. Only a few female ants, the queens, are fertile and lay eggs. The eggs develop into larvae, then pupae, and finally ants. The babies are looked after by worker ants. Whether the young females in the brood will develop into sterile workers or will become queens is a matter of whether the workers bring plenty of properly nourishing food or just meagre rations.

Spider (left)

Worldwide, there are something like 35,000 species of Araneae — the true spiders, to which orb web (or *orbitelous*) spiders and jumping spiders are considered to belong. Jumping spiders lay their eggs in concealed places, such as under tree bark, spin a web over them and then guard them until the new generation emerges.

Orb Web Spiders (below)

The male orb web or orbitelous spiders *(Araneidae)* make contact with females by means of one of the threads that make up their web. After mating, the females lay their eggs, wrapped in silken cocoons, on leaves, tree bark or even garbage. When the young spiders hatch, they are transported away and scattered by the wind — so it is no wonder that orb web spiders are found all over the world, except in the Arctic and Antarctic.

In the Mountains

With its thin air, long months of food scarcity and cold winters, the mountain environment imposes exceptional demands on the animals who live there. In mountainous areas almost all young are born in the spring, so that they can benefit from the warmth and from the abundance of food at that time.

Alpine Marmot *(above)*

This young Alpine marmot *(Marmota marmota)* is about a year old. Together with its family group, it lives in a territory between one and five hectares in size. How big the territory is depends on whether the vegetation offers an adequate food supply. As winter approaches, marmots build up reserves of fat derived from their food. It used to be believed that marmot fat had healing properties, and because of this the 50-cm-long marmot was often the prey of human hunters.

(above right)

The marmot spends its long winter hibernation in its burrow, perhaps three metres underground. During this six to eight month period, its body temperature drops enormously. Young animals have difficulties coping with this, so adults interrupt their own hibernation at intervals to give them some extra warmth.

(right-hand page, bottom far right)

The hibernation is barely finished when male and female Alpine marmots begin mating. A good month later, in a secluded burrow, the female gives birth to a litter of (usually) three babies, which she will suckle for six weeks. A young marmot will not become sexually mature until it is two years old, at which point it will leave its family in order to start one of its own.

(right)

Alpine marmots, which belong to the squirrel family, will stand on their hind legs like this young specimen in order to keep watch. They have a system of whistling to warn each other of danger. As well as having a residential complex of burrows on their territory, they also dig a number of emergency tunnels down from their feeding areas — so that when need arises they can reach safety quickly.

Egyptian Vulture (top left)

The Egyptian vulture (*Neophron percnopterus*) nests high up in Europe's mountains. The two adults share in incubating a single egg, or at most two eggs, for six weeks; then they spend another three months or so rearing the chicks. When they are ready, the whole family flies off to winter in the deserts and semi-deserts of Africa. It is thought that the young birds do not return to Europe until the age of five, when they have reached adulthood.

Moufflon (centre left)

The most striking characteristic of the moufflon (*Ovis orientalis musimon*) is its spiral horns — on the male animal, at least. The moufflon ewe has horns that are simply angled backwards a little, and some females are completely hornless. In the young beasts, the horns are there but undeveloped; a ram's horns will grow between 15 and 20 cm during the first year of life.

Alpine Accentor (bottom left)

The Alpine accentor chick (*Prunella collaris*) guides its parents back to the nest with its cheeping and its bright red wide-open gullet. They will have concealed the nest (made from straw, rootlets, moss and animal hairs) carefully in a rocky fissure or in scree, and the chicks themselves are well camouflaged by their grey and brown plumage.

Golden Eagle (right-hand page, top right)

The golden eagle (*Aquila chrysaetos*) lives in the European mountains, but also in those of North America, Asia and North Africa. The adults build their nest as high up as possible, in trees or on the ledges of crags. They return to it each year, working further on it each time, with the result that nests can grow to 3 m in diameter. This gives adults and young plenty of room.

(right-hand page, bottom)

This golden eagle chick is five weeks old. That means he is just halfway to fledging. Golden eagles generally lay two eggs at a time, but occasionally up to four. The chicks hatch a few days apart, and often the last of the brood will be killed by its sibling or siblings. After they have flown, the parents will continue to feed their young for another month.

Ibex (above)

The ibex or mountain goat *(Capra ibex)* generally stays above the tree-line, at heights where other animals find almost no sustenance. In summer, when the Alpine meadows are in full flower and there is plenty to eat, the ibex's young are born — in most cases, one kid to each female.

(below)

When an ibex kid is born, it has a thick, shaggy baby coat, which it will keep for its first few weeks of life. After that its appearance changes as it grows the shorter-haired adult coat. Ibex practise a kind of segregation: the kid stays with its mother and the group of other mothers and their progeny, while the males are solitary at all times except the breeding season. Ibex are found in the mountainous areas of North Africa and Asia as well as of Europe.

(centre right)

Using their horns, which may be 1.4 m in length, male ibex fight each other in autumn for the females, not stopping until one concedes. After fertilisation takes place, it will be six months before the female ibex gives birth, usually to one kid but quite often to two. After only a few hours more, the little ones will be ready to follow their mother across difficult terrain.

Alpine Ibex (bottom right)

Numbers of Alpine ibex *(Capra ibex ibex)* are estimated at about 20,000, including young. This is quite a large population, given that at the beginning of the 19th century the Alpine ibex was thought to be virtually extinct. Up till then it had been widely hunted, because healing properties were attributed to various parts of its body. Happily, a reserve was established, enabling it to survive.

Chamois *(above)*

For us in the British Isles, no animal is more evocative of the high Alps than the chamois *(Rupicapra rupicapra)*. Its distinctive head markings can be clearly seen even in the kids: the face and the inside ears are white, and two broad black bands run back from the muzzle over the eyes and on to the ears. Fully grown animals have horns about 20 cm long, which hook backwards at the tips.

(left)

Being animals of the high mountains, chamois mate in autumn, and the old bucks plus the male juveniles then separate off from the herd of females. The females give birth in spring, in most cases to a single kid, which initially is reared on milk alone. By the time the Alpine pastures are at their lushest, and the grass at its most nutritious, the baby chamois will be big enough to feed on it.

Urban, Domestic and Farm Animals

Many baby animals, such as birds and mice grow up near human habitation — because that is where the parent animals have found food and suitable homes. But a whole lot of other animals are bred on purpose by us humans because we find them useful. Of course, keeping domestic animals is by no means just a European thing — people do it worldwide.

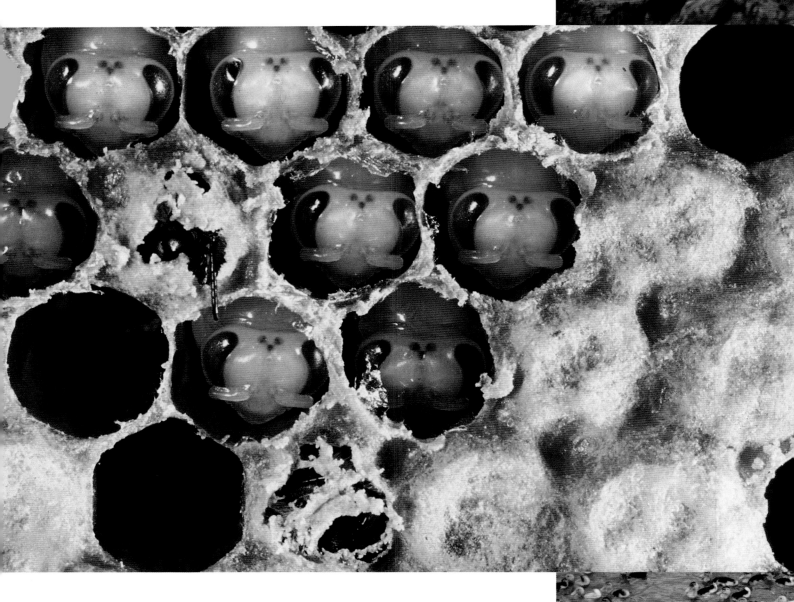

Honey Bee (above)

As social insects living in colonies, the worker honey bees (*Apis mellifera*) share in building six-sided cells from wax that they secrete from between their abdominal sections. The bee larvae are reared inside these cells. Those destined to become queens and so to lay eggs for the future are given different food from the other larvae, which will become workers.

Peking Duck (right)

The Peking duck (*Anas platyrhynchos domesticus*) is a variety of domestic duck which was first bred in China and came to Europe via the U.S. It is farmed for its tasty meat, and very often the ducklings have a much less happy time than those seen in the photo. In many cases they are kept for six weeks in a dark pen with nowhere to swim, and are then killed.

86

Domestic Duck (above)

All breeds of domestic duck (Anas platyrhynchos domesticus) — and so also the duckling sitting so demurely on the tree-stump in the picture — are descended from the wild mallard. Duck-keeping is known to be a very ancient form of animal husbandry, as domestic ducks are to be seen on documents known to have originated in China about 2000 BC.

Domestic Goose (top right)

Domestic geese and goslings (Anser anser domesticus) should always be kept on grassland so that they can graze, just like cows, horses or sheep. But they are also noted for a quality they have in common with dogs: when alarmed they cackle loudly and thus are thoroughly effective farmyard 'watchdogs'.

(centre right)

Domestic goslings — like their wild relatives — have developed far enough by the time they hatch to be able to leave the nest shortly afterwards. They already have membranes between their front three toes, just as their parents do; this means they can swim from the moment they hatch, and so escape from cats or dogs.

(bottom right)

These four goslings are domestic geese, and so are descended from the greylag goose. In winter, the greylag migrates to the south. As domestic geese can't do that, they need to be given a secure indoor pen instead to help them through the cold time of year. Geese are reared mainly for their meat, but their eggs too add welcome variety to the human diet.

Jackdaw (top)

The jackdaw (Corvus monedula) has always followed human civilisation and is found nowadays mainly in built-up areas, where it selects towers, spires, house lofts or trees for its nest. The female lays about five eggs and incubates them, almost entirely by herself, for two to three weeks until they hatch. Then both parents care for the chicks over five weeks or so till they are fledged.

Domestic Pigeon (above)

Newly hatched baby domestic pigeons (Columbia livia domestica) are taken under their parents' wings for a while so that they don't get chilled. Over three weeks or so they exchange their orangey-yellow down for enough plumage to make their first efforts to fly. They will need another one to two weeks to become independent.

(right)

In the case of domestic pigeons, the parents share the task of incubating the eggs, which takes about 17 days. As a rule the clutch consists of two eggs. The baby pigeons or 'squabs' are fed at first solely on the so-called 'crop milk' (or 'pigeon's milk'), a secretion from the parent birds' crop which looks milky but in fact consists mainly of skin cells. Pigeons are the only birds which give their young this special diet.

88

Poodle (right)

Poodles come not only in a variety of colours, but in three distinct sizes. The smallest is the Toy poodle, which stands only 25 cm high at the shoulder, and the largest is the Standard poodle at 58 cm. The recognised intermediate size is known as the Miniature poodle. Whatever their size, all poodles are intelligent, fun-loving and playful family pets.

Fox-terrier (below)

The fox-terrier was bred originally as a hunting dog — it was meant to crawl into the fox-hole and drive the foxes out. Puppies were no sooner born than they were being assessed for their suitability as hunting dogs. The fox-terrier is in fact still used for hunting, but very often it is just a family pet. Even so, the hunting instinct is still innate in every fox-terrier.

Tibetan Terrier (top left)

As the name implies, Tibetan terriers ultimately come from Tibet, the 'Roof of the World'. This is part of the reason for their hardiness and their ability to withstand cold. On average, Tibetan terriers will live for 15–18 years, which in dog terms is a very old age. It means that if you are thinking of getting a puppy you should also think carefully about whether you will want to go on looking after a dog for so many years — or indeed be able to!

West Highland White Terrier (bottom left)

Westies, as their many admirers like to call them, were originally bred as hunting dogs — and bred pure white, so that they wouldn't be mistaken for a fox and get shot. But they have become so popular and appealing as family pets that Westie pups are now bred on a mass basis with no regard for quality.

English Setter (right-hand page, top left)

The name 'setter', like 'pointer', is used of dogs that accompany hunts and have a distinctive trick of stopping and raising a paw while they are tracking game. When the dog 'points', it really looks as if it is pointing towards where it thinks the game bird or animal is hidden. Even the puppies do this — it is an inherited trait.

Bearded Collie (right-hand page, top centre)

Bearded collie pups look like little balls of fur. Their shaggy coat and their 'beard' round their muzzle make it quite hard to see their friendly face and alert, lively eyes. Beardeds are particularly friendly dogs. Once upon a time they were used as sheepdogs. Now, as family pets, they must be given plenty of activity.

(right-hand page, top right)

You wouldn't guess from looking at this bearded collie bitch and her pups that their ancestors were originally bred for sheep-minding duties in the Highlands of Scotland. What was a very practical shaggy coat then is now an outer dress of superfine hair requiring much grooming. What has not changed is the Beardie's character — they need lots of activity and interest.

Boxer (right-hand page, main picture)

The earliest boxer dogs were bred in Germany in the 19th century. The breed is descended from the Brabanter Bullenbeisser, which was used by huntsmen to bring down fleeing game animals. The boxer is an exceptionally muscular, powerful dog, so breeders are very careful to ensure that pups have a stable and resilient temperament.

Samoyed (top left)

Long ago, the Samoyed was used as a herdsman's dog by a nomadic Siberian people, after whom the dog is named. The Samoyed has a magnificent white or creamy coat, very thick even in a puppy and ideal for the cold winters of its Siberian homeland. It is often used nowadays as a sledge-dog.

(top right)

The most famous of all Samoyeds must be Sammy, one of the dogs taken by Roald Amundsen on his expedition to the South Pole. Because of their dense fur, it is only in cooler regions of the world that Samoyeds are well suited to be domestic pets. If the weather is warm, let alone hot, they suffer visibly. Their puppies too have a bad time if the weather is hot.

White German Shepherd Dog (right)

The very first White German Shepherd Dog was recorded in the German pedigree books back in 1913. However, it is mostly thanks to North American breeders that this breed still survives today. This is why it is now called the American-Canadian white shepherd dog. It is very good as a guide-dog for the blind, but for this work it has to be specially trained from puppyhood onwards.

Cavalier King Charles Spaniel *(left)*

Cavalier King Charles spaniels were already popular back in the 17th century — with aristocrats in England. As spaniels go, they are small — they weigh around 8 kg. They reached a peak of popularity at the royal court under King Charles I and later under Charles II. The puppies are of course smaller and lighter still, but — like all animals — they need firm, consistent rearing.

Hovawart *(right)*

The name 'Hovawart' tells us something about the dog, because what it means is roughly 'guardian of the farm-yard'. But to look at the puppies one would not think that such playful animals could ever grow into good watch-dogs. However, even its size is an asset to the hovawart as a watchdog.

Beagle *(below)*

The world's most famous beagle is almost certainly Snoopy in the 'Peanuts' comic strip. In fact all Snoopy has in common with real beagles is high intelligence and a lot of self-confidence. Small as they are, beagle pups need a very firm hand, otherwise they will lead their owners a merry dance.

Azawakh (above)

This pup is an azawakh, a greyhound once used in the African deserts by the Tuareg people. It is an unsuitable dog for anyone other than experienced greyhound-lovers, as it has a special combination of qualities. It must be given far more exercise than most dogs, and carefully trained so as to damp down its wild nature. And yet it is also a particularly sensitive dog and so must never be handled roughly.

Great Dane (left)

The big paws of the puppies give it away: the Great Dane is one of the biggest of all dog breeds, reaching 76 cm (dogs) and 71 cm (bitches) at the shoulder. This giant among dogs was first bred 400 years ago, for hunting wild boar. Today, most Great Danes are either companion dogs or watchdogs.

Lhasa Apso *(top left)*

Keeping Lhasa Apso dogs was once a strictly reserved activity – only Tibetan monks were allowed to have them. It wasn't until the 1920s that this dog, believed to bring good luck, was brought to Europe. It is now popular mainly as a family pet, partly because it is small, but almost certainly also because its puppies look like miniature teddy-bears.

Pug *(top right)*

Pugs have a reputation as particularly lovable and sweet-natured dogs. They originated in China, where they were palace dogs, and are said to have come to Europe some time around 1600. Over here, these fairly small – and not particularly energetic – dogs have won many friends. The pug does however have some problems with breathing, even as a puppy, because of its flat muzzle.

Parson Russell Terrier *(centre left)*

This is the new official name for the popular dog still most widely known as the Jack Russell terrier. These half-grown pups will not get any bigger than 35 cm even as adult dogs, but size is not the point: with their bouncy, quicksilver temperament they will turn any household upside down in no time. If Parson Russells are given lots of freedom to run around, at places like riding stables, for instance, they and their owners will be happy – otherwise, just expect aggro!

Greater Swiss Mountain Dog *(bottom left)*

The greater Swiss mountain dog's puppies are already quite compactly built and muscular. Used in the old days to haul carts for peasant farmers and itinerant pedlars, the greater Swiss mountain dog when fully grown reaches a body weight of 55–65 kg. As a rule it is very good with children and makes an excellent family pet.

95

Pomeranian *(right)*

These two Pomeranian puppies are only six weeks old. Fully grown, they will be 22 cm at the shoulder and weigh about 3 kg. From that point of view they are very suitable for keeping in smaller homes. On the other hand, as they are very alert and vocal in defending their territory, they may annoy the neighbours with their barking.

Short-haired Dachshund *(below)*

The dachshund, of which this photo shows the short-haired variety, is the smallest of the hunting dog breeds that originated in Germany. A newly born puppy will fit easily on the palm of an adult human hand. Small or not, dachshunds are very determined dogs, robust and fearless — they were after all bred to chase foxes out of their burrows.

Red Longhaired Dachshund *(top right)*

When these two red longhaired dachshund pups are grown up, they will have a long coat which lies flat on the body. They should have especially vigorous hair growth round their ears, legs and tail – the experts talk of these parts being well 'feathered' – but one disadvantage of the feathered legs is that they tend to bring in dirt from outside.

Wirehaired Dachshund *(top left)*

With its wiry badger-like coat, the wirehaired dachshund certainly looks the most robust of all the dachshund varieties. However, as one notices with this pair of pups, pedigree dogs of this variety too are expected to show 'attitude' in the way they hold themselves. If the pedigree is a strong one, and if they are to be entered for shows later, this starts early on.

(centre left)

This wirehaired dachshund is only two months old. Because of his short legs and disproportionately long back, he should not be allowed to go up and down stairs during his first months of life. That would put undue strain on his bone and muscle structure, and could cause health problems in later life. But he is a featherweight – so easy to just tuck under your arm!

Short-haired Dachshund *(bottom left)*

Dachshunds come in three varieties distinguished by the type of coat, and in each variety there are three sizes. These short-haired dachshund pups are still very small, but will reach Standard size; Dwarf dachshunds are a smaller variety, and so-called Rabbit dachshunds even smaller still.

Dalmatian (top left)

Ever since ˜01 little Dalmatians like these became film stars, the Dalmatian has been a breed of dog that everyone knows. And yet these striking white dogs with their black spots can be seen illustrated on very old paintings alongside horse-drawn coaches and people on horseback. They need a lot of exercise, and so are excellent companions for those who enjoy riding or cycling.

Cavalier King Charles Spaniel (centre left)

Cavalier King Charles spaniels are ideal family pets, easy to train and always ready for a game. Out walking, they don't pick fights with other dogs but just enjoy the exercise. And if their owner is busy, they will be quite happy to make do with a shorter walk. But it is important to take care over grooming their coat and checking their eyes and ears.

Gordon Setter (bottom left)

These two Gordon setter pups will mature relatively slowly into full-grown adult dogs and will then be powerful animals with a lot of self-confidence. As they are born with a very strong hunting instinct, it is essential to train them properly from the beginning. If this is not done, they will still hunt — but at random.

Cocker Spaniel (right-hand page, main picture)

Cocker spaniels were originally used for hunting snipe and woodcock. They still love finding and retrieving — a very useful characteristic in many sports involving dogs. The name 'spaniel' derives from old words for Spain and Spaniard.

(right-hand page, bottom left)

Anyone thinking of buying a cocker spaniel puppy like these should be very careful to choose a reliable breeder, because these playful, lively dogs are prone to a variety of nervous diseases. Healthy cockers are a joy to own, being quick learners and also friendly and cheerful as companions.

Miniature Schnauzer (right-hand page, bottom right)

These two Miniature schnauzer puppies are definitely not the dogs for anyone who wants peace and quiet — because they will develop into lively, self-confident doggy personalities who don't bark just for the doorbell, but to let everyone know their immediate plans and wants. If you like bouncy, vigorous dogs, you will love the Miniature schnauzer.

Rottweiler *(left-hand page, top)*

The Rottweiler derives its name from its town of origin — Rottweil, in south-west Germany. The dogs were used in the abattoirs there to help drive cattle before slaughter, and they were also handy for hauling loads: these massively-built animals pulled the small carts used for transporting goods. But the puppy in the photo is still enjoying just being a baby animal.

(left-hand page, bottom left)

Puppies like this little Rottweiler are always inquisitive. They are like small children, exploring their world, but doing it with their paws and their nose, their tongue and their teeth. There are bound to be unfortunate results sometimes for a shoe, a table-leg or a sofa. As Rottweilers can easily become over-dominant, it is very important to make sure that the puppies are taught obedience.

(left-hand page, bottom right)

If a Rottweiler pup goes to an experienced and good owner and receives consistent training and plenty of affection, he will pose no greater risk when fully grown than any other dog of 65 cm height and 45 kg weight. Rottweilers are faithful, equable and willing dogs. But to avoid any risk of mischief, they should not be allowed to get bored.

Husky *(top right)*

Husky pups captivate every human heart, with their almond-shaped eyes, mask-like face markings and cuddly fur. They grow up into fleet-footed medium-sized dogs with the stamina to run far and fast. But they must be given work to do: as sled-dogs, that is what they were bred for.

(centre right)

Huskies today are still fulfilling their traditional role as sled-dogs. In races involving several dogs hauling a sled, one of them will take on the role of leader and the others go where the leader goes. It is good for the puppies if they can run together a lot while playing, as it builds up the muscles they will need.

(right)

This Husky pup is eight weeks old and so is likely to be separated from its mother during the next four weeks and handed over to a human owner. This is the best time for the transfer, as the puppy is no longer dependent on its mother's milk, and has reached the phase where imprinting on the human owner is strongest.

Bernese Mountain Dog (above)

This little Bernese mountain cross is a mere five weeks old, still too young to be parted from its mother. That needs to wait until the pup reaches eight weeks. But of course he is not too young to explore his surroundings, venturing a bit further every day.

(centre right)

Bernese mountain puppies like this one love being outdoors, playing and dashing around. However, it is important to prevent young Berners from over-exerting themselves, as this could cause mobility problems in later life. They should also not be forced to exercise when the weather is hot, but allowed to take it easy.

(bottom right)

This panting doggy bundle is a Bernese mountain dog puppy, so he belongs to a popular and easily managed breed of dog — which does, however, require quite a lot of space. Bernese mountain dogs were typically found on farms, where they would normally have watchdog duties, but they were also taken on journeys for their reliable companionship, and yet another job for them was to pull small carts.

Briard (right-hand page, top)

They look like three little balls of wool, these young briards (the breed is also called Berger de Brie) — as if they could not possibly get up to mischief. They are in fact an exceptionally spirited breed of dog, formerly used as a sheepdog. Now that briards have no working role but are only kept as pets, they are not always given enough to keep them occupied — and that can cause a certain amount of chaos in the households concerned!

Pembroke Welsh Corgi

(right-hand page, bottom left)

These tiny Welsh corgi pups will eventually reach about 30 cm at the shoulder and weigh about 11 kg. That makes them ideal dogs for city-dwellers, but on the other hand they are very self-willed, so it is essential to be absolutely consistent in how you train them. This means the corgi is not a suitable dog for a child, nor for anyone new to having a dog.

(right-hand page, bottom right)

This pocket-sized dog will not grow to more than 30 cm shoulder height, but nonetheless a dog for experienced owners only. That is because the Pembroke Welsh corgi was bred for guarding and herding livestock, and its technique for moving cattle along is to nip at their heels. This biting or snapping trait sometimes comes through in corgis sold as pets.

Labrador Retriever *(top left)*

The labrador retriever gets the second part of its name from what it does, namely 'retrieve', or 'bring back', which it does superbly. But it is mostly just called a 'labrador' or even 'lab'. This labrador bitch, seen here suckling her two pups, will enjoy bringing back sticks thrown for her — when she can get time off from her duties as mother.

(top centre)

The labrador's most important qualities are curiosity, friendliness and loyalty. It was originally bred mainly to help hunters who were out after waterfowl. It has a water-repellent undercoat which helps keep it warm after a plunge, even in winter weather. Labrador pups are like all other pups — bouncy and full of fun.

(right-hand page, top right)

At present, labrador retrievers and their puppies are becoming ever more popular, because they are so versatile and because of their rock-steady, unflappable temperament. They are indeed affectionate, cuddly family pets — with a tendency to overeat — but beyond that they also make good guide-dogs and rescue-dogs, and do first-rate work in drug detection and in hunting game. They need thorough, consistent training.

(left-hand page, bottom left)

Labradors love play. This black lab puppy is having fun with a mere stick. But he will find it much more fun if there are two to play, and one can see he will soon be looking for a human playmate. As dogs go, labradors are not hard to look after, but you do have to give them plenty of your time.

Golden Retriever *(bottom centre)*

With those appealing eyes, even adult golden retrievers can melt hearts — let alone the puppies. When grown up, they are still excellent family pets and very good with children. They love play and running about, so are naturals for many sports involving dogs. Unfortunately, there has been mass breeding of Goldies in recent years, and this has led to health problems in many of them.

Pyrenean Mountain Dog *(bottom right)*

Even these young Pyrenean mountain dog puppies have a coat so thick that you can see this French breed was a specialised animal intended for work in high, cold mountain regions. These white-furred giants were originally used by simple herdsmen in the Pyrenees, where France ends and Spain begins. But they were so handsome that it was not long before aristocrats and the wealthy middle-class were wanting them as companions and pets.

Greenland Sledge Dog *(above)*

This Greenland sledge bitch and her two pups belong to the last remaining purebred Inuit breed of dogs — a breed traced back for no less than 4000 years. These dogs can do without water if necessary, as they can eat snow instead. They can go for long periods on nothing but deep-frozen food, and sometimes haul the sledge for days without any food.

German Shepherd Dog *(right)*

This German shepherd pup may be destined for an exciting life of teamwork with humans. German shepherds are now used less as watchdogs, more as guide dogs for people with special needs, and as sniffer dogs in avalanche rescue and police and security work. No machine yet invented can match a German shepherd dog in detecting the presence of concealed drugs, explosives or human bodies.

106

Leonberger (top left)

A really big dog when fully grown, the Leonberger takes its name from the town of Leonberg in Germany. Even in puppy-hood the Leonberger has a certain resemblance to a lion, though a very small one. Some of these dogs have a tawny yellow skin colour, and they are the ones that come near-est to looking like a lion. Others have a red or reddish brown or sandy-coloured coat.

Miniature Poodle (top right)

These are puppies of the intermediate-sized poodle, referred to as the Miniature poodle. Even when fully grown, they stand no more than 35 cm at the shoulder and weigh only up to 7 kg. Their small size makes them just right for home pets. In addition, they are intelligent and quick to learn. With their lively ways and appealing eyes, poodles bring a lot of pleasure.

Pomeranian (centre right)

Originally this breed came from Pomerania, in north-eastern Germany, but for many years it was mainly in English-speak-ing countries that Pomeranians were kept and bred — so much so that back in Germany it is now often called a 'Pomeranian' even though it has a proper German name: 'Zwergspitz'. Its tightly-curled puppy coat develops into thick fur.

English Bulldog (bottom right)

The English bulldog puppy on the grass here has something of a laidback air, typical enough of his breed, because the adult dogs too like to take it easy. They are not very keen on long walks or vigorous games, but always appreciate being cuddled or stroked. The English bulldog's particular bone structure can give rise to some health problems, so it is important to buy only from a reputable breeder.

Crossbreed *(above)*

In this little dog, a cross between Australian shepherd dog and Border collie, the two breeds that have been combined are both very strongly associated with guarding and herding livestock. So from both sides of its ancestry this is very much a working dog who would be an ideal choice as a sheepdog — but would almost certainly be unhappy if he were just kept as a family pet.

(below)

Whenever humans get slack about supervision or fail to keep control, dogs are quick to take advantage. Here a dog and a bitch have mated to produce six fine healthy cross-bred pups guaranteed to give their future owners lots of pleasure, regardless of having no pedigree certificate to show off. And part of the interest is not knowing what they will look like when they get older.

Pekingese *(right-hand page, bottom left)*

The Pekingese dog came from China originally, and is said to be an extremely ancient breed of dog. It used to be kept and bred exclusively in the Imperial Palace there. Even today it still retains its imperious ways, too: it is very difficult to train, can be stroked only if it is in the mood — and if it is not in the mood, it will bite in a flash.

English Springer Spaniel *(above left)*

The English springer spaniel is the ancestral breed that all other hunting spaniels descend from, and it is still bred today, in two separate lines, as a hunting dog and as a companion dog. But no matter whether he is from the hunting line or the pet line, this little fellow will need a lot of exercise and different activities. One that he will certainly delight in is retrieving things thrown for him to run after.

Boxer *(top right)*

The picture of docile good behaviour as they sit here in the field, these boxer puppies will remain beautifully behaved — provided that they go on receiving careful training. Boxers are extremely good with children and as family pets, happy to play for hours on end. They do need plenty of activity and are good when used in practical roles such as protecting their owner, also in various sports.

Shiba Inu *(above right)*

Originally, the shiba inu was a Japanese dog like a Pomeranian and used in hunting. This can be seen in ancient drawings, and it also fits in with the name of shiba inu, which means 'little bush-dog'. North America played a major role in perpetuating the breed. Its pups are lively and enjoy the outdoors — like this one, eagerly begging for a game in the snow.

French Brittany Spaniel (left)

At some time not too far ahead, this French Brittany spaniel puppy will have become a first-rate pointer, unerring in tracking game, and then pointing to show the hunters where to look. The breed is often called by its French name of Epagneul Breton, and the dogs it produces are not suitable as pets, being pure hunting dogs.

(bottom left)

If the hunter trains this Brittany spaniel well, it will help him by finding and fetching downed waterfowl which have fallen somewhere out of sight. It is known for its acute sense of smell, and it loves the water. At the same time, it is said to have a very sensitive disposition and to need gentle handling and lots of affection while being trained.

Chow Chow (bottom right)

The chow chow's blue tongue, clearly seen on the pups in the photo, and its thick fur are two of the main breed characteristics. Its name means 'tasty, tasty', and is a reminder of the fact that in their original homeland of China these dogs used to feature on dinner menus precisely because of their tongue, which was regarded as a delicacy.

Artesian Norman Basset (right-hand page, top)

The Artesian Norman basset is the ancestral French form of the basset hound, popular in Britain. Head, body and paws are as big as those of any long-legged hunting dog, but the legs are distinctly short — the pups will never grow above 35 cm in height. Hunters used to find this low-slung hunting dog easier to follow than bigger breeds.

Siberian Husky (right-hand page, bottom)

The Siberian (or Arctic) Husky with its thick fur is excellently adapted to wintry conditions and loves the snow. It was the Eskimos who first bred this dog, and it became so precious to them that they would bring it into their sleeping accommodation while leaving other sledge dogs outside.

Pygmy Goat *(top left)*

The kids of the pygmy goat (two are seen here with their mother) get up on their feet a mere 20 minutes after being born. Usually they will then immediately seek their mother's udder for a drink of milk. But she will not generally let them suckle until she has licked them clean. When the kids first try to walk, their mother will usually give them a few nudges to help them get going.

Angora Goat *(bottom left)*

Angora goats come from Turkey, or more precisely from the one-time Turkish province of Angora, now called Ankara. The first and second shearings of the kid yield an exceptionally fine wool known as kid mohair.

Domestic Goat *(right-hand page, top left)*

The goat *(Capra aegagrus hircus)* is thought to have been kept as a domestic animal for more than 9000 years. Probably the nannies were milked to feed humans even then, once the kids had been weaned. A modern nanny-goat will give about 1000 litres of milk per year, some of course considerably more.

(right-hand page, top centre)

In Europe, agricultural use of the goat is currently increasing. Goat cheese is becoming ever more popular, and goat milk and goat meat are finding an increasing number of enthusiastic customers. As goats are very frugal animals, they can be kept even where the landscape is relatively barren. There are usually two kids in a litter, but it is not all that rare for four to be born at once.

(right-hand page, top right)

Goats come in a host of different varieties; these two are a Boer goat and a pygmy goat. As its name suggests, the pygmy goat is distinctively small. At the withers it will measure at most 48 cm. The Boer goat is a meat goat, that is to say it is bred largely for the sake of its meat.

(right-hand page, main picture)

It will be about another 18 months before this tiny kid reaches reproductive maturity. At that stage it will also be fully grown, and will be distinctly heavier than now, as adult goats, depending on breed, weigh in at anything between 30 and 80 kg. Goats are happiest living in a herd, but they can also be kept individually.

Domestic Goat *(top left)*

Even the kids of the domestic goat *(Capra aegagrus hircus)* are very surefooted, which is one reason why the goat is so often kept in mountainous areas as a domestic animal. Believed to have been first domesticated in Persia or Palestine, it is now at home all over Europe. A kid weighs about 4 kg at birth, and for its first three months of life is fed solely on its mother's milk.

Wild Goat *(top right)*

The wild goat *(Capra hircus)* can be found almost all over the world. New Zealand and Australia in particular have large herds. The distinguishing features of the wild goat are its exceptionally long horns and its long coat, which does a superb job of keeping it warm even when the weather is cold. In young goats, of course, it still needs time to become really dense.

Smooth-haired Guinea Pig *(below)*

Popular as domestic pets, smooth-haired guinea pigs *(Cavia aperea porcellus)* came to Europe in the 16th century, from South America. In their homeland they had been kept in people's homes since about 3000 years ago. The young are born relatively well able to fend for themselves. They have their eyes open when born, and can already cope with solid food, though they are also suckled concurrently.

European White Stork (top left)

When European white stork chicks (Ciconia ciconia) first hatch, they look quite lost in their little downy coat in the middle of the great big nest. But that does not last long. At three weeks old they can stand on their long yellow legs, and after two months they take to the air, though the parents still supervise for another three weeks after that.

(top right)

White storks, regarded since mediaeval times as bringers of good luck, like to nest on roofs and chimneys. In April/May they lay up to four eggs in their great, cartwheel-like nest, and incubate them for a month until the chicks hatch. By autumn, the young storks must have learnt to fly well, because that is when their journey south to Africa begins.

Guinea Pig (left)

It is extremely difficult to determine the sex of a guinea pig, particularly if the animal is young. This point has been brought home to a large number of guinea pig fans, who have found themselves suddenly landed with unwanted guinea pig progeny. One needs to know that guinea pigs reach sexual maturity in only six weeks, and this means taking early action to separate males from females.

Common Kestrel (top)

These young kestrels *(Falco tinnunculus)* are being looked after and fed by both parents. At first the older birds bring them insects, later on it will be larger animals like reptiles or mice. The kestrel is Europe's most widely distributed raptor. It nests in the abandoned nests of crows, in barns, nesting-boxes, odd nooks in churches and industrial buildings, and once in a while even in a window box.

(above left)

Female kestrels are quite content to lay their reddish-brown, marbled eggs even in nest boxes like this one. Usually they lay from four to six eggs, but on this occasion only two developed fully. The chicks have baby plumage of fluffy white down, but when they grow up they will be brown, with a black tail, and about 36 cm long.

(above right)

These two kestrel chicks are only a fortnight old, and will need as long again before they are ready to fly. Even then they will keep returning to the nest for a while, until they are fully independent and able to survive alone. But first they have to learn to hunt.

Domestic Cat *(top left)*

The adult domestic cat *(Felis silvestris f. catus)* will only turn over to lie on its back in the presence of a human it knows well – because this is a gesture of submission. Young cats behave quite differently, lying down in that position just for fun, then gambolling around, essentially just trying out their young bodies to see what they are capable of.

(left centre)

A tomcat knows through his acute sense of smell when a female cat even several hundred yards away is ready for mating – 'on heat'. Once fertilisation has taken place, it will be 65 days before the kittens are born. An average litter has four young, initially both blind and deaf. Their eyes open after a further eight to ten days.

(below)

Domestic cats notoriously seem to have no difficulty reproducing, often bringing forth charming kittens like this one. Planned breeding of cats is much more difficult. Self-willed and solitary by nature, cats often find ways to forestall the arranged fertilisation of the pedigree cat by the particular pedigree male which the humans have selected for her.

European Shorthair Cat (top left)

It was only as recently as 1982 that the European shorthair gained recognition in Europe as a distinct breed of cat in its own right. Up to then, although bred separately for many years past, it had always been regarded as a subspecies of the British shorthair — and that is exactly how it is still regarded by the cat-breeder organisations of the rest of the world, outside Europe. We can be thankful the breeders' problems don't worry the playing kitten.

Abyssinian Cat (top right)

The Abyssinian cat, often just 'the Abyssinian', had its origins in Ethiopia and there was bred from Ethiopian domestic and street cats, completely avoiding cross-breeding with any other species. It is an inquisitive cat, and never really loses its kittenish playfulness even as an adult. It insists on its quota of stroking and fondling and becomes very attached to its human 'family'.

British Shorthair Cat (right)

Go-ahead by nature like all members of the British shorthair breed, this kitten is climbing on an old tree-trunk, having perhaps spotted a bird and wanting a chase. Its elegant blue is the classical colour for the breed, although British shorthairs are also found with coats of every possible different colour and shading.

Domestic Cat *(below left)*

Young kittens should be suckled by their mother for six weeks before being weaned. It only takes six to eight weeks for them to become sexually mature themselves. As uncontrolled breeding by cats can lead to them becoming a pest, animal-lovers are increasingly adopting the practice of neutering cats to protect them from malnutrition and mistreatment.

(below right)

A domestic cat allowed outside like this kitten will never have a problem finding something to do. But a kitten kept indoors needs something to keep it occupied. If this is not provided by its owners, it will choose its own activities and scratch at furniture, doors and walls. That can be avoided: the owners simply need to play with their kitten regularly and provide a few suitable toys.

(bottom)

For any domestic kitten, a wall is a fine place to spy out 'prey' — which could as well be a windblown ball of wool as a mouse or a butterfly. The key point is that the thing, whatever it is, is moving — that is what excites the hunting instinct in all cats. And feeding the cat does nothing to diminish that instinct.

Colourpoint Longhair *(top left)*

This kitten's long furry coat is good protection against the cold of winter. However, cats of its breed, the colourpoint longhair (in the U.S. it is also called the Himalayan cat), are mainly kept as domestic pussies to cuddle in the family home. It is a role they are well suited for, as they have a serene and friendly disposition. One point to remember is that their long coat requires a lot of grooming.

(centre left)

In some European countries, the colourpoint longhair was known up to the late 1950s as the 'Khmer cat', because it was the result of crossing Persian with Siamese cats. The breed's special feature consists in its so-called 'points': the ears, paws, nose and tail are of a darker shade than the body, but this difference only develops gradually over time.

Maine Coon *(bottom left)*

Only nine weeks old, this Maine Coon kitten already has quite thick and long fur — the Maine Coon breed originated in a cold climate. In spite of its luxuriance, the Maine Coon's fur does not need particularly careful grooming, and it is also water-repellent. And that is a decided advantage in regions where it rains a lot.

(right-hand page, main picture)

The red-hued baby cat perched so appealingly on the stones is a Maine Coon of the colour variety known as red tabby. In judging this cat as a purebred, distinct from any ordinary domestic or street cat, breeders insist that the reddish hue must be a deep red-brown.

(right-hand page, bottom left)

A very old North American breed, the Maine Coon is a relatively large and heavy cat. It is not uncommon for a fully-grown tom to weigh as much as 9 kg. However, it takes Maine Coons about three years — longer than other breeds — to grow from kittenhood to full size.

(right-hand page, bottom right)

This Maine Coon kitten will one day be someone's robust yet gentle companion — not, however, of the kind that wants to be indulged and spoiled. In general the Maine Coon has a dignified and calm demeanour, but it does break into a very distinctive, joyful-sounding mewing when greeting someone, for its admirers a sure sign of the breed.

Persian Cat *(left-hand page, top)*

Persian (or Angora) kittens already have their soft, wavy, long fur coat when they are born, so naturally they look like tiny balls of fur. Persians are bred in almost all colours. The best-known and most sought-after Persian cats are the white ones, but there are others with blue, red or cream-coloured fur.

(left-hand page, bottom left)

The hallmark of the Persian cat is its round, flat face. It is the reason why even adult cats have an almost human, childlike look — probably the main reason for the popularity of this breed. Unfortunately, the flattened nose is associated with a constriction of the tear ducts and nasal passages, and this in turn causes health problems in some Persians.

(left-hand page, bottom right)

This Persian kitten is doing exactly what its owners expect of it: sitting looking at its surroundings. Once it is fully grown, its exceptionally long fur will have to be brushed at least once a day — preferably more often than that — to prevent it from matting. To get round this, some owners just have their Persian's coat clipped short.

(top left)

Like all cats, Persian kittens are real little predators. When they dart after a ball of wool or a spider, and pounce on it, they are training for future hunts — in which the quarry will be small mammals or birds. However, most Persians are prevented from living out their natural hunting instincts, because they are generally kept indoors.

Shorthaired Cat *(centre left)*

More often encountered and more popular than the aristocratic pedigree cats are ordinary common-or-garden shorthair cats — of which this pocket tiger, surveying the world from his branch, is an example. If he spots something interesting down below, it will be nothing at all to him to be down in one bound. It is only in exceptional cases that the fire-brigade has to come with a long ladder and rescue a kitten from its tree.

Siamese Cat *(bottom left)*

The first time a Siamese cat was exhibited at a public cat show was in 1871. The special features of this breed are not just its silky fur and elegant body structure, because Siamese always retain the blue eye colour with which they were born. At most, the blue of their eyes becomes a little darker with the passing of time.

Somali Cat (left)

The Somali cat, also known as the Longhaired Abyssinian, is a relatively new breed, which became known only at the end of the 1960s. But it soon won many admirers. Somali cats are very affectionate animals, yet they also have a great love of freedom. So whenever possible, even as kittens, they should be allowed out regularly to experience the outdoors.

(bottom left)

These two Somali kittens are enjoying each other's company: the Somali is a highly sociable breed. Its alternative name of Longhaired Abyssinian indicates that it was bred from the Abyssinian cat — which was a short-haired breed but from time to time produced long-haired progeny. These then were systematically mated to produce exclusively long-haired descendants.

Siberian Cat (below)

As its name suggests, this cat originated in Siberia. The winters there are cold, and this breed of cat has an exceptionally thick layer of underwool as insulation against the low temperatures. The young of the Siberian cat are born 60 to 70 days after conception, and even then their fur is already quite thick.

Domestic Cat *(right)*

A newly born kitten is tiny enough to fit in the palm of your hand. Its little paws are still quite pink and soft underneath — it is only as the cat grows older that its pads become darker and quite leathery and tough. All the same, no matter how tiny the kitten, it will have sharp claws which one needs to look out for. Babies or not, they can scratch.

(below)

The ancestor of our domestic cat is the wild African cat, which kept human company back in the time of ancient Egypt. The cat's long success story with humans is mostly due to its ability as a hunter of rats and mice. But other things too helped make its success — its looks and its appealing ways. Who can meet the wide-eyed gaze of a kitten and stay unmoved?

(left-hand page, bottom right)

Young kittens love to play, and the ideal toy is something that moves when they put a paw to it, like a ball, or some rolled-up wool. They dart after it and try to grab it. This is how the kittens' play prepares them for hunting mice and other small mammals later on.

Bengal Cat (below)

This sturdy-looking kitten with its dense fur is a scion of the fairly recent breed known as the Bengal. It was bred by interbreeding the wild Bengal cat, which is a native of Asia, with ordinary domestic cats, the Egyptian Mau and Indian street cats – and in some individuals the wild cat element in the Bengal breed comes through clearly.

Siberian Forest Cat (above left)

Looking at these luxuriantly furred kittens as they sit on their mossy log, one gets the impression right away that they are well protected against cold. The Siberian forest cat is in fact a 'natural' breed. The coat has both a strong outer covering layer and warm underwool, and it is both dense to keep out the cold and naturally oily to keep out the rain – and it was Nature that 'bred' the cats this way.

Norwegian Forest Cat (above right)

This Norwegian forest kitten will in time prove itself a true heir to its forebears, the peasant cats of Norway, for it will be just as keen a hunter of mice and birds – and maybe more, as some of these cats will scoop fish out of ponds and streams. If you own a Norwegian forest cat you could have a spot of bother with your neighbours over certain activities at their garden pond...

(above left)

The little tufts at the tip of the Norwegian forest cat's ears make it look like a lynx in miniature. There was a time before these cats associated with people at all — they lived in Norway's forests, and that is why they got their present name. Even the tiniest kittens still have a faint suggestion of wildcat in their appearance.

(above right)

If the Norwegian forest kitten is a tom and grows to full maturity it may tip 9 kg on the scales. But it will still be in perfect balance when it climbs or perches in trees, because a highly developed sense of balance is one of the cat's prime qualities. And even if it should fall off once in a while, a reflex movement will right it in the air so that it is not injured on landing.

(below)

This little Norwegian forest kitten — a red-and-white bicolour — demonstrates well how the cats of this breed enjoy home comforts no less than they love prowling the woods and fields. For a very young animal, a cosy corner to sleep in and feel safe in is specially important — and the leg of a pair of jeans will do just fine.

Turkish Angora Cat *(top left)*

To look at this black kitten, a Turkish Angora, as it poses here, you would think it was the cat equivalent of a lapdog, there to be petted and look beautiful. But appearances deceive. In reality the cats of this long-haired breed are very vigorous, fast-moving and playful. As they are also very vocal, and strong-willed too, they usually get what they want.

Ragdoll *(bottom left)*

Ragdoll cats are born with a pink nose, pink ears and white fur. Soon the fur begins to get darker in certain areas (called 'points') — the ears, the mask, legs and tail. Later on the rest of the fur usually also grows darker. The classical colours for the Ragdoll's 'points' are described as 'seal-brown' and 'blue'.

Somali Cat *(above)*

These five Somali cats, all from the same litter, are being reared as their breed characteristics require — they are allowed plenty of time outdoors for climbing trees and other activities. They have the colour of wild animals and because of it are sometimes called the 'fox cat'. But, more important, they also behave in many ways like wild cats, and are very keen hunters.

Exotic Shorthair *(left)*

At first sight the round teddy-bear face of this pair suggests a litter of Persian kittens. But cat experts will see that their fur is not nearly long enough for that. They are in fact representatives of the relatively new exotic shorthair cat, which is hard to breed and correspondingly uncommon. It was bred from a combination of Persian, American shorthair and British shorthair cats.

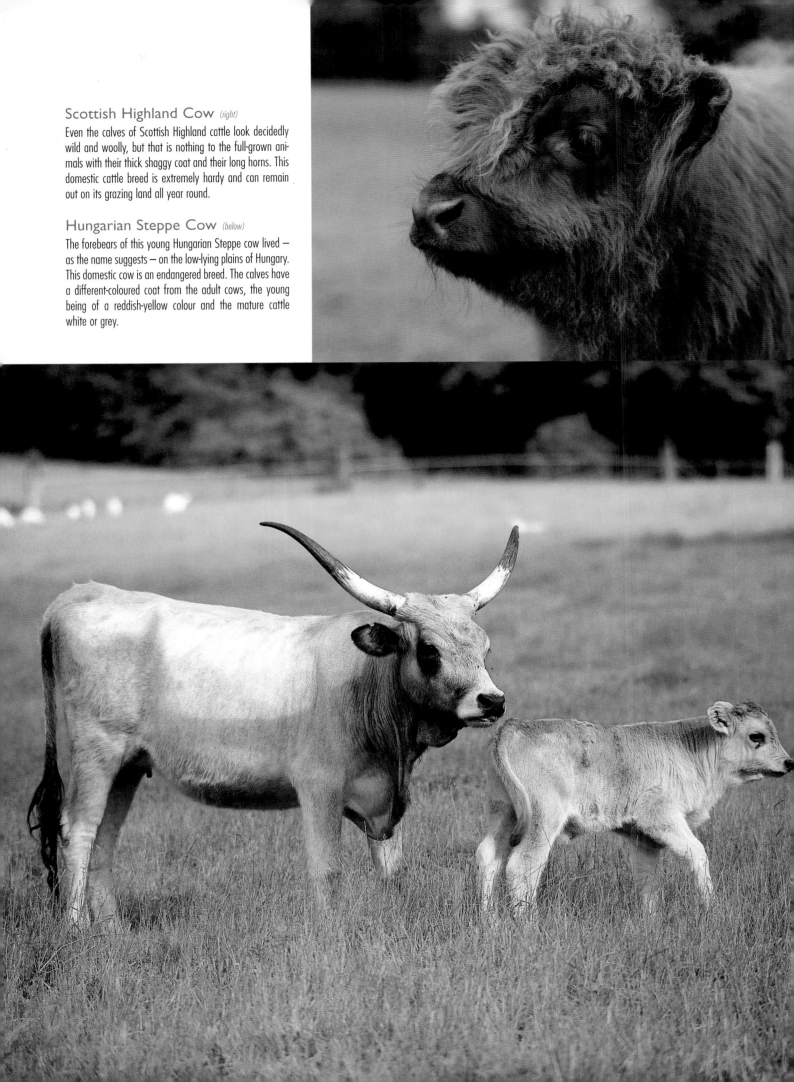

Scottish Highland Cow (right)

Even the calves of Scottish Highland cattle look decidedly wild and woolly, but that is nothing to the full-grown animals with their thick shaggy coat and their long horns. This domestic cattle breed is extremely hardy and can remain out on its grazing land all year round.

Hungarian Steppe Cow (below)

The forebears of this young Hungarian Steppe cow lived – as the name suggests – on the low-lying plains of Hungary. This domestic cow is an endangered breed. The calves have a different-coloured coat from the adult cows, the young being of a reddish-yellow colour and the mature cattle white or grey.

Scottish Highland Cow (top right)

This Highland calf belongs to one of the very oldest and least interfered-with domestic cattle breeds found anywhere in Europe: these shaggy brown meat animals reproduced through centuries without ever being crossed with other breeds. Mature animals have long, slightly upswung horns, and look distinctly like the aurochs, the now extinct progenitor of all domestic cattle.

Domestic Cow (top left)

A cow has to have had her first calf before she can give milk – because it is giving birth to the calf that produces the hormones that in turn ensure the cow's udder will fill with milk. A cow can still give milk for a long time after the calf is weaned, provided she is milked regularly.

(centre left)

Although, looking at this calf, one might not think so, domestic cattle are descended from the aurochs or urus, the last stocks of which were wiped out in the 17th century. In many modern farming businesses, the production of calves is no longer a natural process, as most of them are the result of artificial insemination.

(bottom left)

Up to about five months, the young of domestic cattle are called calves. Above that age, they were sometimes called 'grassers', probably because they get through a lot of grass before becoming productive. The term 'stirk' is now more commonly used. A heifer is a young female cow. A bull is always an uncastrated male, while 'ox' sometimes means a castrated male and is sometimes just a term for a bovine (cattle-family) animal, especially one used as a beast of burden.

131

German Angus Cow *(top left)*

The German Angus cow, illustrated here, one of the domestic breeds, is a particularly good beef animal, and consequently becoming ever more popular with breeders. German Anguses are very often kept out on the fields and also often calve in the open. Bull calves for fattening, like this one, gain weight at about 1 kg per day.

(top centre)

The original Angus was the Aberdeen Angus, which originated somewhere around the year 1800 in the Scottish county of Aberdeenshire. The Aberdeen Angus is a black hornless beast. The calves are relatively light, with a birth weight of 35 kg, but grow very rapidly and reach sexual maturity at two years old.

Holstein-Jersey Cross Cow *(top right)*

Holstein and Jersey cows — the photo shows a young Holstein-Jersey cross — are excellent milkers and bred for their quality as dairy cows. They are among the breeds of cow which calve with relatively few problems, and this is certainly one of the reasons for their popularity with farmers. Holsteins are the most numerous breed of all, worldwide.

Hereford Cow *(centre right)*

Red cow with a white head — those are the most obvious marks of the Hereford, which is mainly found on Irish farms. Herefords are hardier than most other breeds of cattle, and spend most of the year in the open air. This means that many of the calves are reared by their mothers.

Charolais Cow *(bottom right)*

Charolais look rather wild and primitive with their shaggy yellowish or whitish coats. As their name may suggest, they were first bred in France — near the town of Charolles. On good fodder the calves will grow very fast: gains of up to 1.4 kg daily are standard. At the beginning, of course, they are suckled by the mother cow. Charolais make excellent mothers.

Shetland Pony *(below left)*

Hailing originally from the Shetland Islands, the Shetland pony is a very strong and hardy animal in spite of its small size (up to 1.09 m / 10.2 hands at the withers), and can reach the age of 35. The mares can be in season at any time of the year. If a mare has been successfully covered, she will give birth to – usually – a single foal about eleven months later.

(below right)

Not long after they are born, Shetland foals have become as big as their parents – though as they only stand about 1 m at the shoulder one might well say 'as small as their parents'. But such rapid growth is exhausting for the foal, and it needs to be able to rest a lot. Usually it will lie down flat on its side on the ground, and its mother will stand nearby.

Black Forest Draught Horse *(bottom right)*

Back in the 1970s, the Black Forest draught horse was almost completely out of favour for breeding. In the early years of that decade, only 30 foals were born. But fortunately the award of grants designed to support conservation of the species proved sufficient to ensure the survival of this ancient, sorrel-coloured breed. The animals are used mainly as coach- or carriage-horses.

European Domestic Horse *(top left)*

The European domestic horse is thought to be descended from several different types of wild horse, specifically the steppe tarpan, the forest tarpan, and Przewalski's horse. Horses are among the animals that, when attacked, prefer flight rather than fight, and this is why they are among the few mammals that can sleep standing up. Foals learn at a very early age from their mothers that in a dangerous situation it is best to run for it.

Icelandic Pony *(centre left)*

In their native land, Icelandic ponies grow up half-wild, and generally have to survive the hard, bitterly cold winter without human help. This is something that cattle cannot do, and so these truly tough ponies are used by the Icelanders not only as working horses and mounts, but to supply meat.

Norwegian Fjord Horse *(bottom left)*

The Norwegian fjord horse and the Celtic pony are believed to be the ancestors of the Icelandic pony. This fjord horse, raised in Iceland, will need quite a long time to develop to maturity, and should not be ridden before it is four or even five years old. Only then will its bone structure be strong enough to take a rider without damage.

(right, main picture)

The fjord horse, whose homeland is Norway, is one of the world's very oldest breeds of horse. One of its most striking features is that it usually has a dark line (called the dorsal stripe or eel stripe) running down the middle of its back from the head to the tail. Fjords are happiest living in the open, and even young foals are naturally adapted to cope with the harsh Norwegian climate.

Polo Pony *(bottom centre)*

So-called polo ponies are not actually a breed in their own right. Wherever polo is played — it's a bit like hockey on horseback with long croquet mallets instead of sticks — suitable ponies have to be found locally. But a polo pony's foals are left in peace for the first four years of their life, until their bones are mature and strong enough for them to begin polo training.

Welsh Mountain Pony *(bottom far right)*

These ponies come from Wales, where — as their name indicates — they were at home in the mountains. They would also have been a familiar sight on upland moors. At about 1.2 metres (12 hands) in height, they are fairly small animals and most suited to children as riders. Their foals, in comparison to foals of other breeds, tend to look like miniature horses.

Haflinger *(above)*

From its homeland in the mountains of South Tyrol, the Haflinger began to conquer the whole of Europe from the end of the 19th century onwards. It became enormously popular everywhere, especially as a riding horse, but also as a general working horse, and it is still in great demand today for leisure riding and as a family pet. In the 1990s breeding standards became more rigorous, with the result that fewer Haflinger foals are now being born.

(centre right)

This Haflinger foal is one of the lucky ones — it was bred to become, later on, a mount for recreational riders or perhaps to be harnessed in front of a carriage. It is sad to have to record that many Haflinger foals are simply slaughtered soon after birth so that their mothers' milk can be sold for good money as mares' milk — because mares, unlike cows, only produce milk for a short while after giving birth.

(bottom right)

As little as half an hour after it is born, the foal can run about and even gallop. The gallop is its fastest way of covering the ground, and is not a succession of steps at all, but a succession of bounds or leaps. On hard ground they are clearly audible as a regularly recurring triple beat. The distance a really big horse covers in each of these leaps can be anything from 4.35 m to 8 m. Doing this at speed, it is really travelling.

(top left)

Beside its mother, whose height at shoulder is about 1.4 m (14 hands), the Haflinger foal looks quite big already. In terms of size, Haflingers are still small enough to count as ponies rather than horses, even though most Haflinger riders are adult. These horses are robust and willing, and they also have a reputation for being exceptionally surefooted. These qualities help explain why they have long been used by the Swiss army to help with transport and communications in the Alps.

Przewalski's Horse (bottom left)

In the wild, Przewalski's horse *(Equus przewalskii caballus)* became extinct around 1970. That could have been the end of this ancient wild horse, but fortunately it proved possible to keep the line going by breeding from captive animals. Eventually, a herd of them was released in the wild again, in Mongolia. Their young are born in spring.

Foal (bottom right)

If the weather is good, a foal can be allowed outside on the second day after it is born. It needs to be allowed to run about freely in the paddock with its mother, as this makes an important contribution both to its general development and to ensuring it is robust and hardy. If horses are kept in the open year-round — with ponies, this is quite common practice — the mares will often foal out in the open.

Exmoor Pony *(top left)*

Like many other mammals, horses with an itchy place their hooves can't reach will seek out something solid to scratch themselves on or rub against. It might be a fence, or the door or wall of the stable, or it could be another horse or even a human being. This Exmoor pony found itself a suitable tree.

Foal *(bottom left)*

Will this foal grow into a good, physically sound riding horse? That depends on a lot of things. It will need decent living conditions, its training needs to be loving, consistent and appropriate to its breed — but its heredity matters too. Responsible breeders take care when selecting parents to look beyond performance and appearance and insist on the vital attributes of good temperament and physical health.

(right-hand page, top left)

For the first few weeks, a newly born foal will have a very dense, very soft and woolly coat. The mane and tail are still short and curly. The yearling's coat looks shaggy and thick, but fully-grown horses have smooth skins and long hair.

Lusitano *(right-hand page, centre left)*

The Lusitano foal and its mother here belong to a typical Portuguese breed of horse, one that is often seen as a counterpart to the Spanish breed known as the Andalusian. Both were in fact originally bred as cavalry horses, and then later on they were used in agriculture. Of the two, Lusitanos have more Arab blood in their make-up, and have longer legs.

Arabian Horse *(right-hand page, bottom left)*

Biologists reckon the Arabian (or Arab) horse is one of the oldest of all breeds of horse, as it was already in existence around 3000 BC. These noble, strongly muscled animals are mainly sought after as riding-horses. For pedigree foals, horse-lovers pay very large sums.

(right-hand page, main picture)

This Arab foal is already showing his mother's fine head, with the big nostrils and the inward curve of the nose line. The expressive eyes and the small, pointed ears reflect every sensory impression registered by these spirited but gentle-natured horses.

Hanoverian Horse (top left)

For a while yet, this foal will be able to rest for as long as he likes. That will all change when he reaches maturity, because as a Hannoveraner he belongs to probably the most successful of all breeds in competitive horse events. The breed's success is of course in part the result of its outstanding sporting capability, but is also due to its willingness to work, and its sound temperament.

Boulonnais (above)

The Boulonnais breed, to which this horse and her foal belong, has its home in the north-west of France. It is considered to be probably the elite breed among all cold-bloods: its breeding history can be traced right back to Roman times and Julius Caesar. Today, however, this historic animal is hardly bred any longer except to supply meat to the butchery trade.

Palomino (right)

When they gallop together across a field, Palominos look like a golden wave sweeping along. For a horse to be a Palomino, its coat has to have a specific bright gold-red-brown colour, and the mane and tail must be white. 'Palomino' is not a breed name, just a description, as the required colours may be found in horses of a number of different breeds.

New Forest Pony *(above)*

The New Forest home of these ponies lies in the south-west corner of Hampshire. The New Forest breed was recognised as long ago as 1016 and so is nearly 1000 years old. The foals are stud-reared. Most reach a shoulder height of 1.35 m (just over 13 hands). Where many other comparable pony breeds have the reputation of being 'a bit unpredictable', New Forest ponies are said to be straightforward to work with.

Welsh Pony *(below left)*

Welsh ponies like this foal were originally bred from mountain horses and Welsh Cob ponies, with refinement added by some infusion of English and Arabian thoroughbred blood. As working horses, Welsh ponies were used in upland sheep farming and for hunting. Today they are first-rate event ponies with lots of spirit.

(below right)

This Welsh pony foal will not grow bigger than 1.32 m (13 hands) even when fully mature. Its distinctive features are a fine head — indicating the thoroughbred Arabian element in its ancestry — and small, pointed pony ears. As a riding pony later on it will carry itself elegantly, and its long stride and powerful hindquarters will equip it admirably to compete in dressage and showjumping.

Black Forest Foal (above)

When this Black Forest foal has grown up, it will have reached a height of 1.48–1.60 m (14.2–16 hands) at the shoulder. These lightweight coldbloods are only bred as chestnut horses, reddish-brown in colour, though with a lighter mane and tail. They are good-natured animals, used for hauling loads, but also popular for leisure riding.

Quarter Horse (centre right)

A quarter horse like this one will not grow beyond medium size which is 1.43–1.60 m or 14–16 hands. This makes it agile and supple, well suited to cross-country and Western riding. It was the first entirely American-bred horse intended originally for cattle-ranching and is the most popular breed in the U.S.

Appaloosa (top right)

This foal and its mother are genuine Red Indian ponies, because they belong to the Appaloosa breed, a bloodline kept going by the Nez-Percé Indians. In the last years of the 19th century, the Indians and their Appaloosas were almost wiped out by the white man. The very last surviving horses were used in the years before World War II in a programme to re-start the breeding of Appaloosas.

Schleswiger Heavy Draught Horse
(above)

The foal looking so inquisitively over the fence of its paddock here is from a very rare breed of horse. Schleswiger heavy draught horses are a coldblood breed from Schleswig-Holstein and Jutland, originally bred for drawing heavy loads, but now a seriously endangered breed. There are now only 76 breeding animals on the books. Their principal use is for hauling brewery carts or covered wagons.

Mustang *(left)*

Wild mustangs like this mother and her foal may not be captured without official authorisation. Even so, there is licensed breeding of mustangs, because these are very resilient horses with great stamina — and ideal, as they always were, for cowboys. They are reputed to have a great love of liberty, and if placed under duress will react aggressively.

Dartmoor Pony *(top left)*

It's a maddening itch, but this Dartmoor foal knows exactly what to do: back up against a tree, a post or a rock, and just rub. Horses can in fact scratch an ear with a hind leg. However, a foal trying to do this will often overbalance — it needs practice to carry out this tricky manoeuvre successfully.

(top right)

The Dartmoor pony foal in this picture may well have a proud future awaiting it. Dartmoor ponies are extremely popular — especially in the UK — as riding ponies. They jump well, and they also are well suited to dressage competitions, as they do not have a high knee action, and with their long, thick manes they look handsome.

(right)

The Dartmoor pony comes from the south-west of England, an inhospitable, boggy area known — what else could it be? — as Dartmoor. Usually the mares produce a single foal, which when fully grown will measure no more than 1.27 m (12.2 hands). That makes the Dartmoor an ideal breed for a child's first mount, especially as these ponies generally have a very placid temperament.

144

Camargue Horse (left)

By the time this Camargue foal is a few years old, it will have become pure white — this breed produces no horses of any other colour, only white. The white Camargue horses' foals are always born dark-skinned, and every time they moult — which happens in autumn and spring — they acquire some more white hairs. Horses actually born white are known as albinos, and like other albinos have pink eyes.

Dülmen Pony (right)

The Dülmen ponies are a herd of near-wild ponies, in fact the only herd of horses living more or less wild in modern Germany. Their home is in the Merfelder Bruch (Merfeld Marshes) near the city of Münster. Every year a spectacular roundup takes place. The foals are separated out and branded. Then some of them are sold, so that the population does not get too big for the limited area available.

Holsteiner Horse (below)

This young Holsteiner's exuberant capering is an early sign of where its career might take it when it has become a fully-grown riding horse — Holsteiners being a German riding horse breed which has produced a striking number of top showjumpers. They are also very well suited to eventing, with its three disciplines of dressage, cross-country and showjumping.

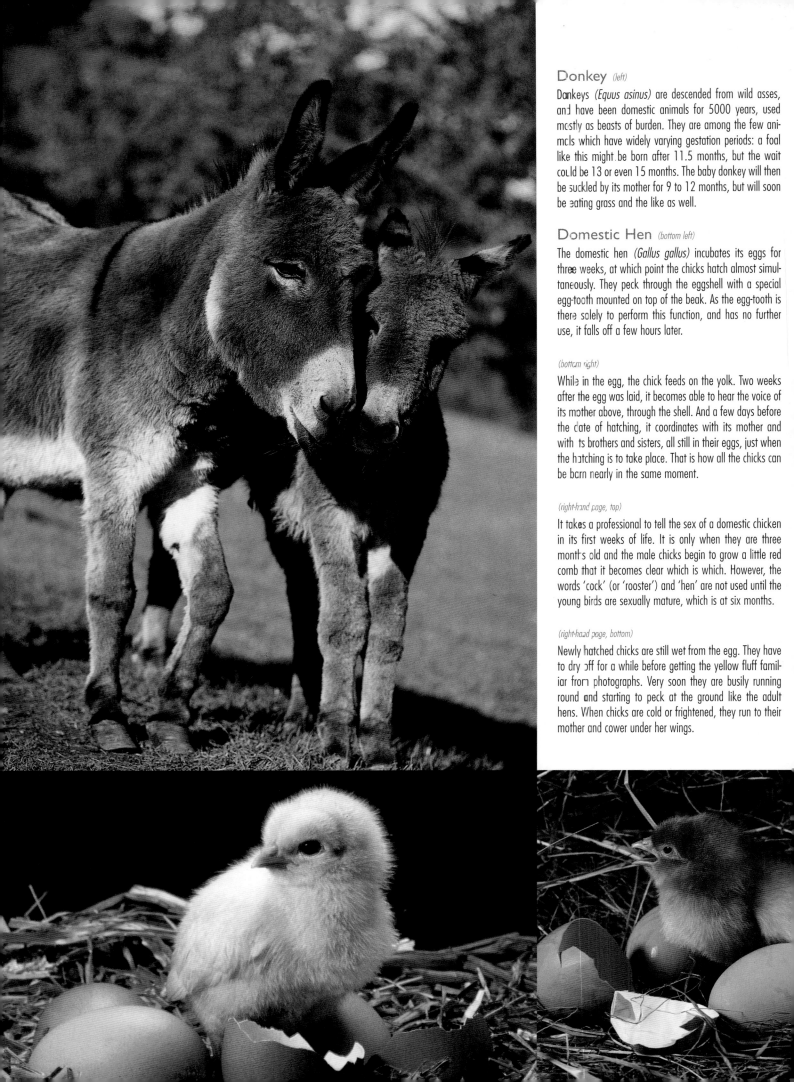

Donkey *(left)*

Donkeys *(Equus asinus)* are descended from wild asses, and have been domestic animals for 5000 years, used mostly as beasts of burden. They are among the few animals which have widely varying gestation periods: a foal like this might be born after 11.5 months, but the wait could be 13 or even 15 months. The baby donkey will then be suckled by its mother for 9 to 12 months, but will soon be eating grass and the like as well.

Domestic Hen *(bottom left)*

The domestic hen *(Gallus gallus)* incubates its eggs for three weeks, at which point the chicks hatch almost simultaneously. They peck through the eggshell with a special egg-tooth mounted on top of the beak. As the egg-tooth is there solely to perform this function, and has no further use, it falls off a few hours later.

(bottom right)

While in the egg, the chick feeds on the yolk. Two weeks after the egg was laid, it becomes able to hear the voice of its mother above, through the shell. And a few days before the date of hatching, it coordinates with its mother and with its brothers and sisters, all still in their eggs, just when the hatching is to take place. That is how all the chicks can be born nearly in the same moment.

(right-hand page, top)

It takes a professional to tell the sex of a domestic chicken in its first weeks of life. It is only when they are three months old and the male chicks begin to grow a little red comb that it becomes clear which is which. However, the words 'cock' (or 'rooster') and 'hen' are not used until the young birds are sexually mature, which is at six months.

(right-hand page, bottom)

Newly hatched chicks are still wet from the egg. They have to dry off for a while before getting the yellow fluff familiar from photographs. Very soon they are busily running round and starting to peck at the ground like the adult hens. When chicks are cold or frightened, they run to their mother and cower under her wings.

Domestic Hen *(top left)*

This domestic hen *(Gallus gallus)* is luckier than most hens living in industrialised countries, because it has been allowed to sit on its own eggs and is free to run with its brood. So-called 'battery hens' can be made to lay 270 or so eggs a year, by means of specialised breeding and constant removal of the eggs, while the hen's direct ancestor bird, the red junglefowl, may lay as few as 36.

Black Rhinelander Hen *(top right)*

Newly hatched chicks like this Black Rhinelander – one of the domestic hen breeds – immediately establish contact with their mother by cheeping. The mother clucks in reply. The person looking after the hens can tell from the pitch and the loudness or softness of the cheeps and clucks how the birds are feeling. Increased sound volume often signals danger – but it may mean they have found food.

House Mouse *(centre right)*

For the first six weeks after birth, baby house mice *(Mus musculus)* are suckled by their mother. Then they begin their real life, as rodents or gnawers. They eat whatever comes the way of their long front teeth – or at least they gnaw at it, because after all it could well be edible. It is in fact this habit of curiosity that has enabled the mouse to spread worldwide, because it enables them to keep finding new foodstuffs.

(bottom right)

One of the greatest menaces to stored food and other supplies is a truly tiny animal, the house mouse, which contaminates food with its droppings and thus makes it useless. It likes to site its nest somewhere handily close to such food stores, and as mice are extremely prolific breeders it is not easy to rid a home of a mouse family once it is established. The female produces four to eight litters a year, each with four to eight young.

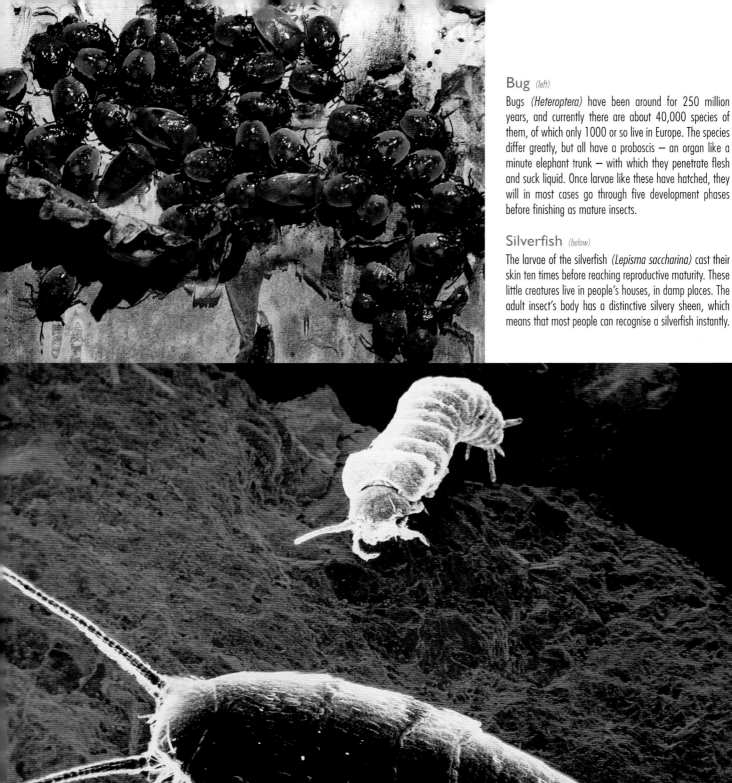

Bug (left)

Bugs (*Heteroptera*) have been around for 250 million years, and currently there are about 40,000 species of them, of which only 1000 or so live in Europe. The species differ greatly, but all have a proboscis — an organ like a minute elephant trunk — with which they penetrate flesh and suck liquid. Once larvae like these have hatched, they will in most cases go through five development phases before finishing as mature insects.

Silverfish (below)

The larvae of the silverfish (*Lepisma saccharina*) cast their skin ten times before reaching reproductive maturity. These little creatures live in people's houses, in damp places. The adult insect's body has a distinctive silvery sheen, which means that most people can recognise a silverfish instantly.

Swallow (above)

The swallow parents (*Hirundo rustica*) feed their young with acrobatic agility, catching the insects in flight and hooking their claws into the nest only for an instant while delivering the meal. They have built the nest out of straw and wet mud, which they attach to a wall in a semi-circular shape, like a bowl with one vertical side.

Dwarf Rabbit (centre right)

Dwarf rabbits are considerably smaller and lighter than ordinary domestic rabbits, weighing only about 700–1500 grams. With their big head — big in relation to the body — and their big eyes, they fit what some scientists call the 'baby schema', meaning that humans see these little rabbits as appealingly childlike and vulnerable. For the same reason, they go on looking like baby rabbits all their lives.

Domestic Rabbit (bottom right)

The domestic rabbit (*Oryctolagus cuniculus domestica*) is bred by humans not because it is a cute little animal but first and foremost because rabbit meat is tasty and the animals reproduce fast. Also, domestic rabbits are very little trouble to look after, by no means fussy about what they eat, and relatively easy to breed from. Rearing the baby rabbits is generally a straightforward matter.

European Wild Rabbit (right-hand page, top)

A European wild rabbit doe (*Oryctolagus cuniculus*) generally has two litters per year. The young are born in a burrow specially excavated for them by the mother, and are initially completely helpless. Three weeks pass before they leave this burrow for the first time.

(right-hand page, bottom left)

The European wild rabbit could be called the ancestor of the domestic rabbit. It is extremely prolific: a female adds an average of eleven young rabbits to the population every year. The figure would be even larger but for the fact that some of the embryos are 'resorbed' — that is, they do not develop but are absorbed back into the mother's body.

(right-hand page, bottom right)

It is possible for a female domestic rabbit to produce young up to ten times in a single year, but breeders usually limit litters to three a year. Just before giving birth, the doe rabbit usually makes a nest for her young and lines it with her own underbelly wool. At about four weeks the young rabbits are beginning to be less dependent on their mother, but they should not be separated from her before eight weeks at the earliest.

Domestic Sheep *(left-hand page, top left)*

The term 'lamb' denotes a sheep *(Ovis ammon aries)* which is less than one year old. Many lambs never complete that year, but are slaughtered. Young ram lambs in particular are taken for meat, because for future breeding purposes one ram per flock is quite sufficient. It will see any other rams as competitors, and this only leads to fights for supremacy.

(left-hand page, top centre)

The domestic sheep invariably lambs in spring. This is the time of year when the meadow grass is beautifully fresh and nutritious and when food generally is plentiful. Domestic sheep are descended from wild sheep, of which the first were domesticated about 10,000 years ago.

(left-hand page, top right)

In Germany, one important use for sheep is as landscape gardeners. In many areas (heathland, for instance), sheep ensure that the land neither degenerates to sparsely vegetated steppe country nor becomes overgrown with bushes. Ewes and their lambs are often put to graze on the dykes which protect low-lying coastal areas from the sea. By trampling the ground they help to consolidate it, strengthening the flood barrier.

(left-hand page, main picture)

The commonest reason for keeping sheep is to ensure a supply of wool, but other sheep products, notably ewes' milk, the cheese made from it, and of course the meat are becoming more and more popular. And lambs at play have long been a symbol of sheer joy in life. You can understand why this should be so if you have ever seen lambs frolicking in a field when allowed out for the first time.

(top right)

The colour of a sheep's coat varies according to breed. There are white sheep, black, brown and grey sheep and mottled sheep. The wool is rather greasy, because the sheep's skin produces an oily secretion called lanolin, which waterproofs the wool and ensures that the animal stays dry even in bad weather. Lambs too produce lanolin in the same way.

Merino Sheep *(bottom right)*

The wool of the Merino sheep is particularly fine and soft, which makes it a natural choice for the manufacture of fine knitwear. To obtain the wool, of course, the sheep has to be shorn. This is done once a year – mostly in spring. Until the wool grows back, the shorn sheep looks pathetically skinny and naked.

Domestic Sheep *(above)*

All domestic sheep – including these pert-looking lambs –
are widely believed to derive from the Oriental moufflon, a
variety of wild sheep which is still extant. One of the very
earliest domesticated sheep was probably the so-called tur-
bary sheep ('turf sheep'), remains of which have been
found in former lake dwellings in Switzerland.

Spectacled Sheep *(right)*

This sheep takes its name from the dark markings round its
eyes which make it look as if it is wearing sunglasses. It is
a mountain sheep from the Alps, bred mainly in Austria. It
is not by any means an old breed, having been first pub-
licly presented in the 1980s. Among its special features is
that an exceptionally high proportion of lambings result in
twin births.

Domestic Pig (top left)

When the sow of the domestic pig *(Sus scrofa domesticus)* farrows, as many as twelve piglets may be born. No wonder there is frequent scrapping for access to the fastest-flowing nipples of the mother. Pigs differ from many animals in that there is no particular time of year for their young to be born — births take place in summer and winter alike.

(centre left)

In Europe and North America, domestic pigs are usually kept in a sty or at least an open-air enclosure and have feed brought to them. The practice is different on the island of Corsica, and in much of Asia, where pigs are often allowed to roam freely and forage for themselves. However, piglets are invariably suckled by their mother during their first three or four weeks of life.

(bottom left)

These domestic piglets are enjoying a free-range life. It is true that they will probably not gain weight as fast as their fellow-pigs undergoing fattening in a sty; on the other hand they are also less nervous, and consequently less at risk of suffering heart-failure. Other differences are that their meat has a finer texture and tastes much better.

Moorish Gecko (bottom right)

The Moorish gecko *(Tarentola mauritanica)* is typical of the animals that move into places where humans have led the way: all over the Mediterranean region, there are Moorish geckos living in house walls. And very useful little lizards they are, too: they hunt at night for spiders and other insects. The female finds four to six out-of-the-way crevices and lays two of her eggs in each. The young geckos hatch in ten weeks, and reach reproductive maturity in two years.

AFRICA

By River, Lake and Marsh

Some African animals — such as the hippopotamus — immerse themselves in water during the day to avoid the greatest heat, and take to the land mostly by night. Young animals of all kinds tend to be born directly after the rainy season, when there is much less risk that they will perish from drought.

African Jacana (top left)

An African jacana chick (*Actophilornis africana*) is not as easily recognised as the adult bird, which has a distinctive blue forehead. Until this develops, it is difficult to tell the African jacana (also known as the African lily-trotter) from other jacanas. With their long, splayed toes and feather-light weight, jacanas are well adapted for running across water-lily leaves on a lake surface.

Ethiopian Wolf (centre left)

Until 1990, the Ethiopian wolf (*Canis simensis*) was known by the name of Abyssinian Wolf, and was believed in some quarters to be a kind of fox. It was given its definitive new name after research proved it to be more closely related to wolves than to foxes. Ethiopian wolves live in packs of up to 13 animals — in which every individual feels a sense of responsibility for any cubs born to the pack and will help look after them.

(bottom left)

A number of factors including the transmission of pathogenic organisms from dogs and human pressure on its habitat have left the Ethiopian wolf's survival as a species critically endangered. Although females do give birth to anything from two to six cubs per litter, this is still not sufficient to stabilise the population while humans go on forcing the wolves to retreat ever further.

Nilotic Crocodile (right-hand page, top)

When the young of the Nilotic crocodile (*Crocodylus niloticus*) hatch from their tough-shelled eggs, they begin to make cheeping noises. Though they are still buried where the mother left her eggs, a pile of 50–80 at a time, in a nest-mound made of plant debris, she hears them and is prompted to excavate the mound and expose the eggs, so that the young crocodiles get air.

(right-hand page, centre)

Young Nilotic crocodiles like this one live in burrows during the first three years of their life as a protection from enemies. They eventually grow so big that the only threat to them comes from human beings and their rifles. They reach a length of 5–6 m when fully grown, and live to the age of about 50.

(right-hand page, bottom)

Like most other crocodile species, the Nilotic crocodile looks after its progeny carefully. The female builds the nest and then guards it, because various small mammal species like to eat the eggs. After the young hatch and the mother has dug them out of the nest, she picks up the tiny creatures carefully in her huge jaws, carries them to the river and looks after them for about a further two months.

Hippopotamus  *(right)*

Water is the natural element for the hippopotamus *(Hippopotamus amphibius)*, and so the baby calves are in fact born under water. Before it can draw its first breath, it has to paddle its way quickly to the surface. Then it has to submerge every time it wants to suckle during the day from its mother's two nipples. It is able to close off its ears and nostrils when under water.

(below)

Baby hippos are suckled for about their first six or eight months by their mother, and they stay with her for as much as five years from birth. During the daytime heat, hippopotami keep their sensitive skin moist by staying in the water.

(top left)

A baby hippopotamus is always a single birth. The mother gestates for 240 days, and after the calf is born will defend it against hyena or the big cats — the only predators that are a real danger to the very sizable calf. By night the hippos climb on to the bank to graze. In one night a full-grown animal will get through 40–50 kg of grass while the young are still being fed on mother's milk.

(top right)

In contrast to most other animals, adult hippopotami may mate at any time regardless of the time of year, so calves are also born year-round. After mating, the adult bull hippos leave the females to themselves and return to their own solitary existence.

(centre left)

Hippos are at home both in water and on land, but it is in the water that they spend most of their time. That too is where the calves are born. Immediately on birth, a baby hippo's first action is to thrust upwards from the river or lake bed towards the surface. Suckling likewise takes place under water.

(bottom left)

For a short while after they are born, hippopotamus calves can walk better than they can swim. During their first few days of life, they escape crocodiles in the water by clambering on to their mother's back — a place of safety, because at about 3.5 m in length she is so big, and the canine teeth showing in her jaws are so impressive, that even a crocodile will keep its distance.

Red Lechwe (above)

The red lechwe *(Kobus leche)* is one of the rare marsh antelopes which are specially adapted to life in the marshes and by water. They only come out of the marsh to calve or to rest. The calving takes place away from the herd, and the mother will continue to keep her calf concealed for about another two weeks.

Lesser Flamingo (right)

This lesser flamingo chick *(Phoeniconaias minor)* is still so young that it stays right by its mother. When it is a little older it will join one of the groups of juvenile flamingos which keep together and are protected by the adult birds. The groups number thousands — not surprising, because the adults congregate in millions. The adults, moreover, not only all perform their courtship rituals at the same time, they even synchronise the movements!

In Rainforests and Other Forests

All year round there are seeds and fruit to be had from the trees of the rainforest, and these provide an ideal nutritional basis for the rearing of young animals. Here, the young live almost exclusively on trees with their mothers. But in more open woodland elsewhere, many species and their young live permanently at ground level.

Jackson's Chameleon (top left)

The East African triple-horned chameleon known as Jackson's chameleon (*Chamaeleo jacksonii*), an animal of the mountain forests, owes its name to the appearance of the male of the species. On its head, virtually on its snout, it has three long horns all pointing forward. It uses them to lunge at its enemies. Here a female is seen carrying her baby on her back. In females, the horns are so shrunken as sometimes not to be visible at all.

Parsons Chameleon (centre left)

The Parsons chameleon (*Chamaeleo parsonii*) of Madagascar is the world's largest chameleon. Every second year, the female lays 20–25 eggs. When the young hatch, they are on their own and have to fend for themselves. Soon they choose a tree and start climbing towards their natural habitat, high up in the rainforest canopy.

(bottom left)

Chameleons (*Chamaeleonidae*) belong to the lizard family, regarded as the most successful of all reptiles, because of the special survival mechanisms they have evolved. The one used by the chameleons is camouflage, a defence system which they have perfected — they have the ability to match their skin colour exactly to the background, whatever it is at a given moment. This means that in the wild they are very difficult to spot.

Eastern Green Mamba (below)

Here an Eastern green mamba (*Dendroaspis angusticeps*) is seen at the moment of hatching. Only the head is showing, but very soon the body will follow — glossy emerald green in colour and about 35 cm long. As a fully grown snake it will be 1.5–2.5 m long, and nobody will say it is 'cute' any longer, because it is one of the world's most venomous snakes. Its colour camouflages it perfectly for living in trees.

Gambian Epauletted Fruit Bat *(above)*

In this picture a mother Gambian epauletted fruit bat *(Epomophorus gambianus)* is seen hanging from a tree with her baby. These two animals belong to the bat family and so are mammals. All day they hang in safety, hidden by dense tree foliage, but as it begins to get dark they venture out in search of food. They do not feed on insects, as European bats do, much less blood, but on aromatic fruits.

Lowland Gorilla *(below left)*

As young lowland gorillas *(Gorilla gorilla)* grow up, they withdraw gradually from their family group. Sooner or later, male juveniles will leave the group altogether and for a while such individuals will lead a solitary existence. Females will in most cases eventually join a male gorilla from a different family.

(below right)

The Western lowland gorilla is an endangered species. These animals reproduce comparatively slowly, so that it takes a long time for dangerously depleted populations to recover. After nine months of gestation, a female will give birth to a baby gorilla which she will suckle for up to 18 months. It will stay with her for up to three years.

Mountain Gorilla *(above)*

The male of the mountain gorilla species *(Gorilla gorilla beringei)* can be a very loving father. It plays with its offspring, but also calls it to order when it misbehaves. The juveniles understand the exact hierarchy within the clan — and in particular that they are right at the bottom and have to obey the adult females and the silverback male.

(below left)

Mountain gorillas live in family clans which have a male, the so-called silverback, as their leader. The clan will generally also have three or four females and the same number of young. In spite of their colossal size and strength, these are exceptionally peaceable animals — and there are only 400–500 of them left in the world.

(below right)

Practical experience is an important factor determining a male's promotion to clan chief, because it will have brought expertise in finding food for the clan and protecting it from hazards, including any threat from humans. It therefore obviously takes a long time for a juvenile to succeed to the position of clan chief — even if the young gorilla is in fact physically stronger.

Barbary Ape *(top left)*

The only ape species with any individuals resident in Europe is the Barbary or pygmy ape *(Macaca sylvanus)*, which has a famous colony in Gibraltar. Most Barbary apes live in North Africa. They are fairly hardy animals, not too bothered by cold weather. The young are not left to the mother ape to rear alone: it can be a touching sight to watch father, uncle and other male relatives involving themselves in child-care.

Ring-tailed Lemur *(centre left)*

The ring-tailed lemur *(Lemur catta)* is a prosimian, and a resident of Madagascar. The females of this lemur species bring forth their young almost simultaneously. At birth, the babies have blue eyes, but these later become yellowish in colour. What we call 'family life' is very important to these lemurs: for example, a clan may all spend the night together on the same tree, and if it is a cold night they will help keep one another warm.

(below)

As its name implies, this lemur's most striking physical characteristic is its black-and-white ringed tail. The tail is quite a bit longer than the body and is used to help the lemur keep its balance. This is particularly important for a mother lemur when she has the added weight of her baby, initially carried against her belly, but later on to be seen clinging to her back like this one.

Okapi *(above left)*

In terms of zoological classification, this young okapi *(Okapia johnstoni)* belongs to the giraffe family, and it is sometimes known as the forest giraffe, a reference to its habitat. While much smaller than the giraffes of the African savannah, it resembles them in a number of ways: its back slopes downwards towards the hindquarters, it has big ears, and the males have skin-covered protuberances or horns.

Mandrill *(above right)*

This female mandrill *(Mandrillus sphinx)* is suckling her newborn baby. Its coat colouring is as inconspicuous as its mother's. If the baby mandrill is a male, its appearance will not change until it is about five years old and attains sexual maturity. At that point its nose will become red, its cheek pouches blue and its throat yellow, while its rear end will take on a brilliant violet colour.

Chimpanzee *(centre left)*

This young chimpanzee *(Pan troglodytes)* is seen playing alone at the edge of the water, but its fellow chimpanzees will not be far away. Chimpanzees live in small groups consisting of females and their young. Several such groups together form a large horde of anything from 25 to 80 animals. Each of them knows all the others, but they do not move around collectively in these larger groups.

(bottom left)

African chimpanzees live both in the tropical rainforests and in the tree savannah areas. Although they are omnivores, their main food is fruit. They will also sometimes hunt, to satisfy a need for meat in their diet. But the young chimpanzee in the photograph has just had a meal and has something else altogether in mind.

Chimpanzee (top left)

The mother chimpanzee *(Pan troglodytes)* starts by carrying her newborn infant held against her belly as she moves around, but once it has grown rather bigger she will prefer it to ride on her back. When the young chimp is hungry it uses its hands to tell the mother, and she responds by feeding it. When the mother is busy fixing up the sleeping-nest in the evening, 10 m up in the tree branches, she will park the baby beside her on the branch until she has finished.

(top right)

Chimpanzees are able to walk upright and to stand as this young beast is doing at the moment, but more often they run on all fours, using their knuckles to take the weight at the front. These anthropoid (manlike) apes spend roughly equal amounts of their time on the ground and in trees. For security while they are climbing, their big toe is set opposite the other toes (like a thumb opposite fingers).

(right)

A very young chimpanzee's face is flesh-coloured, but as chimps age their face colour becomes darker and darker. Mother and child have an exceptionally intense, enduring relationship. Even when the mother has another baby, it still holds good. At night the young animals always build their sleeping-nest near where their mother will sleep.

(left)

Of all apes, chimpanzees are probably the ones that most resemble humans. They are quite similar to humans in that they give birth after a pregnancy of eight months to one baby or occasionally twins. On the other hand, breast-feeding is not a matter of a mere few months, but goes on for all of three or four years, and through all this time the baby gets very close attention.

(right)

With their large round mouth and their slightly thickened lips, chimpanzees always rather give the air of smiling, or at least smirking at some private joke. But that hardly describes this young chimp, which looks as though it is having a hearty laugh. It can even make the same accompanying sounds. No wonder, then, that chimps in zoos always attract crowds of onlookers.

(below)

Chimpanzees use their great lip mobility not just to try everything by mouth and kiss other chimps; they also use their considerable powers of mimicry in order to communicate. To help further, they have a large repertoire of noises and calls. Communication between humans and chimpanzees using these various means of signalling has proved to work remarkably well.

Grey Gentle Lemur *(left-hand page, top)*

This tiny grey gentle or Eastern lesser bamboo lemur *(Hapalemur griseus)* is weighed regularly like a human baby as a check on whether it is developing as it should. At birth it weighed only 40 g. Once fully grown it will weigh a kilogram and have a body length of 34–40 cm. The tail is as long again. In the wild, these animals inhabit the bamboo groves of Madagascar.

(left-hand page, bottom right)

The grey gentle female goes through a five-month pregnancy before giving birth to one baby in winter. She suckles it for six months, but after that it has to change to the adult diet and eat the leaves, buds and shoots of bamboo and reeds. At two years old the young animal is sexually mature. In captivity grey gentle lemurs can regularly reach the age of 12.

Crowned Lemur *(left-hand page, bottom left)*

The crowned lemur *(Lemur coronatus)*, wholly vegetarian in its diet, inhabits the dry forests of Madagascar. In contrast to most other lemur species, which produce only single births, the crowned lemur female is just as likely to have twins as a single baby. The young are born during the rainy season, when food is at its most plentiful.

Red-fronted Lemur *(top right)*

The sole habitat of the red-fronted lemur *(Eulemur fulvus rufus)* is in the broad-leaved forests of Madagascar. After 120 days of gestation the female gives birth to one baby. For the next three weeks she only ever carries it clasped to her belly, but by then it will have grown big enough to ride around in the forest holding on to her back. Fully grown, it will weigh almost 3 kg and be 40 cm long – plus 55 cm of tail.

Blue-eyed Lemur *(centre right)*

Even in a baby blue-eyed lemur *(Eulemur macaco flavifrons)* the blue eyes are unmistakable and very distinctive. The animal is a subspecies of the black lemur. When a baby is born, after 130 days gestation, it weighs only 80 g. The mother suckles it for six months, after which it will feed itself from vegetation. When grown it will weigh 2–3 kg.

Mongoose Lemur *(bottom right)*

The big wide eyes of this baby mongoose lemur *(Eulemur mongoz)* stare out anxiously at the world, but most of it is safely cuddled in its mother's fur. It will need its big eyes most during the dry season, because that is the time when these particular lemurs become semi-nocturnal. During the wet season they sleep at night and feed by day.

Black Lemur (top)

Black lemur (*Lemur macaco*) live only in the canopy of tall trees in the Madagascar forests. The external appearance of the female and the baby does not explain how these lemurs came to get their specific name. It is the males that are black in colour, with a very long, soft coat. The ear tufts and cheek hairs, white in the female, are likewise black in the male.

Grey Parrot (above left)

Because of their ability to mimic human language with uncanny accuracy, grey parrots (*Psittacus erithacus*) are very popular as household pets and for breeding. In the wild they nest in hollow trees, incubating up to five eggs at a time. Sometimes great colonies of nesting parrots develop, with perhaps several hundred mating pairs in close proximity. The noise can be unbearable.

Red-bellied Lemur (above right)

The red-bellied lemur (*Lemur rubriventer*) is so named because the male's belly fur is red, while the rest is brown. The females are different, with a cream-coloured belly. They gestate for about 120 days before giving birth to a single baby lemur, whose weight at birth will be only about 60 g. Fully-grown specimens of this rare lemur weigh in at about 2 kg.

Animal Kingdom of the Savannah

The savannah in Africa is essentially tropical and subtropical grassland, but it has enough diversity of grasses, bushes, trees and thickets to support a wide range of species. Young animals here are avidly sought-after targets for predators, and so have to be either well camouflaged, or well protected by their seniors, or very fleet of foot.

Cheetah *(above)*

The ancient Sumerians used the cheetah *(Acinonyx jubatus)* as a hunting animal no less than 5000 years ago. Other peoples too recognised the qualities of the animal they called a hunting leopard, and made use of the cheetah in the same way. When cheetahs hunt in the wild today, they have to be careful not to have their kill simply carried away by lions. As for learning how to hunt, the cheetah cubs watch their mother and learn from her.

(top right)

These three cheetah cubs are all from the same mother. A cheetah litter will normally have from two to four young. They remain with their mother for two years. Cheetahs do not have a well-defined pattern to their lives. Some are solitary, others live as pairs with their young, others again are happiest in a large family group.

(right)

The coat of the fastest of all land mammals — the cheetah — is a kind of grey-blue when a cub is born. It does not develop its characteristic patterning — black spots on a tawny background until it is older. When this young cheetah is fully grown, it will be capable of running at speeds of up to 75 mph (120kph) when hunting — though it can only hold that speed for 60 seconds at a time.

Ovambo Sparrowhawk (left)

This photograph shows a young Ovambo sparrowhawk (*Accipiter ovampensis*) in the act of calling. This, happily, is not one of the endangered raptor species of Africa. There is a big concentration of them in the Etosha National Park in Namibia. Once this young predator has learnt all the hunting techniques it needs, it will be capable of taking mammals and birds up to about the size of a pigeon.

Coke's Hartebeest (bottom left)

The calves of the Coke's hartebeest (*Alcelaphus bucephalus cokii*), also known as the kongoni, remain close to their mother for about three years. Later, the bucks (males) split off from the mother herd, usually then forming a general group of juvenile animals. The normal kongoni herd consists of from four to 30 animals — but there will only be one mature male, the rest are females and youngsters.

Impala (right-hand page, main picture)

Young impala (*Aepyceros melampus*) have no horns, and only the males will grow them subsequently. The horns, which grow to about 50 cm long and are quite thin, have a distinctive upsweep, so that seen from the front they have the shape of a lyre. These sharp horns go into action in the mating season, when competing males fight violently over the females.

(right-hand page, lower left)

Fragile though its legs may look, they will enable this impala when grown to leap about 10 m forward, and 3 m high. If one of these black-heeled antelopes bounds away, an instant later the entire herd will be on the move too. It can be a memorable sight, as impala often gather in a herd several thousand strong.

(right-hand page, bottom centre)

To look at an impala calf, one might find it hard to believe these elegant gazelles are ungulates, like cows. Only when one hears young impala bleat does it seem more plausible. Often the quarry of predators, impala also call to each other to warn of danger. On hearing the signal, the entire herd takes flight in leaps and bounds.

(right-hand page, bottom right)

Impala young are most often born in the hot midday hours, because then most of the predatory animals who would attack them are asleep. The impala (or black-footed antelope, as it is sometimes called) selects a secluded spot to give birth, away from the herd. She will not return to the herd with it until it has learnt to run properly.

Black-backed Jackal *(right)*

Once a male and female black-backed jackal *(Canis mesomelas)* have bonded as a pair, they will remain monogamous partners for the rest of their lives, hunting together and sharing in the care of their young. Pups — usually three to six in a litter — are born following a gestation period of two months.

(below)

Black-backed jackals (also known as saddle-backed jackals) are members of the wild dog family. In a jackal community, only the alpha female will have young, and these are then cared for by the whole pack. The two names for these jackals derive from the eye-catching dark area on their back, which looks rather like a saddle or saddle-cloth on a horse.

(centre left)

At this stage the two black-backed jackal pups are still only playing, but as they grow bigger, disputes about pecking order within the family group will intrude more and more on the games. Adults of this species are 90 cm long, not counting about 30 cm of bushy tail.

(left)

For the first two months of their life, the young of the black-backed jackal are reared solely on mother's milk. Then they are weaned onto solid foods. Initially they are given semi-digested meat which the parents regurgitate for them. When the young animals are old enough and strong enough to hunt for themselves they will also be able to feed directly off a fresh kill.

Black Rhinoceros (top)

The black rhinoceros (Diceros bicornis) is very much a loner. Even for mating, male and female come together for a few days at the most. The only longer companionship is between the mother rhino and her calf, for about two years. Even at the end of this time, the calf is still suckling. However, it will have begun to supplement the mother's milk diet with browsed plant material only a few weeks after birth.

Square-lipped Rhinoceros *(top left)*

The square-lipped rhinoceros *(Ceratotherium simum simum)* is commonly (but misleadingly) also known as the white rhinoceros. It is not in fact white, but grey. The females and calves live in small groups, while sexually mature males are solitary. Each marks its own territory off by depositing urine and dung-piles. However, juveniles or low-ranking males within the territory may be tolerated.

(centre left)

As a young calf, the square-lipped rhinoceros learns from its mother to stay within reach of a lake — because there are bound to be places where rhinos can wallow in deep mud, something these grey giants love to do. The mud helps cool their skin, and is also a useful protection against troublesome insects.

(bottom left)

Except only for elephants, the square-lipped rhinoceros is the world's largest land mammal. No wonder the unborn calf needs about 16 months to develop in its mother's womb. The suckling period of about a year is also unusually long, and even after it is over, the calf will remain close to its mother for another one to two years.

Vervet Monkey *(right-hand page, top left)*

A newborn vervet monkey *(Cercopithecus aethiops)* can cling on to its mother at once, with its hands and feet, and can even exert some grip with its tail — though that ability disappears as it gets older. Of the breed's other characteristics, one of the more notable is its comprehensive repertoire of warning calls, cries which tell other members of the group about imminent danger, even specifying what kind of danger is approaching.

(right-hand page, top right)

The vervet's most conspicuous feature is its tail. As it can be up to about 80 cm long, it is generally longer than the body proper. Even very young vervets already have an exceptionally long tail for their size. The full length of a grown vervet monkey (including tail) is anything up to 1.3 m.

(right-hand page, main picture)

Vervet monkeys live in quite large communities, usually consisting of several females, their offspring, and a much smaller number of males. The females help each other care for the young.

Vervet Monkey *(top left)*

Females of the *Cercopithecus pygerythrus* variety of the vervet monkey attain reproductive maturity at about three years old. They gestate for eleven months and usually give birth to a single baby. After weaning, the young vervet will feed like its parents mainly on plant materials such as fruit and leaves, but will also eat insects, eggs and birds.

Yellow Mongoose *(bottom left)*

Yellow mongooses *(Cynictis penicillata)* belong to the viverrids family and live in colonies of up to 50 animals, digging extensive underground burrows which are found even in Africa's semi-arid regions. The young are suckled by their mothers for about ten weeks after birth. When grown, they attain a length of 40 cm, with their tail adding at least another 30 cm.

Spotted Hyena *(bottom right)*

There is no fixed annual reproductive rhythm for the spotted hyena *(Crocuta crocuta)*, so young animals can be seen at any time of year accompanying hyena packs. The female usually gives birth to either one or two young at a time. Once the babies' milk teeth have fallen out, they will develop the characteristic immensely strong hyena teeth and jaws, with which they can snap even quite massive bones.

Spotted Hyena *(left)*

Spotted hyenas usually live in groups of from ten to thirty individuals. They use their excreta to mark their territory, in other words as a sign which warns other hyena packs not to intrude. Spotted hyenas also hunt as a pack; the young animals are allowed to go out with the adults once they have reached the age of about twelve months.

(top right)

After a hunt, or when very excited about something, spotted hyenas will sometimes emit noises which sound like humans laughing. These rapid chattering, cackling noises and the hyena's appearance — which many people find unprepossessing — have resulted in the animal acquiring a rather unsavoury popular image. And yet hyenas are exceptionally loving parents, taking great pains to rear their young well.

(above right)

It will be quite some time yet before these two young spotted hyenas go out and kill on their own account. For nine months, the cubs of this largest hyena species are nourished solely on milk from their mothers. Subsequently they feed on game (mainly gnu, zebra and antelope), for which the pack hunts as a single unit, or on carrion.

Topi (top left)

The topi (*Damaliscus lunatus topi* or *D. l. korrigum*) is one of the most abundant subspecies of the *Damaliscus* genus of antelope. Usually a number of females and their young live in a group with a single buck animal, which protects its 'family' from possible attackers. Females normally have only a single calf.

Tsessebe (top centre)

Tsessebe (*Damaliscus lunatus lunatus*) belong to the same antelope genus as topi, and are widely distributed across different regions of Africa. They are among the animals which are most active in the early morning and late evening. The females usually give birth to a single calf after a gestation lasting about eight months.

Korrigum (left-hand page, top right)

Another *Damaliscus* subspecies is the korrigum (*Damaliscus lunatus korrigum*). These animals are sociable, living in small herds of about 15 animals of their own kind, and also associating amicably with zebra and gnu, as well as other antelope species. The calf is hardly born before it is on its feet beside its mother, who is not only its source of milk, but its protector.

Springbok *(right-hand page, bottom left)*

Springbok *(Antidorcas marsupialis)* in full flight from predators have a remarkable habit of leaping high in the air at intervals while they run. Why they do this is still not fully understood. But this is the characteristic for which they are named. Their young do not at first do likewise, but before long they too will be leaping like the herd.

Plains Zebra *(bottom centre)*

Burchell's zebra *(Equus burchelli)* is a subspecies of the plains zebra *(Equus quagga)*, which is found mainly in the southern part of Africa. Its stripes are often rather less clear-cut than those of other plains zebras. The mare and her foal live in a herd made up of other mares and juveniles and a single stallion.

(bottom right)

The plains zebra foals have brown-and-white stripes which are less eye-catching than the black-and-white of their parents. The stripes will gradually change to black as the foal grows older, but for the moment the brown colour is better camouflage for the young animals against the background of the plains. One of the effects achieved by a zebra's stripes is to confuse predators: the patterning makes it harder for the attacking animal to focus on a single zebra in the herd.

Boehm's Zebra (top left)

Boehm's zebra *(Equus quagga boehmi)*, a plains zebra, lives in East Africa and has the clearest striping of all zebra species. Zebras are all different: their stripes vary from individual to individual just as much as human fingerprints. Zebras can recognise each other by their striping. But at the same time the stripes are effective camouflage in the shimmering alternation of light and shade on the daytime savannah.

(above left)

Although both in appearance and genetically Boehm's zebras are very similar to other sub-species, and interbreeding would be perfectly possible, in practice they never do it. The main reason is that interbreeding would endanger the preservation of their own species, because the progeny of a mating with another species would always be sterile.

(above)

In a zebra herd, mares and their foals stay together in family groups which remain together as long as the animals live. Young males, however, once sexually mature, must leave and live an independent life. Initially they form bachelor groups. Then, once they are strong enough, they fight for the right to form their own harem.

(main picture)

Boehm's zebra is one of the plains zebras, whose Latin name, *Equus quagga*, takes its second term from the Hottentot language. 'Quagga' derives from the neigh of the zebra, which for human ears sounds like 'kwa hah ha', and which the Afrikaners wrote down in their language as 'kwagga'. It is a sound with which every zebra foal very soon becomes familiar.

Mountain Zebra *(right)*

Following mating, the mountain zebra mare *(Equus zebra)* is pregnant for a full year before her foal is born. Immediately after it is born, the foal rubs off the amniotic sac and very soon is up on its feet, at first balancing very unsteadily on its long legs. But it only takes a few hours for the foal to learn how to stand and walk confidently on these same stilt-like legs.

Thomson's Gazelle (above)

The young Thomson's gazelle (Gazella thomsoni) is such a recent arrival in the world that it is still not too sure where to find its mother's teats. Another sign that the birth was only moments ago is that the kid's coat is still quite wet. It is normal for the coat of the young animals to be distinctly darker than that of their parents, but two weeks later it will already be becoming lighter in shade.

Hussar Monkey (centre left)

Baby hussar monkeys (Erythrocebus patas) are born after a gestation lasting six months. Once they are weaned, which takes a further six months, they will go out foraging with the other members of their group. However, individuals do their searching more or less independently of each other. The reason is that on the open savannah, with predators on the look-out, a whole group of hussar monkeys foraging together would be too conspicuous for safety and would invite attack.

(bottom left)

Hussar monkeys live in harems consisting of one male and up to twelve adult female monkeys. The young are born towards the end of the year, or early the next year. Hussar monkeys are ground-dwellers, necessarily very agile and fast-moving because of the danger from predators. The adult animals can reach slightly over 30 mph (50 kph) when necessary.

(right-hand page, top)

A Thomson's gazelle kid will be on its feet very soon after it is born; but keeping up with the herd on the move is a different matter, and it will not be ready to do that until it is a month old. Herds of the very abundant Thomson's gazelle often number many hundreds of individuals, even sometimes a thousand. However, within these huge herds the animals group together in much smaller numbers, up to thirty at the most, and within these smaller subgroups real bonding takes place.

Ugandan or Rothschild's Giraffe
(right-hand page, bottom left)

The main distinctive feature of the Ugandan or Rothschild's giraffe (Giraffa camelopardalis rothschildi) — shared by no other giraffe species — is its five horns. It uses them primarily as a weapon, in fights against its natural enemies or against rivals in the herd hierarchy. In the calves, the horns are visible but not yet fully developed.

Reticulated Giraffe (right-hand page, bottom right)

The reticulated or Somali giraffe (Giraffa camelopardalis reticulata) is easily distinguished from other giraffe species by the net-like ('reticulated') patterning of its coat. This is clearly marked even in young calves. Long ago it used to be believed that the giraffe's patchwork skin showed it was a cross between a leopard and a camel. This belief even gave rise to the animal's Latin name, 'camelopardalis', which is made up of the two elements 'camel'-'leopard'.

Masai Giraffe (top left)

The photo shows two young Masai giraffes (*Giraffa camelopardis tippelskirchi*). Giraffes have a most unusual way of walking. They move both legs on one side forward simultaneously, then the two on the other side. This peculiar gait means they walk with a side-to-side rocking effect. The norm among other mammals is to move diagonally opposite legs at the same time.

(above left)

As this young Masai giraffe grows older, its neck will become very long indeed, and this will allow it to eat shoots and young leaves far out of the reach of other herbivores. This is how evolution has ensured that giraffes will always find something to eat and will have to cope with relatively little competition for food supplies. A successful survival strategy!

(above)

The birth of a Masai giraffe is a mid-air event, as the mother giraffe remains standing up, and the amniotic sac with the baby giraffe falls to the ground from a height of about two metres. The force of the fall ruptures the amnion, which will have helped to cushion the impact. During its first year of life the calf stays close to its mother, who also protects it from predators.

188

(left)

Just like humans — and also like all other giraffes — the Masai giraffe has only seven vertebrae. In the giraffe, these vertebrae are enormously lengthened, so that they can support a neck which may be as much as two metres long. In the calves, the neck length and body size are in the same proportion as in adults, and the neck is accordingly shorter.

Reticulated Giraffe (below)

The reticulated giraffe (Giraffa camelopardalis reticulata) is a subspecies of the plains giraffes, in which the white patterning on the coat looks so much like a white net thrown over the brown background. Even in the calf, the typical patterning is fully distinct. In other sub-species of giraffe there is a rather fuzzier borderline zone between the brown areas and the white markings.

Cape Hare *(top left)*

The Cape hare *(Lepus capensis)* is a highly prolific animal, producing up to three litters a year, with anything from one to six leverets being born per litter. For the preservation of the species that is a crucial fact, as the Cape hare has a host of enemies. It is solitary by nature; even the young leave their mother as soon as they have grown sufficiently.

(bottom left)

With a body length of 45–75 cm, the Cape hare is rather smaller than the European hare. But just like its European counterpart it is incredibly fleet-footed and agile. When pursued it takes cover momentarily in a small hollow in the ground, only to explode out of hiding again if the position gets too dangerous. A mother hare will hide her leverets from predators.

African Elephant (top left)

At a weight of between 100 and 150 kg, an African elephant (Loxodonta africana) is a distinctly massive newborn. No wonder its gestation in the mother's womb takes 22 months to complete. This makes elephants one of the longest-gestating creatures in the animal world. After it is born, a healthy elephant calf will put on an average of a kilogram a day, provided that there is enough food available to meet the needs of the herd as a whole.

(top right)

The African elephant calf in the photo will lose its milk incisor teeth or tusks at the age of about six to twelve months. They will be replaced by its permanent tusks, growing at about 16 cm a year. It will use them for a variety of purposes, including ripping the ground up and fighting – the tusks make an effective weapon. Both bull and cow African elephants have tusks.

Giraffe Gazelle (left)

Immediately the baby giraffe gazelle (Litocranius walleri) has been born, the mother animal eats the afterbirth to destroy the tell-tale signs that could alert predators to follow their spoor. Soon after it has been weaned, the young gazelle quickly learns to stand on its hind legs, and so to reach up to the higher branches of trees and shrubs with their crop of fresh leaves and tender shoots, its favourite food.

African Elephant *(left-hand page, top)*

There are a number of differences between the African elephant (shown in the photograph) and the Asian or Indian elephant, and some of them show even in the calves. For example, African elephants *(Loxodonta africana)* have bigger ears than the Asian variety; and African elephants of both sexes have tusks, while female Asian elephants have none.

(left-hand page, bottom)

A newborn baby African elephant's trunk is considerably shorter in proportion to its body size than that of a full-grown elephant. There is a good reason for this: the young calf has to learn how to use its trunk. And in the meantime the trunk is much safer if it is short and out of the way — if it were longer, it would be all too easy for the baby elephant to step on it accidentally, inflicting an agonising injury.

(below)

The sheer size and massiveness of African elephants gives the impression they are lumbering and slow. It's an illusion. Even a colossus standing 4 m high at the shoulder and weighing 6.5 tons reaches speeds of up to 25 mph (40 kph) when in full flight. The calves of course cannot move anything like as fast; if danger threatens, the adult elephants do not run for it, but form a protective circle to face the danger, with the calves in the centre for safety.

(above left)

This baby African elephant has a life expectancy of 50–60 years. When he reaches that age, his last set of teeth (elephants get new teeth six times in a lifetime) will have been worn down, forcing it to seek out swampy areas where the food is softer. There, too, he will probably die. From the fact that elephants always go to certain areas to die, the legend arose that actual elephant graveyards existed.

(above right)

For four years this African elephant calf will be suckled by its mother. However, it will be cared for not by its mother alone, but by the whole herd she belongs to. Most herds are led by a dominant female elephant no longer able to conceive but old enough to have a great depth of experience. It will be she that remembers where water can be found in times of drought, and she will lead the whole herd to the right place.

Hyena Dog (top left)

This young hyena dog *(Lycaon pictus)* is already showing some of the distinctive features of its species, for instance the notably large, rounded ears and a piebald coat in black, white and light brown. It is also known as the African (or Cape) hunting dog. The species habit is to dig a burrow and give birth to the young under ground. There may be as many as ten pups in a litter.

European Bee-eater (centre left)

The European bee-eater *(Merops apiaster)* lives in dry, open country, not only in Africa but also in Southern Europe and in Asia. A mating pair will co-operate in establishing their nest in slopes and banks, pecking at the sand or soil to loosen it and then pushing it out with their feet. Having excavated a burrow perhaps 2 m long, they hollow out a chamber at the far end, and there the naked chicks will hatch.

Zebra Mongoose (bottom left)

So called because of its striped coat, the zebra mongoose *(Mungos mungo)* has a body length (not counting tail) of 30–45 cm, and so ranks within its family, the *Viverridae*, as of good medium size. If a zebra mongoose is looked after by humans from a very early age, it will become very tame. In African households it is a popular domestic pet.

Bat-eared Fox (right-hand page, top)

The young of the bat-eared fox *(Otocyon megalotis)* are decidedly 'cute' in appearance. They have been born to parents which are monogamous — that is, have only one mate for life — and which both work at rearing the babies. The most distinctive feature of the bat-eared fox is its large spoon-like ears, which help it hunt down insects, its favourite food. The big ears also help the animals to shed excess body heat.

African Lion (right-hand page, bottom)

An African lion cub *(Panthera leo)* will never roam on its own: somewhere nearby there will always be its mother or father or perhaps an aunt, keeping a watchful eye on the cub to see that it comes to no harm. Of all cat species, only the lions live in groups and have lifelong bonding with others in the group or pride.

African Lion (above)

The lioness *(Panthera leo)* gives birth to her young — usually a litter of three — in thick scrub, after a gestation period lasting ten weeks. The cubs' eyes do not open for the first ten days, and in every way they are helpless and dependent on the mother. But that phase soon passes, and they soon set about exploring their immediate surroundings — in their own appealingly clumsy fashion.

(right)

The mother lion continues suckling her cubs for about six months. But the rest of the pack also get involved in the rearing of the younger generation. Cubs are allowed to suck from other lionesses in the pride, not just from their own mother. Later on, they will join in the group's hunting, and in the communal feasting that follows.

(main picture)

Lion cubs at play keep their claws sheathed, and do not bite hard. As they get older, however, what was play becomes more and more often a matter of establishing or consolidating or changing the hierarchy or pecking order among their age group or in the pride as a whole. At the age of two to three years, the juveniles are expelled from the pack for good.

(above left)

Even when she is just strolling along, accompanied by her cubs, a lioness has an air of calm superiority that says she has not a fear in the world — and the cubs know well that at her side they are always safe. A swipe from the mother's paw is powerful enough to break a zebra's neck — let alone deal with any hyena that might fancy attacking one of her cubs.

(above right)

Through their play, the lion cubs learn all the things they will need to know later when they are hunting. The most effective way to attack prey, for example: they practise this on each other. Their mother too is a popular practice target for cubs playing the attack game — at least for as long as she puts up with it. When she has had enough, she makes it very clear it is time to back off.

African Lion *(left-hand page)*

The adult African lion *(Panthera leo)* has a uniformly coloured light brown coat, and the males a thick mane. The young, by contrast, have flecks in their fur. Mostly these disappear slowly over time, but they are occasionally still visible in a very old lion. A lion's life expectancy is about 15 years on average; some live to 20, but at that age almost all their teeth have gone, and as a result they starve to death.

(top right)

The cub wants its mother to play – but she needs to rest through the heat of the day, as she has a hard night's work ahead of her. She and the other lionesses of the pack will stalk, pursue and bring down and kill some large animal, perhaps a gnu or a gazelle – so that the whole pride can feast on meat.

(centre right)

Looking at a lioness gently nuzzling her cub, one can easily forget that except for tigers these are the world's largest cat-family predators. Females grow to 1.75 m in length and weigh 170 kg; male lions reach 1.90 m and 250 kg weight. If the pride as a whole is to get all the meat it needs, it simply must have a large territory well stocked with game.

(bottom right)

A mother lioness plays games with her babies just as a human mother does. If the play gets too rough, this big cat reacts just as a domestic tabby would – she deals the youngster a good cuff with her paw. And it is no tabby-size paw… In one important way, lions are quite unlike domestic cats and indeed any other cats: they are sociable and always live in packs, known as prides.

(bottom left)

While the lionesses of the pride are responsible for the hunting, in other words the food supply, the male lions have the task of defending the pride against other, intruding lions. This is no mere matter of roaring their defiance: they will use paws, claws and teeth. When the males of the next generation have come to maturity, they gang up in small groups which are in continuous rivalry.

Anubis Baboon *(left-hand page, top left)*

Anubis baboons *(Papio anubis)*, also known as olive baboons, spend a lot of time at ground level, but they can in fact climb just as well as other monkey species. As they usually prefer to have a clump of trees at the centre of their territory — for the sake of shade during the midday heat — their young have ample opportunity to practise their climbing skills.

(left-hand page, top right)

Fully-grown Anubis baboons have a large head with a dog-like muzzle peering out from a mane-like surrounding mass of fur, but their young look quite different, more like the anthropoid apes. This is because their muzzle is still short, more like a human nose, and the head as a whole looks more rounded. A very young baby baboon's face has pink skin, making the almost-human impression stronger still.

(right-hand page, left)

Anubis baboons are born after a gestation period of six months. The coat they are born with is very dark, but changes to the adult colouring after four to six months. This is the signal for the mother baboon to begin weaning her young.

(left-hand page, main picture)

Like all other baboon species, Anubis gaboons live in troops of about 25–50, though some troops have almost 100 individuals. Until such time as the juveniles grow the olive-green coat of the adult animal, they enjoy all the tolerance they need within the group. But that point brings the big change, with the juvenile males being driven off altogether, and the new generation of females having to fit in at the very bottom of the group hierarchy.

(right-hand page, centre)

During its first few days of life, the baby Anubis baboon clings to its mother's breast or abdomen, where it enjoys convenient access to her teats. But once it has grown rather larger and stronger it changes position and from now on rides around the savannah on its mother's back.

(right-hand page, bottom)

Young Anubis baboons at play are developing both their physical strength and their dexterity. They are trying out what they can do (and not do) with their hands and feet, and they are also learning how the other young baboons in their peer-group react to a given action. Later on, this knowledge will be very valuable to them when rivalry for places higher up the hierarchy begins.

Hamadryas Baboon *(top left)*

The young of the Hamadryas (or sacred) baboon *(Papio hamadryas)* are born after a gestation lasting about five and a half months. For their first eight months of life their mother suckles them, and are relatively slow to reach sexual maturity, at five years old. But the Hamadryas baboons also have a relatively long life expectancy, and may reach 30 years of age unless killed earlier by a predator or disease.

(centre left)

In contrast to many other monkey species, the Hamadryas baboons do not expel their juvenile males from the troop they are born in. These animals gradually begin to challenge the troop leader's authority, or to draw a number of females away from his harem in order to found a new troop.

Yellow Baboon *(bottom left)*

Yellow baboons *(Papio cynocephalus)* can grow to 90 cm in length (not counting the tail) and 25 kg in weight, which for a baboon is decidedly big. They do not reach reproductive maturity until five years old, and even then the troop hierarchy will see to it that males wait several years more before actually mating. However, five is the age at which most females give birth for the first time.

(right-hand page, top left)

The yellow baboon is so named because of its yellowish-brown fur. Each troop will have an extensive territory, usually with a stand of trees at the centre. With this as their base, these omnivorous animals will forage for seeds, grass, insects or snakes. The babies go along too, riding on their mothers' backs.

(right-hand page, main picture)

Looking at the mother yellow baboon with her piggyback baby, it seems hard to believe that baboons are in fact considered aggressive animals. When provoked, the large baboons with their powerful jaws can be very dangerous. If several baboons attack together, they can put even a leopard to flight; however, lone baboons often fall victim to one of the big cats.

Anubis Baboon *(right-hand page, top right)*

The Anubis or olive baboon *(Papio anubis)* is a social animal. It lives in troops of 25 to 100 animals. US researchers have found that the babies' chances of surviving beyond their first year improved in line with the amount of social interaction their mothers got involved in. Baby baboons with highly sociable mothers had 30% better survival chances than those whose mothers were relatively solitary in habit.

Warthog (top left)

The characteristic 'warts' which give the animal its name are clearly visible under the eyes and near the muzzle even when the warthog (Phacochoerus aethiopica) is still very young. The canine teeth which will be used for rooting in the earth and for defence have not yet come through. The piglets are born after a gestation period of just under six months.

(above)

Warthogs give birth to litters of up to eight young, though generally only half at most will survive infancy. The reason is that the piglets depend totally on suckling for several months after birth, yet the mother has only four teats. This means the piglets that cannot regularly secure a teat for themselves will starve. For a comparatively long time – two years – the surviving young will remain with their birth family.

Guinea Baboon (top right)

The Guinea baboon (Papio papio) is one of the monkeys that live mainly at ground level. They suckle their young at ground level, even though the risk from predators is far greater here than in trees. When moving from place to place, a mother baboon will carry a newborn baby clasped to her abdomen, any older offspring on her back.

Slender-tailed Meerkat (top left)

The droll little slender-tailed meerkat or suricate (*Suricata suricatta*) belongs to the viverrid family. It lives in great colonies inhabiting extensive tunnel systems. Their progeny are born after a gestation period of about eleven weeks. The newborn babies are tiny, but it only takes a year for them to reach reproductive maturity.

(above left)

Whenever slender-tailed meerkats leave their burrows, a few remain just outside, on sentry duty. They stand erect on their hind legs and scan the surrounding terrain intently. If they diagnose danger, they give a loud call which warns the other members of the colony to seek safety, together with their young.

African Ostrich (above right)

The chicks of the African ostrich (*Struthio camelus camelus*) hatch out from their huge eggs after just less than six weeks. Several females lay their eggs in a shared nest, which may have up to thirty eggs in it. It is a male that does most of the sitting to incubate the eggs, and again a male that looks after the young birds until they can fend for themselves.

Eland (above)

For young eland (Taurotragus oryx or Tragelaphus o.), the best protection against predators is the herd of adult eland. This is why they never stray far from the herd. A given herd might number anything from five to fifty beasts, but during dry spells eland herds often amalgamate into mass herds of about 200.

African Buffalo (centre right)

The African buffalo (Syncerus caffer), Africa's only wild bovine, can be found not only in the savannah, but also in the rainforest, near rivers, and in marshy areas — its only essential requirements are drinking water and a mud wallow. During the main heat of the day the animals rest, like this cow and calf, or take a mud-bath.

Vervet Monkey (bottom right)

Young vervet monkeys (Cercopithecus aethiops) face a whole range of different perils: from the big cats, from birds of prey, and also from the big yellow baboons. Adult vervets have a sophisticated system of calls to warn each other which of these predators is approaching. The young monkeys have to learn the system so that they too know what they need to do in a given situation for the best chance of survival.

Slender-tailed Meerkat *(left)*

The gregarious meerkats *(Suricata suricatta)* often have to relocate several times in a single year because food supplies are exhausted. This is a fairly laborious operation, as they have to dig an entire new tunnel system, and of course moving with the whole colony involves taking a large number of animals along, young as well as adult.

(below)

Slender-tailed meerkat babies are fed exclusively on their mother's milk for their first three or four weeks of life. From then on they begin to take solid foods. Their 'favourites' include insects, vegetation of various kinds, scorpions, lizards, small mammals and birds, and birds' eggs.

In the Deserts and Other Arid Regions

These areas have extreme climates, and the animals and their young that live there have to cope with drought, high winds and huge temperature variations. The regions concerned are not all sandy deserts like the Sahara; some are dry stony wastes, others are semi-desert with some sparse vegetation.

Caracal *(top left)*

The caracal, or desert lynx *(Caracal caracal)* seems not to have a fixed mating season, as young caracal are encountered all year round. They are born, usually in a litter of three, after a gestation period of 69–78 days. The mother suckles them for at least ten weeks following birth and then progressively transfers them to a meat diet.

(above left)

This young caracal will not grow bigger than 60–90 cm in length, and a weight of 20 kg at most. Even so, it will then be capable of preying successfully not just on rodents and birds but on small antelopes. Caracals can leap 3 m vertically from the ground and can thus for instance kill a bird in mid-flight with a well-aimed swipe of the paw.

(above right)

The affinities between this juvenile caracal and the whole cat family are apparent at first glance. It can hiss just as menacingly — and it even looks very like a young cat, because caracals do not have a mottled coat like most other wild feline predators, but a same-all-over colour somewhere between yellowish-brown and reddish-brown. However, it does have small ear-tufts.

Domestic Donkey (top left)

Donkeys – the one in the photograph is just six days old – are generally regarded as obstinate, because they will not always do what their owner wants them to do. In fact, what that shows is that they are intelligent. If at all possible a donkey should never be kept on its own, because they are herd animals, and without company will feel terribly lonely.

African Wild Ass (top right)

All our domestic donkey breeds derive from the African wild ass *(Equus africanus asinus)*. It is an exceptionally frugal animal, which does not starve even during the dry season, when the only grass to be found is bone dry: it makes do with what is available. However, naturally enough, fewer foals are born then than at other times of year.

(above)

This feral domestic donkey foal will almost certainly not be quite as alone as it looks. Its mother will be somewhere close by, because mother donkeys seldom allow their foals to be out of sight for more than a moment or two. The mother also keeps up close physical contact with her young for quite some time after it is born, even helping to groom its coat.

Sand Cat (top left)

The sand or barchan cat *(Felis margarita)* is much the same size as an ordinary domestic cat. It lives in very inhospitable regions, mostly sandy or stony deserts. At birth, a kitten weighs only 40 g. The young are suckled for a while, but later their only source of liquid — essential for life — is the bodies of their prey.

Barbary Sheep (top centre)

The Barbary sheep *(Ammotragus lervia)* lives in inhospitable, rocky, arid mountain regions. With its iron-hard hooves it is well able to keep its footing — for instance, it is easily nimble enough to outdistance a pursuing leopard or similar predator. Their young too are also exceptionally sure-footed. Very soon after the young animal is born, its mother moves off, and it has to follow.

Somali Wild Ass (right-hand page, top right)

With the greyish to sandy colour of its coat, the Somali wild ass *(Equus africanus somaliensis)* wears the ideal camouflage for living in the arid regions of Africa. Another feature they have — this one shared by many other wild ass species — is the dark so-called 'eel stripe' along their spine. The Somali wild ass is in imminent danger of becoming extinct, one of the contributory reasons being that it normally gives birth only to a single foal.

African Spurred Tortoise
(left-hand page, bottom left)

The African spurred tortoise *(Geochelone sulcata)* is found mainly in the Sahara region. During the greatest heat of the day the tortoise hides under bushes or in cavities in the earth, to protect its body from dehydration. It is active only in the early mornings and towards evening. Its young need to be particularly vigilant, as they have many more enemies than the adult tortoises.

Asil Arabian Horse *(bottom centre)*

'Asil' means pure, and Asil Arabian horses *(Equus caballus)* are purebred desert Arabian horses that have never been interbred with other Arabians. This foal already has the Arabian horse's unmistakable head with the concave (inward-curved) nose line, the big nostrils, and the wonderful big dark eyes.

(bottom right)

Purebred Arabians are regarded as the noblest of all breeds of horse. Certainly they are one of the most ancient and physically most resilient of all breeds, for their original home was in the deserts of Africa and Arabia, where they had to keep going on little water and scanty food — quite unlike this mare and her foal. Arabian horses are now used worldwide as riding horses, enjoying tremendous popularity in Europe and Africa in particular.

Chacma Baboon *(left-hand page, top)*

A baby chacma baboon *(Papio ursinus)* is initially fed solely on mother's milk and grows rapidly, as this food is highly nutritious. Then, out of sheer curiosity, it will sample the various titbits it sees in what the adult baboons are eating. Their diet includes vegetarian foods such as roots, grasses and plant bulbs as well as animal-source foods such as eggs, insects and small vertebrate animals.

(right)

Typical features of the chacma baboon are a black or at least dark face — as on this youngster — together with black hands and feet and a lighter, almost yellowish coat elsewhere. All baboon species are rated intelligent and capable of learning relatively complex things. For instance, they show great skill in using tools to get access to their food.

(left-hand page, bottom)

During the first six months of their life, baby chacma baboons ride around on their mother's back and from this safe viewpoint learn the topography of their home area. Home is not necessarily the savannah country of South Africa, Zimbabwe or Namibia: these baboons can also be found in stony deserts, in mountainous areas, and close to the coast.

(below)

The chacma is the largest of all baboon species. But it will be quite some time before this baby animal reaches its ultimate body length of almost a meter. By then its tail will have grown to 50—80 cm in length, and the animal will weigh 15—30 kg. Females will be nearer 15 kg, the males nearer 30 kg, as they are bigger and heavier.

Gelada Baboon *(above)*

The gelada baboon *(Theropithecus gelada)* has two hairless areas on its neck and chest which go bright red when the animal is on heat. After a successful mating, gestation will last for about six months, then one baby, or on rare occasions twins, will be born. The young are suckled for a relatively long time, one to two years.

Scorpion *(right-hand page, bottom right)*

Scorpions *(Scorpiones)* are arthropods, and partly viviparous – i.e. they have a segmented body and jointed appendages, and bear live young. Most of the baby scorpions emerge before egg-laying takes place, some during it and a few subsequently. Some species of scorpion carry their newborn offspring around with them for a while. Scorpions are found on almost all continents, as they are well adapted to cope with diverse environments.

Cape Rock Hyrax *(above right)*

The Cape rock hyrax *(Procavia capensis)* is found on the Arabian peninsula as well as in Africa. These little herbivorous mammals are – believe it or not – the nearest living relatives of the modern elephant. Their young can feed partly on solids from only a few days old, but suckling continues as well until they are six months old.

(right)

The Cape rock hyrax, which reaches a maximum size of 55 cm, has a number of dangerous enemies, above all leopard and jackal, but large birds of prey are also partial to the flesh of these small mammals. Because of their vulnerability, the hyraxes always have one of their number acting as sentry for the whole colony, ready to warn the others of the approach of a predator. At the warning signal, all the hyraxes scurry back down their burrows.

North America

By River, Lake and Marsh

The immense tracts of freshwater in Canada and the USA provide great numbers of animal species large and small with everything they need to sustain life and reproduce their kind — fish, amphibians, mammals, reptiles, insects and birds.

Wood Duck (top left)

Like all ducks, the young of the wood duck (*Aix sponsa*) leave the nest early. Their mother begins the move soon after they hatch, by calling to them in a special way. When the ducklings hear this call, they start scrabbling upwards to get out of the hollow tree they began life in, digging their tiny claws into the wood too get a hold. Once they have made it to the exit hole, it's a quick hop down.

(above left)

The rather dowdy-looking ducklings will grow into handsome adult wood ducks, though the females — as always with ducks — are by no means eye-catchers. The richness of the drakes' plumage is all the more striking. They have a long crest and very obvious white flashes on their head, neck and wingtips, while the rest of their plumage is greenish-brown.

(above right)

Wood duck are a familiar sight in Europe too, where they are bred as ornamental waterfowl. They often nest in hollow trees, or in nesting-boxes. They line the nest with down and deposit eleven or more cream-coloured eggs in it. These hatch after 30 days to produce a brood of ducklings — the males grow into handsome, richly-coloured drakes, the females remain predominantly a sober brown in colour.

Mississippi Alligator (top left)

Mississippi alligators (*Alligator mississippiensis*) climb out onto the banks sometimes, but as land animals they are lethargic and slow-moving. Back in their freshwater habitat, they are both fast and agile. They only attack their prey in or from the water. And the first thing a female does after her babies hatch out is to carry them down to the water in her jaws.

(top right)

An unusual phenomenon can be seen here: of the two young alligators in the photo, one has the normal colouring, while the other has quite different colours. This is a genetic mutation brought about by a variation in the animal's heredity.

(main picture)

Mother alligators are very protective of their young. This starts the moment she lays the eggs — between 30 and 65 of them. She will cover them over in a large nest-mound that she has built in readiness. Then she guards the nest, defending it against egg-thieves such as raccoon and pig. When she hears the baby alligators croaking inside their eggs, she uncovers them and helps the babies to hatch.

Great Blue Heron (top left)

The great blue heron (Ardea herodias) makes its nest in a tree near water. Usually there will be between three and seven eggs in the clutch. Once the young have hatched, they will need caring for until they are fledged. That generally takes about two months.

Snowy Egret (centre left)

The snowy egret (Egretta thula) belongs to the family Ardeidae, which also includes other long-legged wading birds like the bittern and the heron. Tracts of marshland are the snowy egret's favourite nesting terrain, and here it selects a bush or a tree. Once there are eggs in the nest, it will be about another two and a half weeks before the chicks hatch. The two parent birds share in incubating them.

(bottom left)

The first snowy egret chick to hatch is also invariably the most successful one when it comes to begging for and receiving food — and thus quite naturally also grows the fastest. This has now been proved scientifically. The reason for the difference is probably that the oldest chick has had a slight start over its siblings in terms of life experience.

Pacific Heron (right-hand page, top)

The Pacific heron (Ardea pacifica) may nest as a solitary pair or in a colony with other herons or different species of waterbird. It builds a flat nest like a platform from branches and twigs, perched in the fork of a tree — preferably a dead one — or actually in the water. In this way the supply of fresh frogs, other amphibians and aquatic insects for feeding the progeny is assured.

American Bittern (right-hand page, bottom)

In the case of American bitterns (Botaurus lentiginosus), the female bird is wholly responsible for the business of rearing the brood. She begins by selecting a site where she will construct a nest — well concealed in among the reeds — about 5 cm above the level of some shallow water. After four weeks of incubation the young hatch out. They leave the nest after a week or two, but even after this they will be fed for a further fortnight.

Canada Goose *(left-hand page, main picture)*

The Canada goose *(Branta canadensis)* is a sizable bird, with a body length of a full metre. It is widespread in Europe too, where it has the status of an ornamental bird. It produces an annual clutch of about five eggs. To keep the eggs warm, and ensure the future nestlings will have a soft bed, the nest — in a ground depression — will be lined with goosedown. The infant goslings hatch out after about four weeks of incubation.

(left-hand page, bottom left)

The Canada goose hatchling needs barely two days in the nest before it is ready to follow its parents onto the water. The gander plays an active part in rearing the brood; earlier on, it had guarded the goose and nest while she incubated the eggs. The goslings do not become sexually mature until their third year, yet by then the mating pairs will have been together for a year — and they will stay partners for life.

Painted Turtle *(left-hand page, bottom centre)*

This little creature is one of the freshwater turtles known as painted turtles *(Chrysemys picta)*. They start life in a clutch of up to twenty eggs, laid by their mother in a special chamber hollowed out in the sandy soil. The warm sun beating down on the sand produces the right uniform temperature for the embryos to develop.

(left-hand page, bottom right)

Here a baby painted turtle is just hatching. Its sex is not a matter of chance, but determined by the ambient temperature at the time of hatching. Females are only born if the temperature is above 30 °C. Only if it is cooler than that will males be born. When the shell reaches 10–18 cm in size — this takes several years, and the females will generally have grown faster than the males — the turtles will be sexually mature. They go on slowly increasing in size until the shell reaches a length of about 25 cm.

Sandbill Crane *(above left)*

Sandbill cranes *(Grus canadensis)* are monogamous, staying together for life, and the cock and hen bird always share in the rearing of their chicks. Even so, they never fail to go through their elaborate courtship ritual every year before mating. They build their nest on land, but always near a lake or other standing water, to ensure food supplies. After the young cranes hatch, the family will stay together for another ten months.

(left)

Any minute now, this young sandbill crane will probably hear its parents calling to it. This species of crane is well known for its insistent, loud, trumpeting calls. The calls that matter most for the chicks are of opposite types, one an encouraging call and the other a warning of danger. It is quite a thought that these calls may have rung out across the Earth as much as 55 million years ago — because the sandbill crane is believed to be the world's oldest living species of bird.

223

Red-spotted Newt (left)

The red-spotted (or Eastern) newt (Notophthalmus viridescens) begins life as a 7 mm larva, yellowish-green with red spots, hatched in the water. About three months later, after its metamorphosis, it will have become a juvenile newt, red in colour and initially 5 cm long. For about three years it will be a land-based creature, but it will then return to the water, change back into an aquatic creature, and reproduce.

Four-toed Salamander (below left)

In early summer, after fertilisation, the female four-toed salamander (Hemidactylium scutatum) lays 15–25 eggs in moss overhanging the water, and keeps watch on them until they hatch. The emerging larvae drop off into the water. In late summer they will assume the totally different shape of the adult salamander and become a land-living creature.

Bald Eagle (right-hand page, top)

The bald or American eagle (Haliaeetus leucocephalus) lives near water, which can be lakes and rivers or the sea. Young eaglets of this species are difficult for anyone not an actual expert to identify positively, as the head and neck have not yet developed their distinctive white plumage, but are still brown. This way the nestlings are better camouflaged.

(right-hand page, bottom left)

A young bald eagle is brown all over. The white colouring on head, neck and tail feathers characteristic of these large raptors is a mark of the adult bird. The chicks in the nest attack each other as well as competing fiercely for food, so it is quite normal for the weakest of the brood not to survive.

(right-hand page, bottom right)

Bald eagles have a body length of over 90 cm, and their wing-span may be as much as 2.5 m. They build huge nests, some measuring 3.5 m in diameter. Here, each year, the female bird will lay two or three eggs. The nestlings, once hatched, are looked after for a period of some weeks, with both parents sharing the work.

North American Bullfrog (above)

This tadpole of the North American bullfrog (Rana catesbeiana) is halfway through its metamorphosis from larva to adult animal — in other words, from tadpole to frog. It has already developed frog legs, but also still has its tadpole tail. In the grown North American bullfrog, with a body length of 20 cm, the stretched hind legs will be 25 cm long.

Red-legged Frog (centre right)

This photo shows a tadpole of the red-legged frog (Rana aurora) in the final stage of its metamorphosis. This North American native species of tailless amphibian is recognised easily by its red legs. Now becoming very rare, it has been added to the list of endangered species. The main cause for its decline is the destruction of its habitat by human encroachment.

Pickerel Frog (bottom right)

The female pickerel frog (Rana palustris) lays its eggs between March and May, on aquatic plants under the water's surface. Ultimately these eggs will develop into frogs 4.5 to 9 cm in length, with dark flecks. The tadpole is seen here at the beginning of its metamorphosis — the frog head is already clearly recognisable. These frogs produce a skin secretion that makes them unappetising to potential predators.

Roseate Spoonbill (far left)

These three young chicks already have enough pink plumage to show why their species name is roseate spoonbill (Ajaja ajaja) — and their beak has also had its distinctive spoon shape right from the beginning. This species builds its large, deep nests in mangrove swamps if possible, because the water there is rich in food.

Brown Pelican (left)

The brown pelican (Pelecanus occidentalis) is so named for the brown plumage of the adult birds, but the juveniles are white. It is the smallest of all pelican species, and also the only one that dives from a height to secure its prey; the habit of all the others is to ladle their catch out of the water, using their beak like a spoon.

(below)

The brown pelican likes to nest near others, in trees or bushes, or — as here — in mangroves. Until the chicks are ten days old, the parents regurgitate pre-digested food for them onto the nest floor, but from that age up the young birds are able to eat the caught fish direct from the throat pouch under the parent's bill.

Kodiak Bear (above)

The Kodiak (or Alaskan brown) bear (*Ursus arctos midden-dorfii*) is the largest subspecies of brown bear, weighing up to 800 kg. These two cubs have a lot of eating to do before they reach that weight – including plenty of highly nutritious salmon. Here by the river they can watch their mother fish, or have a splash themselves, as all brown bears love the water.

Northern Leopard Frog (right)

This Northern leopard frog (*Rana pipiens*) is clearly only a juvenile, as it lacks the full adult colouring: there is no sign of the two or even three bands of flecks which run down the animal's back and give the species its name. Like the leopard's spots, these patches are dark with light edges, and irregularly shaped.

In the Mountains

Well adapted for life at high altitudes and on steep rocky ground, the baby mammals here are sure-footed climbers. But many of them become the food which the big raptors swoop down on and bring home to their own young.

Deer Mouse *(above)*

The little deer mouse *(Peromyscus maniculatus)* is probably the most abundant North American mammal. It is highly adaptable, making itself at home almost anywhere. Furthermore, it is a prolific breeder: it is not at all uncommon for a female to produce four litters in a year, with from three to six baby mice each time.

Rocky Mountain Goat *(above left)*

The Rocky Mountain goat *(Oreamnos americana)*, which is related to the chamois, has its kids in May and June. It only takes about an hour for the newborn kid to be able to move nimbly through the rough terrain of its mountain home. With their dense white coat and multiple layers of subcutaneous fat, Rocky Mountain goats are superbly adapted to cope with life in this inhospitable habitat.

(left)

The Rocky Mountain goat's kids stay with their mothers till the next batch of young comes along. They are weaned off their mother's milk after three to four months, reaching sexual maturity at the age of two and a half. In winter, the Rocky Mountain goats come together in big herds, but in summer they roam the mountains in groups of only a few animals.

Dall Sheep *(above)*

It is not usually until she is three to four years old that the female Dall sheep *(Ovis dalli)* will bear her first lamb. Outstandingly agile climbers, Dall sheep (also occasionally called thinhorn sheep) prefer to live in high mountain areas of Canada and the USA. Once they are 24 hours old, the lambs just have to follow their mother wherever she goes.

(below left)

In summer, the Dall or thinhorn lambs live close to their mothers on the rather lower mountain slopes where the grazing is abundant and nutritious. The rams spend this period among the crags and stony wastes of the mountain tops. They are distinguished by their impressively curving horns — which they use as weapons when they fight to establish the herd hierarchy.

(below right)

If you go on a high mountain trek in Alaska, you have a very good chance of encountering wild Dall sheep. There are estimated to be between 60,000 and 80,000 of them roaming the mountains there. A group like this, with ewes and lambs, may take flight when visitors appear, or may be quite unconcerned — depending on what happened in any previous encounters the adult animals may have had with humans.

Bighorn Sheep (above)

Bighorn sheep *(Ovis canadensis)* are exceptionally foot-sure, and can also jump powerfully and accurately. These skills naturally fit them ideally for the mountain environment. The various groups tend to follow paths whose routes they have learnt from preceding generations of bighorn. This is how they find — for instance — the best grazing and the safest spots for lambing.

(bottom far left)

During summer, bighorn live in same-sex groups. The ewes take their lambs to the meadow grazing in the more accessible, lower-altitude areas of the mountains, while the rams come together to forage on the higher slopes. This is a period in which status disputes between the males virtually never happen.

(left)

Bighorn sheep have horns which are twisted spirally and on the rams may reach a length of 115 cm and weigh up to 13 kg. On a very young bighorn there is still not much sign of the formidable weapons it is destined to have, but it is not in fact long before the horns start to grow, on females as well as males.

Puma (bottom left)

Mammals up to the size of a stag are the preferred food of the puma *(Profelis concolor)*, an animal referred to in some areas as the cougar and in others as the mountain lion. Even before weaning her cubs at the age of six months, the mother puma will have taught them how she stalks, chases and kills prey animals. But of course it will take them a long time to become equally adept themselves.

Hoary Marmot (top left)

The mountains of Alaska and Siberia are the home of the hoary marmot *(Marmota caligata)*. The ash-grey coat is good camouflage for this animal against the background of the stony heights. It lives in an extended family, the members of which whistle to warn each other of impending danger. Guard duties in a hoary marmot tribe, however, are mainly the responsibility of father animals.

Yellow-bellied Marmot (top right)

The young of the yellow-bellied marmot *(Marmota fla-viventris)* are born in a grass-lined nest inside the residential burrow. After three weeks they emerge into the open air for the first time and start inquisitively exploring their surroundings. By the time a further two weeks have passed, they will be weaned and feeding like their parents on a mainly herbivorous diet.

On the Prairie

The natural grasslands of North America have been taken over to a large extent as arable land for agricultural development. But even today there are still vast tracts of almost virgin land where the young of bison and coyote can grow up as they always have.

Harris's Hawk (above left)

Harris's hawk (Parabuteo unicinctus) is found not only in the southern states of the USA but in Central and South America, living in desert, semidesert and steppe country. It is a tough environment, and these birds co-operate both in hunting and in rearing and guarding their young. The females usually raise three broods every year.

American Goldfinch (above right)

The tiny American goldfinch nestlings (Carduelis tristis) seen here will grow only to a body length of 12 cm, which is smaller than a sparrow. They will have hatched from pale blue eggs — the usual clutch is four — after two weeks of incubation. Once they reach adulthood, the males will have brilliant yellow plumage with black wings and tail and a black cap.

Squash Bug (left)

The squash bug (Anasa tristis) has no pupal stage, and the nymphs look very like the adult insect itself while they go through several moults. Squash bugs can wreak havoc on North American crops of cucumber, pumpkin and other gourds, grape and peach. They are members of the corei bugs group, feeders on plant sap.

Colorado Beetle (left)

Twice to three times every year, a Colorado beetle lays almost 2500 eggs on the leaves of solanaceous plants, which notably include potatoes and tobacco. The tiny red larvae deposited there, which can easily be mistaken for ladybird larvae, and in due course the beetles themselves, will ravage the crops if not checked. They are understandably a much feared pest.

Killdeer (below)

The killdeer (*Charadrius vociferus*), or killdeer plover, makes its rudimentary nest on the bare earth and typically incubates a clutch of four eggs. When it leaves the nest temporarily it camouflages the clutch of eggs so skilfully in a stony background that they can only be seen with difficulty. In most cases the parents take turns to sit on the eggs, which need four weeks to hatch.

Monarch Butterfly *(above left)*

The monarch butterfly caterpillar *(Danaus plexippus)* hanging here on a leaf is about to enter the pupal stage. Since hatching it will have been feeding on leaves of the milkweed plant, in this way absorbing toxic substances which will make the future monarch butterfly inedible from the point of view of potential predators.

(above right)

The monarch is a brilliant orange-brown butterfly with a black body, black veining on its wings and white spots on black edges to its wings, one of the 'true' butterflies. It is noted for its long-distance migration to winter feeding areas 2000 miles away — areas in which deforestation is now a severe threat to the butterfly's survival.

Seventeen-Year Locust *(centre right)*

This periodical cicada *(Magicicada septendecim)* is so named because of its life-cycle: it spends no less than 17 years underground while progressing through successive nymph stages. When the insect finally leaves its underground fastness and comes to the surface, it will attach itself to a branch or similar object and develop rapidly — over only four or five days — into a fully mature cicada.

Harlequin Bug *(bottom right)*

The female harlequin bug *(Murgantia histrionica)* lays its eggs, twelve or more of them, in a double row on the underside of the leaves of cruciferous plants such as cabbage and broccoli. The eggs look like tiny barrels. Once the nymphs hatch, they will feed on the plant's sap, and they are capable of causing considerable damage to fields of vegetables.

Pronghorn *(above)*

This pronghorn fawn *(Antilocapra americana)* only needs to grow a little older before it will no longer need its mother's protection — because by then, like the adults, it will find safety from its enemies in flight. Pronghorn have no problems in running at a sustained 25 mph (45 kph), easily enough to outdistance wolf or coyote. Over short distances, up to a few hundred yards, they can sprint at 60 mph (100 kph), which makes them one of the world's fastest-moving mammals.

(centre right)

Among the hoofed mammals, the pronghorn is in a family of its own, and is the only species within this family. The two juveniles in the picture, when grown, will be 1 m long and weigh up to 70 kg. Their horns rest on bony spurs, and are hollow like antelope horns, but are shed annually like deer antlers. This combination is unique in the animal kingdom.

(bottom right)

A pronghorn only a few days old might seem easy prey for wolves or large raptors, but this is not in fact so unless it has lost its mother. Female pronghorn will defend their young fanatically, lashing out at attackers with their front hooves.

Green Lynx Spider *(top left)*

Green lynx spiders *(Peucetia viridans)* are hunting spiders, which means they do not spin webs to catch prey, but attack it directly. The only web they make is a cocoon that the female spins for her eggs. Inside it, an average of about 200 orange eggs hatch after four weeks or slightly over, releasing a brood of tiny spiders. Having guarded the nestful of eggs since laying them, the mother spider now watches over the hatched babies.

Burrowing Owl *(top right)*

Burrowing owls *(Athene cunicularia)*, of which these are two young specimens, must be among the strangest of all birds anywhere, because in all respects they are a complete contrast to their relatives, the nocturnal owls. They hunt by day and even spend time sunning themselves; they often run from place to place — though they can fly perfectly well — because they find their food on the ground; and they live and nest underground in old rabbit-holes.

Swallowtail Butterfly *(left)*

The swallowtails *(Papilionidae)*, which are found in all the world's warmer regions in about 600 species, lay their eggs on the food plants needed by their caterpillars. The caterpillars can then begin feeding immediately they are hatched. As a protection against predators, the caterpillars have a forked scent gland which secretes a substance with a smell that deters birds, for example, from eating them.

Ringtail *(bottom left)*

The ringtail *(Bassariscus astutus)*, with its big eyes, is a typical nocturnal animal. It is resident in the United States and Mexico, and has the distinctive ringed tail which earned it its name. Young ringtails only keep company with their mother for about four months. After that they go off to lead a solitary existence — except at mating times.

(above)

This little ringtail seems to be frightened and calling out fearfully to its mother. She may perhaps be in the process of moving her young to a new nest, with this baby the last to be moved and sensing its aloneness. From the time a ringtail litter is two weeks old, the mother will move all the babies once in a while to a new nesting place, for added safety.

(bottom right)

Pregnant for hardly even two months at a time, the ringtail has the shortest gestation period of any of the raccoon-like animals. This ringtail baby weighed a mere 30 g when it was born in a rock cavity or similar place. Usually there are two or three in a litter, sometimes four, sometimes there is only one baby. Ringtails can fend for themselves from the age of six months, and they reach reproductive maturity at two years.

Bison *(above)*

Today, many of the bison *(Bison bison)* in North America are kept on large ranches and are farmed for their meat. However, there are still some free-roaming herds in such areas as the Yellowstone National Park. Ranch-bound or free, bison live outdoors all year round, and they themselves manage the rearing of their young.

(bottom left)

During the mating season, the bull bison often fight violently over access to a particular cow or cows in the herd for mating. In the course of this warfare a bull may lose a fifth of its body weight. Yet once the calves are born, the bulls show no interest in their progeny. The bison one sees moving over the prairie will most often be groups of cows with their calves.

(bottom right)

A bison calf is born following a gestation period of about nine months. Very soon after first seeing the light of day, it will be ready to move on across the prairie with the herd. By the beginning of the 20th century, humans had nearly wiped out the bison as a species, but since then it has recovered, and now the bison population has grown to about 350,000 animals.

Bison *(left)*

A newborn bison calf *(Bison bison)* weighs between 10 and 15 kg. But very quickly indeed this weight multiplies many times. A fully grown bull bison will tip the scales at up to 1000 kg; however, females only reach about half that weight. One can well see why generations of American Indian hunted the bison for its meat.

Black-tailed Prairie Dog *(centre left)*

The black-tailed prairie dog *(Cynomys ludovicianus)* is a rodent, a member of the ground squirrel family. These little nibblers live in colonies, and within the colonies the individual animals or individual family groups live in separate burrows. Here the babies are born. At a mere 7 cm long, and weighing only about 15 grams, they are truly tiny.

(bottom left)

Any males among these three young black-tailed prairie dogs will have to leave their family behind once they attain sexual maturity at about two to three years of age. But such juveniles generally establish themselves right next to where their elders are living, and as a result, with successive generations, prairie dog colonies can become enormous.

Coyote *(right-hand page, top left)*

In an average-sized litter, the female coyote *(Canis latrans)* will give birth to six whelps. The young coyotes soon learn from their parents how to hunt: it is not true — as widely believed — that coyotes feed exclusively on carrion, because they take any small mammals they can get, such as hares or mice. Although their diet is mainly carnivorous, coyotes also eat fruit.

(right-hand page, top right)

The coyote, like the wolf, is one of the ancestors of the domestic dog, and this is the reason why it can mate with dogs — some matings even proving fertile. However, such couplings are relatively rare, and only feral domestic dogs (dogs that have gone wild) are involved. Coyotes otherwise mate only with their own kind.

(right-hand page, main picture)

Coyote belong to the canine or dog family. They look rather like a wolf in miniature, which is why they are also commonly called the prairie wolf. Another way in which they are like wolves is that they live in a family group — admittedly smaller than a wolf family, often just as a pair living on their own — and have a strong family instinct. For instance, the male coyote will initially bring food to the female and the babies — there may be as many as ten in a litter — after the birth has taken place.

Long-tailed Weasel *(above)*

The long-tailed weasel *(Mustela frenata)* occurs in North America and in north-western regions of South America too. In the north, the weasel's coat changes colour in winter from brown to white. This is better camouflage amid snow and ice, and in these conditions only the black tip of the weasel's tail stands out perkily from the winter landscape. The winter colour change occurs even in juveniles.

Striped Skunk *(right)*

The striped skunk *(Mephitis mephitis)* is notorious above all for the stink of the secretion it can fire from its anal glands when threatened. This is also the reason its enemies are so few in number: its main predators are owls, which have no sense of smell. However, at birth its young — three to five in a litter — are blind and helpless. Their eyes do not open till they are about 20 days old.

Mule Deer *(top right)*

One of the identifying characteristics of the mule deer or black-tailed deer *(Odocoileus hemionus)* is its coat, which has a reddish sheen in summer and looks if anything blue-grey in winter. However, the fawns — of which there are one to three in a litter — have a spotted coat, which makes it more difficult for predators to see them.

Mustang *(top left)*

The wild mustangs *(Equus caballus)* of North America are not true wild horses, being descended from horses that lived under human protection. The present-day mustang's ancestors were brought to North America by the Spanish in the 16th century. Today, mustangs are rare. This means that every foal born is an occasion to be celebrated by conservationists trying to ensure the survival of the mustang.

(centre left)

Mustangs are North America's wild-living horses. They are the origin of many American breeds of horse, and are themselves descended from horses brought across the Atlantic by the Spaniards during their conquest of America. The Indians and, later, white Americans valued the mustang as a tough, resilient riding horse and packhorse. It is now a protected animal, which means that this foal may never have to carry a rider on its back.

(bottom left)

As long as her foal is lying resting or asleep, the mustang mare will graze alongside it to keep it safe. To get up from the lying position, a very young foal has to make a terrific effort. Its legs are very long relative to its body size, and so the foal must also concentrate hard on placing and angling them just right so that it can spring to its feet — and not topple back to the ground a second later.

243

Western Harvest Mouse *(left-hand page, top)*

The Western harvest mouse *(Reithrodontomys megalotis)* lives in Mexico and the western United States. When first born, following about 23 days' gestation, the tiny baby mice are completely helpless. Their eyes do not open until about 11 days later. That is also the point at which they get their first solid food — and just a few days later still they will have been weaned off their mother's milk.

Deer Mouse *(left-hand page, bottom)*

The deer mouse *(Peromyscus maniculatus)* belongs to the vole family, but unlike most other vole species has large external ears. As regards fertility, it is a match for any of them. Usually it digs itself a burrow and makes a nest by lining the far end with hairs, moss and the like. That is where the young will be born.

Uinta Ground Squirrel *(right)*

The Uinta ground squirrel *(Citellus armatus)*, like other ground squirrels, is a relative of the marmot. It has cheek pouches which it uses for moving food from place to place, or clearing earth out of its burrow. After hibernating for up to eight months, ending in April, it produces its young in May. There may be as many as ten babies in the litter.

American Badger *(below)*

The word 'badger' in the name of the American badger *(Taxidea taxus)* is misleading. This predatory animal, which feeds mainly on smaller mammals, birds and insects, is not a badger, but belongs to the same family as the martens. A solitary-living animal, it brings forth its young in spring. By autumn they leave their mother and disperse.

In the Forests

The Canadian forests, with their colourful autumn foliage, are among the best-known in the world. They cover vast areas of the North American continent, providing space and cover for wild animals, including several large predators, to reproduce their kind.

Great Horned Owl (top left)

The parents of these two great horned owls *(Bubo virginianus)* provide for them not only until they are fledged, but for some six weeks afterwards. This ensures the owlets have enough time to become good hunters, able subsequently to forage for themselves. Their standard technique is to perch on a tree, keeping a sharp look-out for prey, which they then swoop down on directly from their tree.

(above left)

As a nocturnal raptor, the great horned owl utters its characteristic 'whoo-whoo' cry mainly during the courtship and breeding season, and then in the gloaming or at night. Young birds like the one in the picture will not begin calling like this for quite some time yet, gradually picking it up later on. Chicks hatch in a nest situated as high as possible — though not built by the parent birds, as they take over the old nests of other large species.

(above right)

By the time it is two months old, a young great horned owl like this one will have exchanged enough of its original down for feather plumage to be able to begin flight trials. A young bird perched on a branch will often spread its wings and puff out its feathers in order to make itself look bigger and deter potential predators.

Spotted Salamander (bottom left)

The creature that will soon emerge from these blotchy-looking eggs, and grow eventually to 20 cm or so in length, is a spotted salamander (*Ambystoma maculatum*). Its underside is plain grey, but its back is marked by yellowish-brown spots of varying size. In their spawning-grounds, the salamanders mate in spring, following which the female lays her eggs.

Wapiti (bottom right)

The wapiti (*Cervus elaphus* or *Cervus canadensis*) belongs to the elk, deer and moose family and is the North American elk. When fully grown, this animal is an impressive sight. It can weigh up to 450 kg, of which the antlers alone may account for nearly 30 kg. Newborn, a wapiti will weigh up to 14 kg, less than half the weight of the antlers carried by the fully-grown beast.

Polyphemus Silkmoth (below)

This vividly green caterpillar will metamorphose in due course into the polyphemus silkworm moth (*Antherea polyphemus polyphemus*). It leads a solitary existence, in which its first act was to eat the eggshell from which it had hatched. Then it will have turned to devouring leaves. The caterpillar is not particularly fussy about which tree's leaves it eats: oak will do just as well as willow or birch.

Opossum *(above left)*

The Southern or common opossum *(Didelphis marsupialis)* is a nocturnal, omnivorous animal which lives in trees and bushes. The opossum is a marsupial — meaning that it has a pouch on its body, into which its young crawl immediately after being born. But of course as the babies grow bigger the pouch very soon becomes too small for them. At that point they clamber out, and from then on the mother carries them on her back.

(above centre)

Baby opossums are born roughly twelve days after conception. At this point the tiny marsupials actually weigh less than two grams and are still very immature. So their first move is to crawl into the pouch of their mother and suck from her teats for the next 50 to 65 days.

North American Porcupine

(right-hand page, top right)

'Take it easy, what's the hurry?' describes the movements of the North American porcupine *(Erethizon dorsatum)* — which can afford to take it easy, as its dangerous spines ensure that it has few real enemies. Even so, there are a few predators (e.g. lynx, puma and wolf) which will tackle porcupine, especially the young animals, which are less formidably armed against attack.

The North American porcupine, a nocturnal animal which is also referred to as an urson, has barbed spines on its back which in the event of a fight or attack would come away and stick to the skin of the attacker, causing festering wounds. Ursons live in ground cavities or hollow trees. Females have a relatively long gestation period of seven months before giving birth to a single baby — already equipped with spines, though at this stage they are soft.

North American porcupines like these two young animals might easily be confused with Old World porcupines, at least by the casual observer. But the American animal's spines are shorter, and also only grow on its back and tail. The belly has no spines, only bristles.

The preferred food of the North American porcupine consists of tree bark and leaves. Where possible it will spend an entire winter on a single tree, steadily eating the bark. This naturally kills the tree. Young porcupines too, when weaned, are trained by their mother to expect the same diet of bark and leaves.

Eastern Hognose Snake

The Eastern hognose snake *(Heterodon platyrhinos)* is a mildly venomous snake which grows to about 1.15 m in length. Its colour varies from yellow to brown to reddish, always with blotches. The female lays a clutch of eggs which may contain as few as 5 or as many as 60. The picture shows young Eastern hognoses at the moment of hatching.

Fallow Deer (right)

Fallow deer *(Dama dama)* live in herds consisting of family groups, the family groups in turn consisting of mothers and fawns. The bucks only join the herd during the rutting season, when they use the impressive palmate (shovel-shaped) antlers characteristic of their species to fight each other for the possession of the does. Then, a good six to seven months after the rut, the next generation of fallow deer is born.

250

Canadian Lynx (top left)

Broad, well-furred paws are among the distinctive features of the Canadian lynx *(Lynx canadensis)*. These have a purpose — in winter they function like snowshoes, so that even when there is snow on the ground the Canadian lynx can move fast, without sinking in. Its young are born after a relatively short gestation period of nine weeks.

(top right)

When fully grown, these Canadian lynx kittens will stand 60 cm at the shoulder and have a body length of 90–120 cm. The males reach a weight of anything between 10 and 17 kg. But they look bigger and more massive than that because their coat is so thick. As with all other lynxes, the tail of the Canadian variety is fairly short.

(centre left)

These two Canadian lynx kittens are still just enjoying a carefree game. But it will not be long before the serious business of life starts for them. Once they are about ten to twelve months old, they will have to fend for themselves, which means catching their own prey. When these two indulge in rough games, they are in fact engaging in a kind of training for strength and agility which will stand them in good stead when they begin hunting.

Pacific Treefrog (bottom left)

Even when fully grown, the Pacific treefrog *(Hyla regilla)* is almost as inconspicuous as its second developmental stage, the tadpole. A widespread species on the North American Pacific coast, this amphibian has been occasionally found living in the wild in Europe because some specimens kept in captivity escaped or were simply released.

Canadian Lynx *(top right)*

The Canadian lynx's principal prey is rabbits and hares (whereas the Eurasian lynx mainly hunts deer). The Canadian lynx population in any given year will accordingly depend in part on the size of the rabbit and hare populations in the current year. Whenever these food animals are scarce, there will usually also be a fall in the Canadian lynx birthrate.

(centre right)

Canadian lynx kittens are assiduous in practising climbing, an activity for which their supple build and their claws equip them well. These razor-sharp little hooks can be unsheathed in a flash, the lynx holds on by digging them into the bark of the tree and then uses muscle power to haul itself upwards. From the crown of the tree it has a good view of all the various activities going on underneath.

(bottom left)

During the moult in spring and autumn, the coat of the adult lynx will look just as tousled as that of this young kitten lynx. So that they don't overheat in summer and get too cold in winter, they lose their thick under-wool every spring, only to grow a new winter coat again in the autumn.

(bottom right)

The Canadian lynx's thick fur equips it marvellously for sub-zero temperatures. It is also extremely long-legged, which means it can run effortlessly even in deep snow. However, so that the kittens are not exposed too early to extremely cold temperatures, they are born in late spring or in summer, usually during May and June.

Hissing fiercely and showing its teeth, this young lynx is leaving no doubt at all that it belongs to the cat family. As an adult animal later on it will use exactly the same behaviour to defend its territory. The territory can be as much as 1000 square kilometres — depending on the amount of food that can be gleaned from it — and the lynx marks it out by spraying.

(left)

To actually see young lynxes in the wild, one has to be extraordinarily lucky. The lynx is a largely solitary animal, and rare enough to be an endangered species. Female kittens reach sexual maturity at a shade under two years, while it takes the males just under three years to reach the same stage of development.

Bobcat *(above)*

Eight to ten weeks after a mating between bobcats *(Lynx rufus)*, which will have taken place any time from February to June, the female produces one to (rarely) six young. Kittens are blind when born, and during their first eight weeks of life are fed solely with their mother's milk. Then they are gradually weaned on to a diet of meat.

(right)

The bobcat has reddish fur with flecks which may often be almost invisible, or located mostly round the legs and on the belly. As a rule it is a solitary animal, but there are quite frequent exceptions, some males choosing to remain with the female after mating. These males do still roam, but keep on returning to their mate with food for the kittens.

(top left)

Though only a kitten, this bobcat is already showing the ear tufts characteristic of the lynx family — though they are smaller than those of the Eurasian lynx. A further difference from the European cousin is that the bobcat has a circular moustache of semi-erect hairs framing its face.

(centre left)

A bobcat kitten like this one needs to practise for quite some time before it is skilled enough as a hunter to be able to fend for itself. A bobcat is a pure carnivore, preferring rabbit, hare, birds and any available mammals up to the size of a small deer. Its hunting technique is to stalk the victim, get within close range, pounce and — if it has caught the prey — to kill with a bite to the back of the victim's neck.

(bottom left)

Mating often takes place only after savage fighting between males and the emergence of one as the victor, who has established his right to mate with the female concerned. However, once the kittens have been born — in most cases three of them — the male has to leave. Usually the mother bobcat chases him off and rears her young alone.

Woodchuck *(bottom right)*

The young of the woodchuck *(Marmota monax)* — a North American resident — stay close to their parents for their first summer only. Born in spring, they have to move out of the parental nest in autumn because at that point the father animal chases them off. From then on, they forage independently for roots, bulbs and seeds.

White-tailed Deer *(top left)*

To help camouflage them, newborn white-tailed or Virginia deer *(Odocoileus virginianus)* have white flecks on their coat. They are called white-tailed deer because of the white colouring of the underside of their tail — they raise their tail when alarmed, and the resulting white flash acts as a signal for the rest of the herd, even over quite a long distance.

(top right)

It takes about 18 months from birth before a white-tailed or Virginia deer becomes sexually mature. Certainly, these two juveniles are giving each other a good sniffing-over, but of course not yet as a preliminary to mating, it is far too soon for that. In winter they feed mainly on leaves and small branches.

(right)

The white-tailed deer originated in North America, but has also been introduced in a number of European countries, including the Czech Republic, and most notably Finland. Ii is an impressive-looking deer, whose fawns can run very soon after they are born, but stay behind, hidden in thickets by their mother, when she goes off to forage for food.

Raccoon *(left)*

One of the most versatile members of the *Procyonidae* family (a group often regarded as smaller cousins of the bear family), the raccoon *(Procyon lotor)* is an omnivore and a regular scavenger in areas where waste is tipped. It is thus frequently seen near human habitations. Also, raccoons breed rapidly: the females have three to five young every year, and it only takes one to two years from birth for them to reach the mating age themselves.

(right)

This young raccoon weighed a mere 70 g or so at birth. It was reared solely on its mother's milk for the first few weeks, then gradually weaned onto solid foods of both vegetal and animal origin. Since reaching the age of eight weeks, it has been accompanying its mother as she searches for food. When four months old it will become independent.

(below)

A young raccoon adopted by humans and well cared for can become extremely tame. Being both omnivorous and exceptionally adaptable, a raccoon is not a problem to look after. However, as they have to be allowed some freedom, anyone keeping a raccoon may well find that a single animal has suddenly become a raccoon family — and that could well be something of a problem!

Raccoon *(left-hand page, top left)*

Very young raccoons *(Procyon lotor)* manage to look not only particularly cute but also very like adult raccoons. Partly this is because of their strikingly marked face, their thick and exceptionally long coat and their ringed tail. But it is also because young and adult alike have a behaviour pattern that explains why these animals are known in some cultures (especially German-speaking) as 'wash-bears' — they take their food to water and dip it in as if they were washing it.

(left-hand page, top right)

This young raccoon makes an appealing picture as it sits munching corn — and it always looks droll when these miniature bears pick up their food in their paws and lift it daintily to their mouths. Looking at an attractive image like this, one wonders how it is that some people can enjoy actually wearing these beautiful animals as part of a fur coat.

(left-hand page, main picture)

Baby raccoons are born, after a gestation lasting about 65 days, in a nest that the mother has fitted out in a safe place. That might be a hollow tree, a rocky outcrop or even a house. The raccoon's origins lie in North and Central Americal, but as a consequence of fur farms in Europe and the escape or release of some animals they are now present in the wild on our side of the Atlantic too.

Lodgepole Chipmunk *(top right)*

The lodgepole chipmunk *(Tamias speciosus)* is a native of North America. It has cheek-pouches which it uses for carrying food from place to place. Its babies are born blind and helpless, and it is a month before they open their eyes. But after that they develop rapidly, and by the age of seven months a lodgepole chipmunk is fully grown.

(centre right)

Chipmunks are essentially solitary animals. It is only for the first few months of their life that they stay with their mother and siblings. Then each young chipmunk will look for a burrow of its own, near which no other chipmunk will be tolerated. The only exception they make is for purposes of mating.

Grey Squirrel *(bottom right)*

This baby grey squirrel *(Sciurus carolinensis)* is sitting in its nest in a hollow tree. Its mother suckles it in the nest for about three months before it can be weaned onto solid food such as fruit, mushrooms and the like. It differs from the European squirrel in having white underparts and a grey (rather than red-brown) back. Also, its ears are not tufted. In Britain, the introduction of grey squirrels in the 19th century has led to a dramatic decline of red squirrels, to the point where these are now an endangered species.

Grey Fox (top right)

Uniquely among animals of the dog family, the grey fox (*Urocyon cinereoargenteus*) can climb trees. No tree-trunk is too steep for it, no treetop too high. Up there in the dense forest foliage, the grey fox can hide from its enemies and search for nourishment. Grey foxes are believed to form monogamous pairs. A litter will have up to four cubs.

Black Bear (centre right)

This young American black bear (*Ursus americanus*) probably has one or two siblings somewhere, because unlike most other species of bear, which have single births, a female black bear produces either two or three babies on most occasions. Once this bear-cub has been weaned, it will nourish itself on food from both plant and animal sources.

(bottom right)

The black bear — so called even though some animals are brown or even quite light-coloured — produces its young during the long winter recess, in a hideaway well protected from snow and excessive cold. The cubs have a birth weight of only about 300 g, but once they have grown somewhat they are free to romp in the snowy paradise outside the den.

(right-hand page, top left)

A muzzle that is lighter-coloured than the body fur, and relatively sharp-pointed ears — those are the main characteristics differentiating the black bear from the brown bear. In other ways, depending on region, the two species may be very similar, both in size and in predominant colour. However, the black bear is much more widespread than the brown, and so it is the black — like this young specimen — that one is much more likely to encounter.

(right-hand page, top right)

After looking at the appealing face and attitude of the little black bear in the photograph, it is not difficult to decide against wearing things made of its fur. It was in fact the trade in furs that almost finished the black bear as a species for ever. The famous bearskins of Her Majesty's Guards used to be made from its fur. Fortunately the black bear has now become fairly abundant once more.

(right-hand page, main picture)

From the time when they are about twelve months old, black bear cubs begin to cut the ties with their mother and live more independently. They reach reproductive maturity when they are three. Not particularly large as bears go, black bears are very agile and quick-moving, and even when fully grown are adept at climbing trees.

Black Bear (bottom left)

An adult black bear *(Ursus americanus)* climbs just as nimbly as a young one: this is a species admirably adapted to life in the American forests. And it has no problem at all in standing up on its hind legs to demonstrate its full stature.

(bottom right)

At the age of about a year, a North American black bear will stop keeping company with its mother and become self-reliant. It will have its own territory, which may be up to 300 square kilometres in area. At three years it reaches sexual maturity, and between May and July will be seeking a mate to have cubs with.

Grizzly Bear (above)

When a grizzly bear cub *(Ursus arctos horribilis)* is born, it is hard indeed to imagine that this little thing will one day be a huge and dangerous bear measuring as much as 2.5 m in length — because the cub has a weight at birth of only about 350–400 g. It is born during the winter retreat period, which ensures that the little cub, initially blind and helpless, is not exposed too early to real danger.

(above)

As it plays with its mother or its siblings, the grizzly cub is developing its muscular co-ordination and its skills, and picking up all kinds of useful knowledge. One of the most important things it learns is to read the signals in their behaviour which enable it to judge their state of mind and also how they react to things as they happen.

(bottom left)

It may not look like it, and he does not know it, but this grizzly cub is in the process of training to become a hunter. Every year at a certain time, salmon migrate upriver to their spawning grounds. It's a feast delivered to the grizzlies' front door. They simply wade into the water and with their huge paws and powerful talons they swipe at every passing salmon, they see, killing and eating as many as possible.

(bottom right)

Like most of the larger mammals, a grizzly she-bear goes on caring for her young for a long time. This is not just a matter of suckling them and subsequently feeding them with solid foods. She also guards and defends her progeny, and shows them what plants are good to eat and how they can catch and deal with prey. As the young bears begin to try out what they can do for themselves, the mother will watch attentively.

Collared Lizard (above)

Collared lizards (Crotaphytus collaris) hatch from eggs which the female will have laid in a safe place under rocks or in a cave or recess. At this time the female lizard has red flecks, but otherwise these lizards are well camouflaged in the desert environment by their brownish-beige body colouring. The only time the collared lizard is active is the time when other desert-dwellers are resting — in the fiery heat of the midday sun.

Mourning Dove (centre right)

This young mourning dove (Zenaidura macroura) — the species is also referred to as the Carolina dove — will surely be taking to the air soon like its parents. The name 'mourning dove' was given to it because of its sad-sounding, flute-like call, which in fact is the mourning dove's way of communicating with others of its kind. Another of its identifying features is a black fleck underneath each ear.

Black-throated Sparrow (bottom right)

Three chicks of the black-throated sparrow (Amphizpiza bilineata) are seen here waiting and begging loudly for food in their nest. The yawning expanse of bright red gullet thus exposed triggers the parents' feeding instinct and also helps to ensure accurate delivery when the food arrives. The clutch laid by the hen black-throated sparrow generally comprises three or four eggs. The nests are commonly built in bushes, low down near the ground, and very well lined.

In the Alaskan Tundra

In the bare, treeless country bordering the Arctic, with permafrost deep in the soil and only scanty vegetation in the form of lichens and hard grasses, baby animals are not born until late spring, when there will be enough food for them and for the adults nurturing them.

Arctic Fox *(above left)*

The two Arctic fox cubs *(Alopex lagopus)* seen playing here still have their juvenile brown coat. Once grown up, they will have a summer coat consisting of relatively thin, grey or brownish fur, which changes completely at the autumn moult. The fox then grows an extremely thick winter coat, the colour of which will depend on the camouflage needed for the particular habitat — for foxes living on the snow-bound tundra it will be snow-white, but for those whose range is along the Arctic coasts with their blue shimmer off the sea, the coat will be a pale grey-blue.

(above centre)

As it plays, this Arctic fox cub is unwittingly practising a hunting skill — how to pounce on your live quarry. Only by practising and refining its techniques will it one day become capable of providing for itself by catching lemmings, fish and birds. And for each of these three types of prey the fox needs to know a different hunting technique.

(top right)

The number of cubs an Arctic fox will have depends on how much food is currently available. At times when the fox's preferred food, the lemming, is abundant, Arctic fox litters may contain as many as 16 whelps — but a much more usual figure is half that. Newborn fox cubs remain safely in their parents' extensive burrows until partly grown, when they are allowed out into the open.

(right)

The Arctic fox is found not only in northern Canada and Alaska, but also across Greenland and northern Europe and into northern Asia.

Rough-legged Buzzard (top left)

The rough-legged buzzard *(Buteo lagopus)* is a winter visitor in Europe, that being the time when there is no food for them up in the Arctic tundra. In spring these birds return to the Arctic, and there they lay and incubate three or four eggs during May/June. The female guards and feeds the young, while the cock bird hunts for food and delivers it.

(top right)

How many chicks a hen rough-legged buzzard rears to maturity will depend on how much food there is. If lemmings and mice are plentiful, it will lay up to seven eggs, against an average of four. If there is not enough food, the buzzards will move somewhere else. In the tundra they often build at ground-level, but sometimes also in small trees or in a rocky crevice.

Eastern Timber Wolf (right)

The Eastern timber wolf or grey wolf *(Canis lupus lycoon)* is the commonest wolf species in the United States. It occurs throughout the Eastern states, right down to Florida. Like all other wolves, the timber wolf communicates by means of varied calls. For instance, even the cubs are expert in the characteristic howls with which timber wolves summon others from far away.

266

Eastern Timber Wolf (left)

The timber wolf's coat may be any of a whole range of colours. Some are dark grey, others nearer light grey. In common with all other wolves, timber wolves live in groups of related animals in which — so far as is known at the time of writing — only the alpha male and alpha female, that is to say the pack leaders — produce progeny together.

Wolf (right)

Worldwide, the biggest wolf population today is to be found in North America. In Europe, by contrast, the wolf (Canis lupus) has become a rare animal, although some conservationists are attempting to re-introduce it. It has to be borne in mind that once again presumably only the alpha animals will mate and reproduce, so that herd numbers will be slow to grow. There are generally about four to six cubs accompanying every pack.

(below)

This little chap looks as though butter would not melt in his mouth, and yet the wolf is portrayed in many a fairy-tale and in other literature as a man-eater and figure of dread. In reality, no wolf is known ever to have attacked a human being. The main reason for wolves' unpopularity with humans is that they kill not only wild prey but domestic animals too, such as sheep.

Alaska Tundra Wolf *(top left)*

At birth, an Alaska tundra wolf *(Canis lupus tundrorum)* weighs about 500 g and is blind. It will usually have about five siblings, but there can sometimes be ten or more. It can be regarded as fully grown only when it has reached the age of two; by then, as the wolves of this subspecies are particularly large, it will stand a metre high at the shoulder and weigh 75 kg. And yet, with its dense, snowy-white fur, its looks are more reminiscent of a big dog than of a wolf.

Wolf *(top centre)*

Wolf cubs *(Canis lupus)* at play growl often, just as dogs do. They growl most of all when fighting among themselves, or when tugging with their sharp teeth at the coat of older pack members. Basically, growling at other pack members is a threat signal, but when young cubs do it they are only issuing a playful challenge.

(right-hand page, top right)

Newborn wolf cubs are particularly helpless. They are blind, and dependent on their mother. It is about a fortnight later that they open their eyes; and roughly a further week after that they are ready to leave the den and go out into the open for the first time. But their mother continues to keep them under her watchful eye.

(left-hand page, bottom left)

When the pack has been able to supply good quantities of meat following successful hunting, the well-nourished cubs will only need to be three to five months old before being able to accompany the pack wherever it goes. As wolves are not simply predators but sociable and intelligent animals as well, they hunt as a pack and so are able to bring down animals much bigger than themselves, such as caribou.

(bottom centre)

At birth, a wolf cub weighs no more than 300–500 g. The weight reached by a fully-grown wolf will depend on its sex and on what subspecies it belongs to — out of the 40 or so that have been identified — but will be at least 15 kg and can be as much as 65 kg. In the same way, a wolf's body-length may be anything between 1 and 1.5 metres, to which the tail adds a further length of between 30 and 50 cm.

(bottom right)

Cubs are suckled for from four to eight weeks from birth. After that, the whole pack shares with the parents in feeding them — by regurgitating meat they have eaten themselves. Wolves never eat plants if meat is available. The meat is made more digestible for the young cubs by having been partly predigested in the stomachs of the adult wolves.

Caribou *(top right)*

The caribou *(Rangifer tarandus)* is the wild North American reindeer. It belongs to the same genus as deer, and is the only member of the genus to have females as well as males bearing antlers. The female gestates for about 240 days before giving birth to either one or two calves — which are born already well adapted for life in cold climates.

Musk Ox *(centre right)*

The musk ox *(Ovibos moschatus)* may look like a buffalo, but in fact it is not related to the cattle family, but to goats and sheep. Musk oxen can defend themselves and their young very effectively. If the herd is attacked by predators — wolves, for instance — the calves hide behind the grown animals, and these organise themselves in a chain from which individual animals strike at the attackers with their horns.

Arctic Lemming *(bottom left)*

The Arctic lemming *(Dicrostonyx torquatus)* is a small animal, not reaching more than 15 cm in length. With its white winter coat and the double claws which grow every winter on the third and fourth toes of its front paws, it is splendidly adapted for the inhospitable climate of the polar regions. The females can produce between two and five litters a year, so the species' survival can be regarded as secure in spite of the numerous predators that target it.

Semi-palmated Plover *(bottom right)*

In the case of the semi-palmated plover *(Charadrius semipalmatus)*, the younger birds can be told apart from the adults by the different colour of the plumage. Both young and adults have a white breast with the white interrupted by a dark ring encircling the neck. In the older birds this ring is black, but in the juveniles it is brown.

Wolverine *(above)*

For a short time after they are born, baby wolverines *(Gulo gulo)* have a light-coloured coat, but it soon darkens towards its adult brown to blackish-brown shade.

(centre left)

The wolverine is known to have lived in the north of Canada, the United States, mainland Europe and Scandinavia for some 400,000 years. Regrettably, there are no longer very many living specimens of this animal, a member of the marten family. In Scandinavia, for example, the estimated wolverine population is no more than about 500. Also, the fact that a wolverine litter has no more than two to four babies does not do much to boost numbers.

(bottom left)

The wolverine is a solitary animal. The only exception is in the breeding season, when male and female animals come together for a short time. The young, born after a gestation period of seven to nine months, stay with their mother for all of two years — even though they will have grown virtually to their full size by the time they are about three months old.

271

South America

By River, Lake and Marsh

The rich stores of nutrients contained in these freshwater areas are the reason for the great variety of species that live here: these foods provide a good basis for the rearing of the young animals. As many of the wet areas in this part of the world dry out at certain times of year, the animals' reproductive timetable is geared to the natural seasons.

Broad-snouted Caiman *(top left)*

In the absence of their mother, these two baby broad-snouted caiman *(Caiman latirostris)* are just as much at risk in the water as they would be on land, or indeed as they were earlier on while still inside their eggs. While adult crocodiles — to which caiman are related — need fear no animal other than man, their eggs are a favourite prey for small mammals and large lizards, and the young caiman are targeted by snakes, fish and herons.

Common Caiman *(above left)*

The female common or spectacled caiman *(Caiman crocodilus)* before laying prepares a nest of leaves and aquatic plants on the river-bank and deposits in it a clutch of up to 40 eggs. As the plants decompose, they generate the warmth that the embryos must have if they are to develop. Two or three months later the baby caiman hatch. For most of this time the mother animal has been there to guard the nest.

(above right)

These two young common caiman will eventually grow to be 2 m long when they are adults, but before they reach that size they will have to eat their way through a lot of aquatic insects, crabs, fish, frogs and also mammals. The common caiman has bony ridges near its eyes which make it look as if it is wearing spectacles: hence the alternative name given to this caiman, the 'spectacled caiman'.

Muscovy Duck (bottom left)

While the young of the Muscovy duck (*Cairina moschata*) are still either yellow or light brown and black in colour and covered in down, the adult birds' plumage is white where birds have been bred like the wild variety. However, Muscovy duck have been bred in many other colours as well. As the wild birds like to perch on tree branches, they have sharp claws on their toes which enable them to get a good grip.

(bottom right)

The natural home of wild Muscovy ducks is on the rivers, lakes and salt lagoons of South and Central America. However, because of their handsome plumage and interesting face — the drakes have a kind of 'mask' of fleshy wart-like appendages round their eyes — they are bred all over the world as ornamental ducks, like the duckling in this photo.

Broad-snouted Caiman (below right)

For just under three months this little broad-snouted caiman was developing inside its egg which was lying with 20 to 80 others in a nest-mound of plant material. As the plants decomposed, the temperature inside rose to about 32 °C, warm enough to incubate the eggs. Then the baby caiman hatched, and now, together with its siblings, it will be looked after for a while longer by the mother caiman.

Muscovy Duck *(above)*

The Muscovy duck *(Cairina moschata)* is a very old breed of domestic duck. Over the course of a year it will lay between 200 and 300 eggs, from which ducklings hatch after a period of 28 days. After the first week they are allowed into the water, but they also like foraging on grassland, plucking out dandelion leaves, small nettles and fresh young grass.

American Flamingo *(bottom right)*

By the time an American flamingo *(Phoenicopterus ruber)* has roseate plumage to rival that of its parents, it will be three years old and will itself have reached the reproductive age. When first hatched, after being incubated in its egg for four weeks, it was covered in whitish-grey down. In its first weeks as a chick, the baby flamingo was fed by its parents with a regurgitated mess of pre-digested food.

Chilean Flamingo *(below left)*

Chilean flamingos *(Phoenicopterus chilensis)* breed in huge colonies in the swamps of temperate South America. They build their conical mud nest only 1.5 m from the next one, and lay a single egg, which both parents incubate and guard. Once the chicks have reached a certain age, they continue to be fed by the parents, but form their own juvenile groups consisting of many hundreds of young flamingos.

Black Caiman *(above)*

Only just hatched, the baby black caiman *(Melanosuchus niger)* surveys its surroundings. Its mother laid between 35 and 60 eggs here, and will almost certainly still be somewhere nearby. During the incubation of the eggs she will have guarded the nest against egg-eating predators, and she continues to protect the young caimans after they have hatched.

American Flamingo *(below left)*

The American flamingo, also called the Caribbean flamingo or simply the greater flamingo, is found virtually anywhere warm except for Australia and New Zealand. However, in the Old World, its plumage is usually white, while in the Caribbean it is red. The young are fed by their parents for rather over two months, until their bill has developed enough for them to be able to strain water through it for the food it contains.

Chilean Flamingo *(below right)*

This Chilean flamingo chick, just a week old, will be very new indeed to the world outside the nest, as baby flamingos need from four to seven days for their legs to grow strong enough for standing and walking. The parents still stay very close by, as the chick needs their protection.

Bare-throated Tiger-Heron (above left)

The bare-throated tiger-heron (Tigrisoma mexicanum) nests in trees, laying greenish-white eggs that are sometimes lightly flecked with brown. After the chicks hatch, they develop into semi-nocturnal birds, which when fishing often stride through the water, wading where it is deeper.

Giant Neotropical Toad (above right)

This toad (Bufo marinus neotropical) is also variously called the cane toad or marine toad. The young specimen in the picture is perfectly camouflaged in among the brown foliage. The females sometimes reach over 20 cm in length, considerably more than any of the males. Giant neotropical toads are venomous and are also voracious feeders. They have been introduced by humans to many parts of the world to combat pests, only to become regarded as pests themselves.

Capybara (right)

From the photo it may be hard to imagine it, but these young capybara (Hydrochaeris hydrochaeris) will grow into animals of up to 1.3 m in length: capybara are the world's biggest rodents. Although they forage for their food on land, their true element is water, and that is where they seek refuge from their enemies.

In the Mountains

The Cordilleras of the Andes, regarded as the world's most multifariously formed mountain ranges, provide a habitat for a correspondingly wide range of animals and their progeny. One particularly notable area is the vast, desert-like plateau known as the Altiplano, home of the New World's various camelid species.

Llama *(top right)*

Llama foals *(Lama guanicoe glama)* are born into a family group consisting of one male animal and several females with their young. Though they are domestic animals in the Andes, they are not kept wholly or partly indoors like European domestic animals: they live outside all year round. They are kept mainly for meat and wool, but are also used as beasts of burden.

Guanaco *(above left)*

The native peoples of Central and South America made use of the guanaco *(Lama guanicoe)* in various ways. They ate its meat, they made clothing from its wool — and its dung when dried made good fuel. They gradually tamed the guanaco species and with its help they bred the llama. However, most guanaco now live in the wild, like the young beast in the photograph.

(right)

The guanaco, found in Central and South America, is a member of the camel family. Every other year, and only after eleven months' gestation, females at the reproductive age will produce a single foal — which then grows up in a herd consisting of up to ten females and a single male. Exceptionally frugal and undemanding animals, guanaco are at home even in the inhospitable high upland terrain of the Andes.

Mountain Viscacha *(left-hand page, main picture)*

This young mountain viscacha *(Lagidium viscacia)* lives with its relatives in a colony containing from 20 to 50 individuals. The deeply fissured mountains offer them any number of hideaways, and mountain viscacha families live together in caves or cavities. Females are pregnant two or three times a year, but only produce a single baby.

Vicuña *(left-hand page, bottom left)*

If this young vicuña *(Lama vicugna)* happens to be living in Peru, it may well be in for a traumatic experience at some point in the future: like the ancient Incas before them, the modern Peruvians round up the individual animals of this camelid species annually and shear them for their ultra-fine, much sought-after and expensive wool. But after shearing is complete, the vicuña are released and can return to living wild in their family groups.

Degu *(left-hand page, bottom right)*

At birth, which comes after the mother has gestated for 80 days, a degu *(Octodon degus)* is at a relatively advanced stage of development. It will find itself living in a colony, inside a complex warren, and will have anything from one to nine siblings from the same litter. Its tail suggests a similarity to mice, but degus are in fact related to the guinea-pig, and are about the same size. They are sometimes kept as domestic pets, but are not suitable for cuddling.

Black-chested Buzzard-Eagle *(top right)*

The black-chested buzzard-eagle *(Geranoaetus melanoleucus)* has plumage of a generally grey-blue colour with a metallic sheen. However, young birds look different, with much lighter-coloured plumage. It does not acquire the adult colours until it reaches reproductive maturity itself.

Alpaca *(bottom right)*

The alpaca *(Lama guanicoe pacos)* is a New World camelid, but considerably smaller than its Old World relatives, the dromedary and the Bactrian camel. In fact, its small size and its general appearance have led to it sometimes being called the sheep-camel. The alpaca is a subspecies of the guanaco, and in the Andes alpaca are kept as domestic animals for the sake of their warm, soft wool.

In the Rainforest

The rainforests are an extremely species-rich region of the world, yet in our time fewer and fewer baby animals are being born there, because the continued clear-felling of the rainforests is destroying the habitat that many of the species need if they are to survive. The Amazon basin is particularly badly affected, and in spite of many attempts to save it for the future, the destruction goes on — with the object of exploiting the area's mineral resources.

Red-eyed Treefrog *(above left)*
The female red-eyed treefrog *(Agalychnis callidryas)* grows to about 7.5 cm in length, bigger than the male. It fixes its eggs — bright green in colour, and delivered in bundles of 25 to 75 eggs surrounded by masses of jelly — on branches or the underside of leaves hanging above water. From there, the tadpoles drop into the water, where they spend a little less than 12 weeks developing into more frogs.

(above right)
The baby red-eyed treefrog already has the adult frog's shape and also its large toes with the sticky pads which enable these frogs to cling so securely to slippery leaves and twigs. It has already got the red eyes for which the species is named, and the leaf-green body colour — both of these are marks of the adult animal.

Three-toed Sloth *(right-hand page, top left)*
This baby three-toed sloth *(Bradypus tridactylus)* has lost its mother and is making its way all alone down a forest track, when it should be clinging securely to its mother's warm belly. Here, it is helpless, wholly at the mercy of bigger animals and snakes. Normally, sloths never come down from the rain forest canopy except to defecate.

Red Uakari (top right)

Red uakari *(Cacajao rubicundus)* live in mixed-sex groups of 10 to 20 animals, but may also merge to form troops of 100 individuals. In their daily search for nutritious fruits and seeds — and also small animals — they use arms and legs to swing their acrobatic way through the branches of the forest canopy. Mothers carry their young with them, holding tight.

Black-handed Spider Monkey (above left)

The black-handed spider monkey is not confined to the rainforests of Central and South America, being found also in the mangrove swamps. It is an endangered species. Before the baby in the photograph reaches the roughly 60 cm body size and 8 kg weight of the adult monkey it will have to wait quite some time and consume a lot of nutritious fruits and leaves.

(above right)

This baby black-handed spider monkey still has its mother carrying it with her as she moves about. But once it has grown rather bigger, it will have to swing itself along from branch to branch. It is physically well adapted for this, as its hand has a rudimentary thumb and long fingers which can be used as hooks. In addition, its tail has a hairless tactile area which the monkey can use as a fifth hand.

Strawberry Poison Dart Frog (above)

The strawberry poison dart frog *(Dendrobates pumilio)* has a unique approach to rearing its offspring. The male frog visits the clutch of 4-6 eggs regularly to keep the eggs moist. Ten days after the tadpoles have emerged, the female takes the tadpoles, on her back to the water-filled inside of leaf-cups made by bromeliad plants. There she feeds each tadpole on specially produced infertile eggs until it metamorphoses to frog form.

Green Iguana (right)

Green iguana babies *(Iguana iguana)* hatch from a clutch of up to thirty eggs after 10 to 16 weeks. The emerging iguanas are only 20 cm long, and their diet will initially consist of insects. Fully grown — which means 1.5 to 2 metres long — this largest of American lizards will switch to a mainly herbivorous diet. They are sexually mature from the age of three.

Two-toed Sloth (top left)

The two-toed sloth (Choloepus hoffmanni) has just two curved claws on each foreleg and three on its hind legs, and uses these claws to suspend itself securely from tree branches. And in this upside-down position the animal carries out all the activities of its everyday life, from eating to sleeping to mating. Even their babies arrive upside-down.

Titi Monkey (top right)

The titi monkey (Callicebus moloch donacophilus) lives in the Amazon region. A species threatened by human encroachment, the titi monkeys usually live in a social unit of two to seven individuals. A particularly interesting peculiarity of the titi monkey is that the father monkey takes on the job of providing for the offspring — usually a single baby — once the mother has stopped suckling it.

White-throated Capuchin Monkey
(centre left)

A white-throated (or white-faced) (Cebus capucinus) capuchin monkey is born at the end of a gestation period lasting a good five months, and for the moment is entirely dependent on its mother. After its first six to twelve months the baby will have been weaned and is well on its way from its 250 g birth weight to its adult status as a 3–4 kg capuchin monkey, which can use its long prehensile tail for far more than merely holding on to branches.

Bushmaster (bottom left)

It almost defies belief that the little snake hatching so innocently from its egg will terrify any human it meets, once it is fully grown. This is because it is a bushmaster (Lachesis mutus), the largest American venomous snake and the second largest anywhere. Its poison fangs reach a length of 3.5 cm. Fortunately the bushmaster is so shy by nature that confrontations with humans are rare.

285

Ocelot *(above left)*

The alert young ocelot *(Leopardus pardalis)* captured in this photograph was born blind, like all cat species' babies, but it did already have the characteristic ocelot coat colours and patterning, with its lines of irregular dark flecks. An ocelot cub will be reared by its mother and father jointly. The juvenile animals reach their own reproductive maturity at two to three years old.

Jaguar *(above right)*

The jaguar cub *(Panthera onca)* in the picture looks as if it has just had a good meal and is contentedly licking the final morsels off its lips. If so, they are probably the remains of a fair-sized mammal that its mother will have hunted and killed — perhaps a capybara, but it might even have been a fish. Jaguars take to the water readily themselves, and most of their kills are at the waterside.

(below left)

Just as some leopards are black (and commonly known as black panthers), so too there are occasional 'melanistic' (black-coated) jaguars, like this six-week-old cub. Rather more heavily-built and stockier than the leopard, the jaguar is widespread over the whole area stretching from South America to Mexico and Louisiana. But the melanistic animals are especially frequent in the Brazilian rainforests.

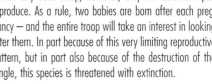

Cuvier's Dwarf Caiman (above)

This still young Cuvier's dwarf caiman (Paleosuchus palpe-brosus) was photographed swimming harmlessly in the waters of the Orinoco river. Like all caimans, it is classed as a crocodile. Crocodiles in turn are regarded as the last survivors of the great saurians – a type of animal whose design has remained essentially unchanged throughout roughly the last 65 million years.

Giant Ant-eater (left-hand page, bottom right)

When female giant ant-eaters (Myrmecophaga tridactyla) go foraging for food, any young go with them, riding on their mother's back. The adults use their long slender snout to hunt underground for ants' nests, which they first smash with their big claws and then lick virtually clean, using their long flexible tongue. The extended tapering snout can be clearly seen on the baby giant ant-eater also.

Golden Lion Tamarin (left)

Some golden lion tamarin monkeys (Leontopithecus rosa-lia) live in pairs, others in troops of up to twelve individuals. Within any such troop, however, only the dominant pair reproduce. As a rule, two babies are born after each pregnancy – and the entire troop will take an interest in looking after them. In part because of this very limiting reproductive pattern, but in part also because of the destruction of the jungle, this species is threatened with extinction.

Lowland Tapir (above)

The natural habitat of this young lowland tapir (*Tapirus terrestris*) is either forest or thick underbrush. In such surroundings, the spotted and striped coat of the young animals provides them with superb camouflage. Lowland tapirs are particularly apt to frequent areas that have lakes or other standing water — and are even capable of walking under water.

Bush Dog (right)

Bush dogs (*Speothos venaticus*) are reared mostly in litters of seven animals. The first period of their lives is spent entirely inside their burrow, with the mother. She nurses her young — born after 67 days of gestation — and has food brought to her in this 'lying-in room' by the male bush dog. Later, they will live together in family groups and also hunt together.

White-faced Saki (top left)

In the case of the white-faced (or Guianan) saki (*Pithecia pithecia*), it is not only the babies and young animals that look appealingly cuddly — even the adults look for all the world like soft toys. However, there are marked differences between the sexes. Females have a brown coat with white tips and a dark face, while the males have a black coat and a tawny-coloured face.

Southern Tamandua (top right)

For the female Southern tamandua (*Tamandua tetradactyla*) and her young, a termite mound like this is just what they were looking for. First the big claws rip the mound apart, then the family set to with their long intrusive tongues, licking up the termites from the recesses inside. However, they do not devour every last termite, always leaving some in the nest so that the insects can rebuild their population.

(above)

The Southern tamandua, which is a medium-sized ant-eater, lives — unlike the giant ant-eater — on trees, searching them during the night for ants and termites. A baby tamandua is born after five months of gestation, and is suckled by its mother for three months until it is ready to feed itself. During this time, the mother carries it around with her.

In Forest and Woodland

Whether the trees are coniferous or broad-leaved, their branches and leaves help to provide a number of species with the basics of existence — and so does the forest floor. So it can be said that the various species resident here rear their young in every 'storey' of their forest home.

Amazon Tree Boa (above, main picture)

This baby Amazon tree boa (*Corallus hortulanus*, formerly *Corallus enydris*) like other tree boas, spends its entire life on trees. These snakes have scales near their mouth which react extremely sensitively to a change in temperature in their surroundings. This information enables the snake to locate its prey (such as a bird or small rodent) accurately. Then, hanging from its branch, it launches itself with a snap at the prey.

Emerald Tree Boa (top right)

Baby emerald tree boa (*Corallus caninus*) may be coloured brown, orange, red or yellow. It is not until they are about one year old that they acquire a brilliant green hue on their upper side to rival that of their parents. The small white flecks are usually already present during the earlier stages. These snakes will grow to 3 m long. A female usually produces from 3 to 15 liveborn young each year.

Patagonian Mara (top left)

The Patagonian mara (Dolichotis patagonum) is also known as the Patagonian cavy or, misleadingly, Patagonian hare. The mara's way of rearing its young is unusual: the female sits up while suckling, rather than lying down like most other mammals. This South American native animal is related not to the hare but to the guinea-pig. The young remain with their mother for a good nine months.

Turkey Vulture (top right)

For this turkey vulture chick (Cathartes aura), the hardest year of its life will be the first one. If it survives that, it should have a life span of about 15 years. Turkey vultures have an exceedingly keen sense of smell which enables them to find food anywhere and everywhere, from thick forests to built-up areas. Being carrion-eaters, they often hang around in areas where they can get the benefit of roadkill.

Woolly Opossum (above)

Woolly opossum (Caluromys) grow to between 18 and 29 cm in length and up to 500 g in weight. The babies are of course much lighter, especially the embryos, which have to be carried in their mother's pouch during the period immediately following their birth. The woolly opossum is a nocturnal animal, and spends most of the daylight hours in a tree, either in a hollow inside the tree, or in a nest.

Armadillo *(top left)*

Armadillos belong to the edentates, animals whose lumbar vertebrae have extra articulating surfaces. This gives additional strength which is useful to the armadillo in its digging activities. The skin scales on young armadillo are still soft. As it grows, the scales on its back begin to ossify, getting harder and harder till they form a rigid protective armour.

Nine-banded Armadillo *(centre left)*

However much its appearance suggests a tortoise, a lizard, or even a fantasy animal out of science fiction, the nine-banded armadillo *(Dasypus novemcinctus)* is a mammal and suckles its babies during their first weeks of life with mother's milk just as dogs, cats and humans do. The nine bony bands round the middle of their body, from which they take their name, allow the armadillo greater mobility than it would otherwise have.

(bottom left)

The reproductive physiology of the nine-banded armadillo is decidedly unusual. Following fertilisation, the egg proceeds to the uterus, but instead of lodging in one place right away, it drifts around freely for about another 14 weeks. During this time the egg splits into four identical embryos, which eventually do lodge firmly in the uterus. Four months later still, the four babies are born.

Margay *(right-hand page, top left)*

This is a young margay *(Leopardus wiedi)*, a predator cat which looks very like an ocelot and is in fact often called a tree ocelot. Unlike many of the other smaller members of the cat family, margays are always single births, and this means that the early bonding to the mother is unusually close. Even as adults, margays have enough elasticity in their joints and paws to be able to climb almost as well as monkeys.

Hoary Zorro *(right-hand page, top right)*

In September, the hoary zorro female *(Pseudalopex vetulus,* formerly *Dusicyon vetulus)* gives birth to a litter usually containing two, three or four babies. Even so, these small fox-like mammals with their short-haired tawny coat are a threatened species, not just in the wild in Brazil, but also in zoos. As yet not much is known about the behaviour patterns of hoary zorro, which are active mainly in the twilight and after dark.

Swallowtail *(right-hand page, main picture)*

Worldwide, there are something like 200 species of swallowtail butterfly, so named because their rear wings look like a swallow's tail. The caterpillar of the Thoas swallowtail *(Papio thoas)* and its relatives has an orange, forked organ at the back of its neck, which it extrudes when alarmed. This action also releases an odour perceived as unpleasant by potential predators.

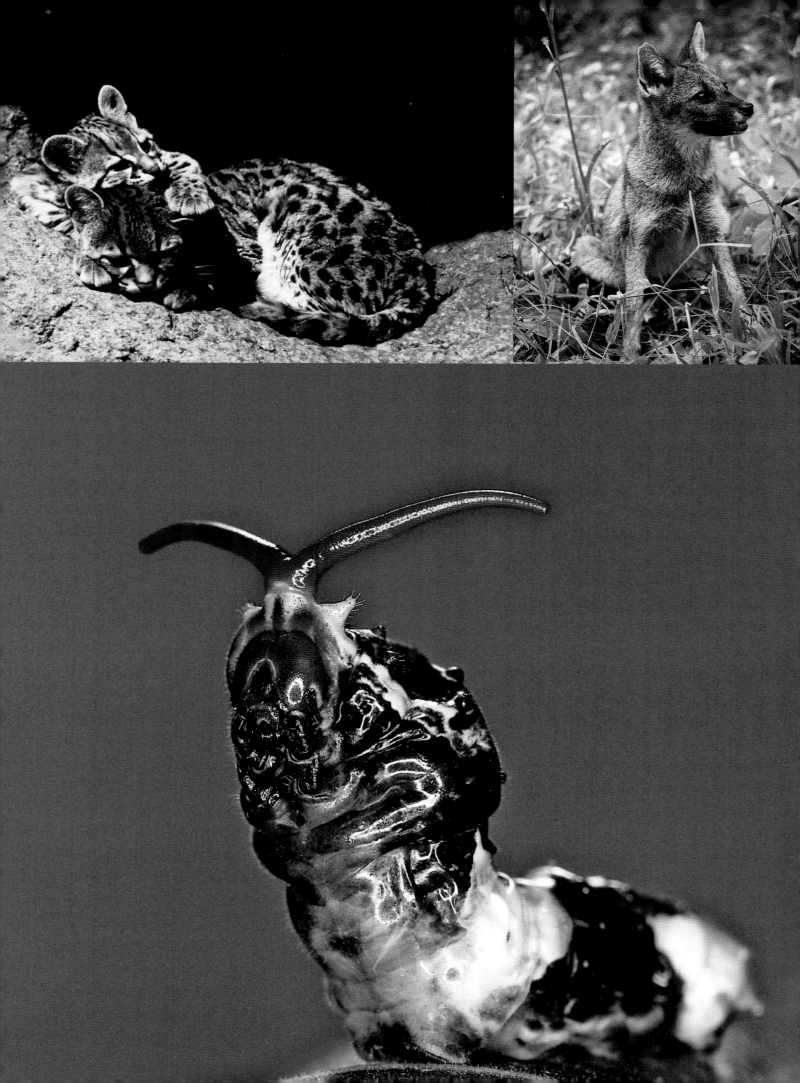

Squirrel Monkey *(left-hand page, top left)*

From birth, baby squirrel monkeys *(Saimiri sciureus)* are used to hubbub and crowds, because these New World monkeys form troops of up to 300 animals. They all join in scouring the jungle for nutritious small fauna such as insects, frogs and crabs. A baby clutches its mother's back and is never in danger of being thrown off, no matter how long the leaps as she bounds along.

Collared Peccary *(left-hand page, bottom left)*

The collared peccary *(Tayassu tajacu)*, also known as the javelina, lives in different habitats in South America and the southern U.S. On their back they have a special scent gland, and when the animals rub against each other a scent is released telling the animals that they belong to the same family. However, when two peccaries rub heads, like mother and baby in this picture, each is simply cleaning up the other's face.

Azara's Zorro *(above)*

Azara's zorro *(Pseudalopex gymnocercus,* formerly *Dusicyon gymnocercus)* give birth to four young on average at a time. Eight weeks on, the cubs leave the den, which the parents will have made in a rock crevice or an abandoned burrow. But they will remain with their parents and siblings for a further three months, learning all the things they will need to know in order to ensure reasonable chances of survival, before finally heading off on their own.

(bottom centre)

Fully grown collared peccaries have a dark coat relieved only by a white ring running round at the point where neck and body meet. However, young peccary look quite different, as they have a reddish coat, with a black stripe down the back. Collared peccary are omnivorous, and live in family groups of about 15 animals.

Asia

By River, Lake and Marsh

Water, the basis of all life, is so important for some species that they live there, give birth to their young there, and rear them there. For some, water is more than just a source of food — the water buffalo, for example, needs mud for its skin.

Red-crowned Crane *(above left)*

This red-crowned crane chick *(Grus japonensis)* belongs to the largest and heaviest of all species of crane. The adult bird looks extremely elegant in its black-and-white plumage with the red fleck on its head. The red-crowned crane is an endangered species, and as pairs are believed by ornithologists to breed only once every four years, it is clear that the prospects for an increase in this bird's numbers are not good.

Chinese Water Deer *(above right)*

The Chinese water deer *(Hydropotes inermis)* in the photograph is a young animal, not yet strong enough to move around with the adults. So while its mother grazes, the fawn lies in its hiding-place and waits for her to return and suckle it. Fully grown, it will reach a height at the shoulder of 50 cm. The males develop long canine teeth which protrude from the muzzle.

Long-tailed Macaque *(top right)*

Baby long-tailed macaques *(Macaca fascicularis)*, also known as crab-eating macaques, live with their parents in groups which join together into large troops. These are among the most abundant monkey species in South-East Asia, and are found in the rainforests, by rivers, and in marshy areas and mangrove swamps. Appropriately for their habitat, they are good climbers and good swimmers.

Asiatic Water Buffalo (top left)

Water buffalo (Bubalus arnee) are not called water buffalo for nothing, because whenever they are not actually foraging for food they are evidently happiest lying in water with only their head showing above the surface. Water buffalo calves — which are suckled for a whole year by their mother — likewise quickly become accustomed to life in and near the water.

(top right)

In China, Asiatic water buffalo were being domesticated as long ago as the 3rd millennium BC. Today they still serve the human population in many countries as beasts of burden, and often they are used to help in cultivating crops. In particular, they have always been used by rice growers. A further advantage is that they are relatively easy to breed.

Dalmatian Pelican (above, main picture)

A new Dalmatian pelican hatchling (Pelecanus crispus) like this one comes into the world featherless. Gradually it begins to sprout a coat of white down. Later, as a juvenile, it will exchange its baby down for the plumage of the half-grown bird, brownish-grey on top, with off-white underparts. Only when it is fully grown will it wear the predominantly white plumage of adult Dalmatian pelicans.

In the Mountains

Although the mountains of Asia are a hard and unforgiving environment, the animal species that live there are in one respect less threatened than in many other habitats worldwide: particularly on the highest slopes, the young animals can grow to maturity and live their adult lives free from human interference.

Himalayan Griffon *(top right)*

Named after its habitat, the Himalayan griffon *(Gyps himalayensis)* or snow griffon incubates its eggs far above the tree-line, in an enormous nest made from branches. This griffon plays an important role in Tibetan culture, for at the end of all funeral ceremonies the body of the dead person is taken to a place where the griffons will devour it. For most of the year the ground is frozen and far too hard for burial; and wood is far too scarce and precious to be used as fuel for cremations.

Cinereous Vulture *(right)*

The cinereous vulture *(Aegypius monachus)* is the largest Old World vulture and likes to build its eyrie on a tree high up on a mountainside where there is plenty of updraught. The rising air helps the chick at fledging time at the age of four months when it is making its first attempts at flight. As the cinereous vulture lays only a single egg at a time, there is not much prospect that this severely endangered species can recover.

Japanese Macaque *(right-hand page, top)*

In some cultures, this species of monkey is named for its striking red face, but its alternative name in English, 'snow monkey', refers to its habitat. The Japanese macaque has adapted successfully to the very harsh, cold climatic conditions of the Japanese Palearctic (far north). Even in winter, mother and baby don't think twice about taking a swim.

(right-hand page, bottom left)

This young Japanese macaque — a member of a strictly protected species — is busily and inquisitively exploring the world around it. Like all monkeys, it is intelligent and an apt learner, well able to remember what it has learnt. Its hands are adapted for holding things, and with them it can use sticks, stones and other objects skilfully as tools for a particular purpose.

(right-hand page, bottom right)

Among Japanese macaques or snow monkeys, the mother-child bond is exceptionally close. At the same time, mother and child are just one unit in a large troop of monkeys, numbering as many as a hundred individuals. And within the group every individual has its assigned social position. These macaques feed primarily on plants, and sleep in caves or on trees.

Giant Panda (right)

These giant panda cubs (Ailuropoda melanoleuca) belong to a species which is so rare and appealing in its black and white coat that it has become the emblem of the international World Wide Fund for Nature (WWF). In the wild, young giant pandas become independent at the age of a year and a half — but it is rare for two cubs to survive.

Snow Leopard (below)

Snow leopard cubs (Uncia uncia) are born, after 100 days of gestation, in a litter of from 2–5, eyes still closed. From the moment the cubs' eyes open, however, they begin to explore their surroundings — at first clumsily, then with ever greater agility, until they are no less skilful climbers and hunters than their parents. The dense, woolly, light-coloured pelt protects from the winter cold, but also from heat in summer.

In Forest and Rainforest

Forests and rainforests, with their lush vegetation, provide a highly supportive living environment for many animal species and their young. Unfortunately, though, many of these species have now become rare because of the continuing destruction of their habitat by humans.

White-handed Gibbon *(above left)*

White-handed or lar gibbons *(Hylobates lar)* live as pairs in the canopy of the broad-leaved rainforest. After fertilisation takes place, it is seven months before a white-handed gibbon is born. The parents look after their baby for about three years – that is, until a new brother or sister takes its place. But the older sibling is still allowed to stay with the family, until it reaches the reproductive stage itself.

Malayan Sun Bear *(top right)*

After only 96 days developing in its mother's womb, the Malayan sun bear cub *(Helarctos malayanus)* is born, weighing only 300 g. Once it is old enough, it will eat a mixed diet, in which plants and eggs are supplemented by the honey and various grubs that the bear can fish out of tree crevices with its long tongue – 25 cm long in the adult bear.

Indian Moon Moth *(above right)*

The Indian moon moth *(Actias selene)* is one of the moths that entomologists often breed in captivity. The eggs hatch into minute caterpillars only half a centimetre in length. Once they have eaten their way to fifteen times that size, at 7.5 cm, sloughing off their skin several times during the process, they spin themselves a cocoon in which they will pupate. About four weeks later the mature moth emerges.

Proboscis Monkey (top left)
Definitely one of the world's most unusual-looking monkey species is the proboscis monkey (Nasalis larvatus), found only in the rainforests and mangrove swamps of Borneo. In the young animal, the characteristic nose is not yet as fully developed as in the mother. Adult males have an even longer nose, long enough to get in the way sometimes as they are feeding.

(top centre)
Proboscis monkeys live in 'harems', groups consisting of a single male with about seven females and their young. Once the males among the young have grown to juveniles and then reach adulthood, they disperse from the group and for a while live alone. In due course each male will form his own harem. All proboscis monkeys prefer to live near fresh water and also love swimming in it.

Clouded Leopard (top centre)
This clouded leopard cub (Neofelis nebulosa) already has a tail almost as long as its body – and the tail is a constant encouragement to play and to chase, as it is constantly there teasing the cub and close enough – almost – to catch. Later on, the tail will still stand the 70–100 cm long adult clouded leopard in good stead as a kind of stabilising rudder when it is climbing trees, perhaps to rob a bird's nest.

Leopard *(above)*

As a rule, the leopard *(Panthera pardus)* is a solitary animal, but sometimes a pair will live together amicably. The young usually separate from their mother at about two years old, by which time she is usually pregnant again and the birth of the next litter is imminent. The mother readily tolerates the half-grown females around her, but the males have to disperse and seek a territory of their own.

Slow Loris *(left-hand page, main picture)*

The slow loris *(Nycticebus coucang)*, like this mother with her baby, is an arboreal animal, one that lives its life among the branches of trees. It has specialised gripping hands, with which it can hold on so securely that it never falls off even when fast asleep. The hands of the loris are also well adapted for climbing, but not for leaping, nor for hand-over-hand locomotion with the body suspended.

(left)

A look at the big saucer eyes of this young slow loris is enough to tell us: this prosimian species is a wholly nocturnal animal, one that spends the daytime sleeping. The slow loris is an omnivore, and nourishes itself on leaves, fruit and smaller animals, e.g. birds — which it catches by creeping up and then grabbing its victim with its forepaws.

Leopard *(above)*

Leopards *(Panthera pardus)* are powerful, accurate long-jumpers and agile climbers — as this young acrobat is demonstrating. They dig their claws into the bark and haul themselves upwards. They also like to drag food they have killed up a tree with them so as to be able to devour it in peace, undisturbed by jackal or hyena.

(below left)

After a pregnancy lasting a hundred days, a she-leopard will give birth to — usually — two to four cubs at a time. They are born with their eyes still closed. The mother does all the rearing of the young by herself, suckling them for the first three months. At this age, the cubs begin feeding from the meat killed and brought to them by their mother.

(above)

Among leopards, the mother animal alone sees to the rearing of the cubs, and one of her roles is playing with them. The male leopard is presumably prowling his territory alone, as leopards are generally solitary animals. It is not unknown, however, for a pair to stay together even outside the mating season.

(below left)

Leopard cubs stay with their mother until well into their second year. As a species, the leopard is highly adaptable, and this is why it is so widely distributed. It occurs in Africa as well as Asia, and in both continents it is found living in extremely diverse habitats — in rainforests, in the mountains, in stony deserts and on grassland — and as a result of this several varieties of leopard have evolved.

(below right)

Not all leopards have a brown-spotted coat. Some baby leopards are born black; these are referred to as black panthers. The different colour is due to a genetic mutation, and statistics show that the mutation occurs more commonly among Asian leopards than among those in Africa. In fact, looking in good light from a particular angle, one can make out the spots still there even in the black fur.

Orang-Utan *(left-hand page, main picture)*

Young orang-utans *(Pongo pygmaeus)* remain with their parents and siblings for eight years from birth. During this time they learn that, while leaves and tender twigs and honey are very tasty, they can also enjoy food from animal sources. They learn to steal from birds' nests, taking eggs and even chicks, and they catch and eat young reptiles and termites. As adults, these animals are notably solitary.

(left-hand page, bottom left)

Thin and delicate at birth, the skin of a baby orang-utan develops into a dense reddish-brown matting of long fur. The long hairs of this coat ensure that the water from tropical downpours runs off quickly, so that the orang-utans are protected as if by a raincoat. Once the rain has stopped, the animals can get rid of the remaining water by shaking themselves vigorously.

(left-hand page, bottom centre)

Riding on its mother's back, the baby orang-utan gets around everywhere, learning its own way round its environment, the trees of the Sumatran or Borneo rainforest. Baby and mother also have their sleeping-nest up there in the canopy, a nest strong enough to support their weight of about 70 kg. Orang-utans are active mainly at cooler times of day, in other words morning and evening.

(left-hand page, bottom right)

In their first weeks and months, baby orang-utans clutch their mother tightly when she swings her way through the canopy in her forage for food. But once they have grown rather bigger and stronger, they begin to find that, while their short legs and hand-like feet are not very good for running on at ground level, they are all the more excellent — in combination with long arms and relatively big hands — for climbing and swinging one's way through the trees.

(top right)

The term 'orang-utan' is from the Malay and means 'man of the forest'. Male orang-utans do in fact grow to 1.9 m (or 6 feet) like a human. Another similarity with humans is that gestation lasts for nine months. The mother gives birth to her baby high in the forest canopy, in a nest made of branches and twigs, and suckles it for a long period before gradually weaning it onto a plant diet.

Douc Langur *(bottom right)*

The douc langurs of Vietnam and Cambodia *(Pygathrix nemaeus)* are in danger of becoming extinct. Only a few zoos breed them, and these are in practice the only places where it is feasible to photograph their young. Also, although these langurs have splendid markings and attract a lot of attention in the zoo, the same markings lend them perfect camouflage — which means near-invisibility — in the play of light and shade in the forest.

Sika Deer (top right)

The sika deer *(Cervus nippon)* from Eastern Asia is of course often seen, with its young, in our animal parks, and is also not uncommon in the wild in parts of Britain. Yet in its homeland it is a seriously endangered species. The sika's antlers do not have complex branching; in fully-grown animals they may have three to four points. The coat is dark in winter, but lighter and spotted during summer months.

Stump-tailed Macaque (bottom right)

The young of the stump-tailed macaque *(Macaca arctoides)* have pale skin on their face, but in the adult the face is reddish with black speckling — and in cold weather it takes on a bluish tinge. A striking feature of these macaques (also known as bear macaques) is the expressive forehead wrinkling, which changes constantly as the animals interact with each other. As well as gesture and expression, stump-tailed macaques use loud calls as a further means of communication.

(right-hand page, bottom left)

As ground-dwellers — in the forests of Myanmar (Burma), South China and Malaysia — stump-tailed macaques rarely sit up on trees, but they can of course climb perfectly well, as these two animals show. A baby stump-tailed macaque is always a single birth, and will be suckled by its mother for between six months and a year. The main predators it has to fear are python and leopard.

Rhesus Macaque (right-hand page, bottom right)

Rhesus macaques *(Macaca mulatta)* live together in large troops made up of juveniles, females and a few adult males, and often inflict severe damage on growing crops. When the mating-season comes round, the faces and genital areas of receptive females take on a distinct red coloration. For procreation they frequently switch male partners, but among these some will be favourites.

(right-hand page, top)

Rhesus macaque babies are born in May and June, and for the first two weeks of their life they cling tightly to their mother's breast. It is not until they have begun to be less dependent that they also begin experimenting with foods other than the nutritious milk they get from their mothers. As they grow bigger, more and more seeds and fruits find a place in their diet.

Crested Black Macaque (right)

The light-coloured face and rear end of the baby crested black macaque *(Macaca nigra)* stand out against the otherwise jet-black coat. When the young animals grow up — they will reach 55–66 cm, and 10 kg in weight — their coat colouring becomes lighter. It also becomes clear why these animals are called 'crested' macaques. The quiff of hair on their heads now stands erect rather like the bristles of a brush.

Ailanthus Silkworm Moth (below)

This ailanthus silkworm moth *(Philosamia cynthia)* has just come out of its chrysalis and is waiting on its twig to gather more strength for its next move. While in its caterpillar stage it had fed off the tree of heaven, *Ailanthus glandulosa.* Being one of the silkworms, the caterpillar produces a fibre called eri silk. This silk is obtained from the cocoons before the moths emerge.

Entellus Langur *(left)*

This young entellus langur, also referred to as a hanuman *(Presbytis entellus)*, lives in a family unit made up of several females with their offspring and led by a dominant male. Once a young male entellus has reached adult age, it is forced to leave the family group. It will then join a bachelor troop until such time as it can found a family of its own

(below)

After a relatively long gestation period of 200 days, baby entellus langurs are born as 'only children'. They live in the mountains of Asia, sometimes also in forests and in areas of human habitation. Here they often do a lot of damage to gardens and fields. But they are not chased off, because they are venerated as descendants of the monkey-god Hanuman.

Brown Bear (top right)

Once upon a time, brown bears *(Ursus arctos)* were common in the forests, marshlands and mountains of Europe, but their sole enemy, man, has enormously reduced bear numbers there, first by hunting them and latterly by destroying their habitat. So the sight of a mother brown bear playing with her cub is one that Europeans are much more likely to see in a zoo than in the wild.

(centre right)

It is hard to imagine that this little brown bear cub — here about two months old — may one day reach a height of 2.3 metres or over seven feet. When first born it was tiny, weighing only 300–400 g, but it puts on weight rapidly and when fully grown will weigh hundreds of kilograms. Brown bears live in Russia as well as in Canada and Alaska.

(bottom right)

From the time when brown bear cubs are about two months old, they can start accompanying their mother on longer and longer expeditions in search of food. In the course of these trips, they learn a great deal and also develop and train their muscles. But as they of course do not have anything like as much stamina as the huge, powerful she-bear, the cubs just have to have a breather every so often.

(right-hand page, top)

While brown bears are certainly classed as predators, they are by no means specialised carnivores. The truth is quite different: in fact what they eat is mainly from plant sources, with a strong preference for berries and sweet ripe fruit. This taste is imprinted on them when they are cubs. However, they are not averse to discarded human food, and this results time and again in aggro between bears and humans.

(right-hand page, bottom)

Like all brown bears, this cub was born during the winter recess — with a birth weight, already hard to credit, of only about 500 g. But in some regions the fully-grown brown bears can reach weights of up to 800 kg. Brown bears are found not only in northern Asia but also in Europe and North America. They are often forest animals, but some live on the relatively barren wastes of the tundra.

In Taiga, Tundra and Steppe

In these wide, bare habitats the only baby animals which can be slow developers are those whose size or whose formidable parents are a serious deterrent to predators. All others are typically able to look after themselves after their first few months or even weeks of life.

Indian Elephant *(top left)*

This Indian elephant calf *(Elephas maximus bengalensis)* is taking its daily mud-bath — an important routine, as it keeps the elephant's skin in good condition. Getting in and out can be tricky, and its mother or other cow elephants often help. These 'nanny elephants' support the mother in other parental tasks too, like minding the calf or playing with it.

Sri Lankan Elephant *(above left)*

Sri Lankan elephant calves *(Elephas maximus maximus)* live together with their mother and older siblings in small family groups in the tropical forests and rainforests of Sri Lanka; some of them are found higher up too, in the mountains. Their fathers, the adult bull elephants, are solitary, rejoining the families only when the females are in season.

(above)

A cow elephant will have been pregnant for almost two years by the time her calf is born. When a herd of Sri Lankan elephants has a number of calves with it, these eventually form a kindergarten group looked after by several cow elephants. It takes about twelve years from birth for an elephant calf to reach the reproductive age itself.

Great Indian Rhinoceros (top left)

In young and adult rhinoceros (Rhinoceros unicornis) alike, strengths and weaknesses are plain to see: their large ears enable them to hear well, and their big nostrils are a reminder of their superb sense of smell – but, in keeping with their tiny eyes, their eyesight is relatively weak. If threatened, rhino can move quite astonishingly fast, and if cornered they will not hesitate to attack with their horn.

(above, main picture)

An Indian rhino calf is born only after a gestation period of 16 months, but from then until a sibling is born – usually a period of about three years – it will remain close to its mother. After that it becomes a solitary animal, coming back to others only to mate. The rhino feeds off long grasses, which it tears off with its lip.

Asian Wild Ass (top right)

The kulan subspecies of the Asian wild ass (Equus hemionus kulan) used to be widespread on the steppes of Turkmenistan and Kazakhstan, but is now so rare that even in a zoo one of these animals will be regarded as a special treasure. The kulan can be distinguished from Przewalski's horse mainly by its long ears and tufted tail.

Tawny Eagle *(above)*

Tawny eagles *(Aquila rapax)* are ground-nesting birds. They return every year to the same site and rebuild their nest. Then the female eagle lays two eggs and sits on them for 40 days. During this time the male bird brings food for her. Once the chicks hatch, both parents look after them for about three months, until they are fledged.

Snowy Owl *(centre right)*

Snowy owls *(Nyctea scandiaca)* prefer to feed on a diet of lemming, and lemming is what they typically bring to a chick such as the one in the photograph. Young birds are predominantly grey-brown in colour, not developing the snow-white adult plumage until they are independent of their parents. Even then, the females' plumage is always brown-speckled on the upper wing surfaces, so that it is better camouflaged while nesting on the ground.

(bottom right)

After snowy owls have mated, the female lays her eggs in a small depression which she has scraped out in the soil and lined in a rudimentary way with any materials available. While she is incubating, the male bird brings food for her. After the chicks hatch, the snowy male is still responsible for hunting and delivering lemmings, while the female bird takes care of the young.

Great Grey Owl (top left)

The great grey owl *(Strix nebulosa)* is found in the tundra of North America and Scandinavia as well as in the Siberian taiga. The female uses an abandoned raptor nest, laying from three to six eggs and incubating them alone over a period of just a month. The chicks will begin clambering around in nearby branches once they are about three weeks old, but it takes a further three weeks for them to learn to fly.

Snowy Owl (bottom left)

The three snowy owl chicks in the picture are 18 days old, and will leave the nest in about another week. However, that does not mean they will be fledged, which will take at least as much time again. With only three chicks in the family, the clutch of eggs has been on the small side; the average figure is about six, and in fact significantly more eggs will be laid if lemmings — which make up the staple diet — are currently abundant.

(bottom right)

The snowy owl begins incubating immediately she has laid her first egg, and this means that the chicks do not hatch more or less simultaneously — as happens with many other bird species — but with a time-lag between first and last. How many eggs a snowy owl lays is directly related to the number of lemmings available in the relevant year as fodder for the chicks.

Bengal Tiger *(top left)*

To clear six metres in a single bound is a matter of course for the Bengal tiger *(Panthera tigris tigris)*, which is native to India and South-East Asia. Sadly, this formidable animal has now become rare in its own territories because of the steady human encroachment on its habitat. But at least almost every pregnancy results in the birth of two more tiger cubs, which helps to maintain the population.

Sumatran Tiger *(above)*

Like all tigers, the rare Sumatran tigers *(Panthera tigris sumatrae)* which live in the jungles of the island of Sumatra are solitary. However, male and female live together for a while at mating-time. About 100 days later, the female will give birth to two or three cubs, and will have sole responsibility for teaching them the hunting skills essential to their longer-term survival.

Siberian Tiger (left)

Tiger cubs are born, their eyes not yet open, after a gestation period of just under four months. Born weighing only a kilogram, they rapidly grow bigger and stronger on their mother's milk. The mother animal is scrupulously careful in looking after them, and if need be will often carry them in her mouth to a safer place, which is what this Siberian tiger (Panthera tigris altaica) is seen doing in the photograph.

(above)

Tiger cubs are very often born as twins, so each young animal has a playmate from the beginning. In the first year of their life they are wholly dependent on their mother, who initially only suckles them but later shares her kills with them. Only when the young generation have reached two years of age are they strong enough to hunt and regularly kill.

(top right)

This tiger cub belongs to the exceedingly rare tiger sub-species known as the Siberian (or Amur) tiger, of which there are believed to be only 200 individuals still surviving in the wild. This is also the biggest of all tigers. The little male cub in the picture should one day reach a length of 4 metres! And the Siberian tiger also has the densest and the lightest-coloured coat of all tiger sub-species.

321

In the Deserts and Other Arid Regions

To escape the heat, many animals in arid regions are nocturnal and/or live underground. Many species reproduce only when food is available in adequate quantities. As a result, the reproductive cycle is subject to major irregularities.

Syrian Hamster *(above left)*

The Syrian (or golden) hamster *(Mesocricetus auratus)* seen here suckling six young, carried them for only sixteen days before giving birth. Three weeks on, the young hamsters of this litter will already be independent of the mother, and she for her part may well already be pregnant again. She has the capacity to produce eight litters a year, each with from six to ten babies.

(top right)

The Syrian hamster is the ancestral form of our popular pet hamsters. In the wild it is found only in Syria, and is also difficult to observe: it is nocturnal by habit and leaves its 2 m deep burrow only to eat and to forage for food. Tiny though they now are, the baby hamsters in the picture will reach reproductive maturity in ten weeks' time.

Bactrian Camel *(above)*

The Bactrian camel *(Camelus ferus bactrianus)* is born after a gestation period lasting 406 days. There are only a few animals of this species still living wild in the Gobi Desert. There, the young animals and the females live together in small groups protected by one male. When the juvenile males reach adulthood, they initially form bachelor groups.

Dromedary (top left)

Like all camels, the dromedary calf (*Camelus dromedarius*) has very thick, fleshy lips and a split in the upper lip. This enables it when foraging to get a better grip on the often tiny or ephemeral plants growing in the stony deserts. It has the ability to close off its nostrils to keep out the whirling grains of sand hurled against it in a sandstorm.

(top right)

As mammals, dromedary calves enjoy the privilege of drinking nutritious mother's milk. Even so, they have to get used very early to the scanty nourishment that is all the desert provides — much of it in the form of plants which are salty or thorny. In its single hump, the dromedary can store water for several days, greatly reducing the risk of its dying from dehydration out in the desert.

(above, main picture)

As a wild species, the dromedary is extinct: the only dromedaries still living are domesticated. In the calves, the eyelashes look particularly long. They grow in a double row as a better protection against flying sand. The dromedary's thick coat is a good protection against the cold of the desert night, but also against the great heat of midday

Indian Gerbil *(right)*

The Indian gerbil *(Tatera indica)* occurs mainly in India, but is found also in other parts of Asia and as far west as Syria. It is one of the animals that follow in the wake of human civilisation and tends to become a pest — one reason being that Indian gerbils need only 60 days to grow from birth to reproductive maturity, following which a further 28 days will be sufficient for a female animal to produce a litter of up to seven babies. And so on.

Gerbil *(below)*

The gerbil family *(Gerbilinae)* has about 70 different species, most of them native to one or other of the world's arid regions. At birth — usually in a nest or a burrow — young gerbils are still hairless and pink. Once weaned off their mother's milk, they feed exclusively on seeds.

Mongolian Gerbil (top left)

When a litter of Mongolian gerbils (Meriones unguiculatus) is born — the ones in the picture are nine days old — the father needs to keep right out of the way, not approaching the nest at all. If he does, the babies' mother will send him packing. She does not need to do it physically, her body language suffices. However, after about a week has passed, she relaxes and allows the father to come and 'inspect' the litter.

(centre left)

By the age of two months, Mongolian gerbils are sexually mature and ready to reproduce. So if you are keeping them as pets, you need to be careful only to keep animals of the same sex together, unless you actually want and can cope with the (admittedly very cute) next generation that will certainly arrive. The animal shown here is a 25-day-old juvenile. When about to mate, the male chases after the female and drums its hind legs on the floor.

(bottom left)

Mongolian gerbils in the wild live in areas where the temperature can fall to minus 40 °C in winter and rise to a scorching 50 °C in summer. This is one of the reasons why they make their nests in caves: it is the best way to protect their newborn young both from cold and from heat.

(bottom right)

For some time now, Mongolian gerbils have enjoyed great popularity as home pets. Like almost all mice, they are very prolific and relatively easy to breed from. They are active by day as well as by night, very fast-moving, and inquisitive — as one can see from this young gerbil photographed as it investigated a flower-pot.

Australia

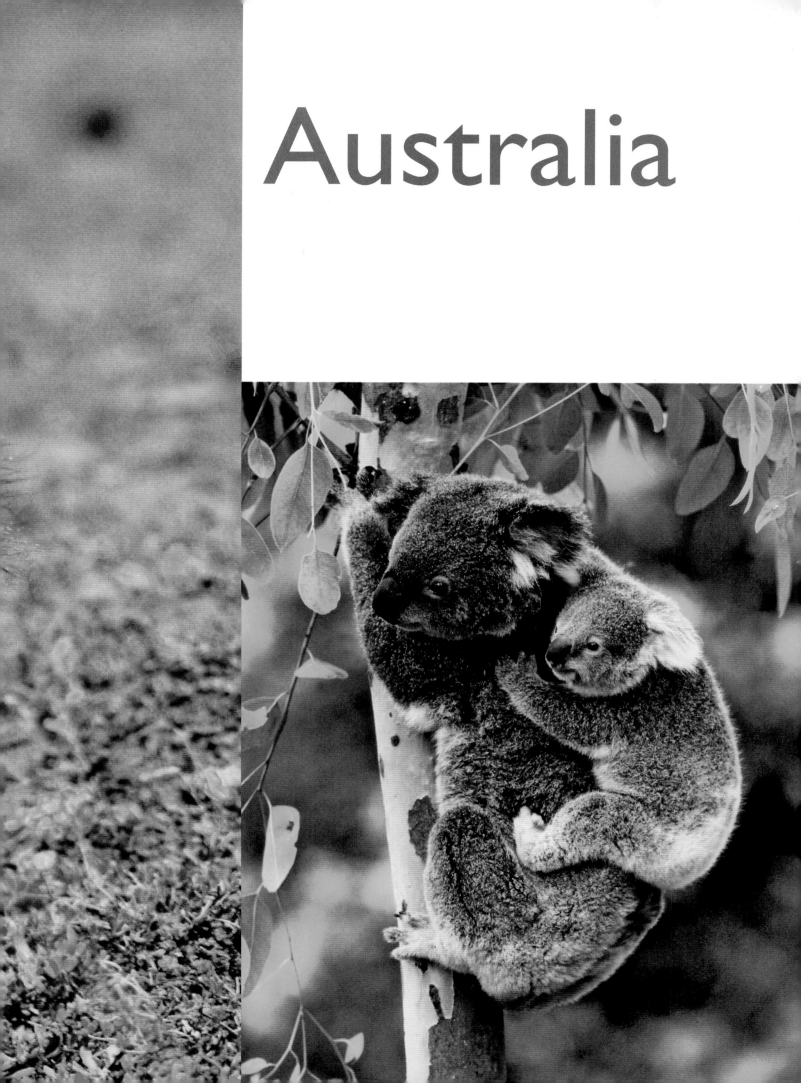

In Grass Country

In the dry and flat parts of Australia there are great tracts of grassland, interspersed here and there with trees and shrubs. In these areas, large numbers of marsupials are born and grow up. The young, riding inside their mother's pouch, are well protected from the blazing sun.

Agile Wallaby *(left)*

Most agile wallabies *(Macropus agilis)* are born in the four months May to August. Fully grown, these small tan-coloured kangaroos weigh from 12 kg (female) to 20 kg (male). They feed exclusively on plant material, mostly grass. However, during the dry season they dig for roots, which contain a considerable amount of useful moisture.

Red-necked Wallaby *(below)*

After a gestation lasting 30–40 days, the red-necked wallaby *(Macropus rufogriseus)*, which is also known as Bennett's wallaby, crawls at birth into the pouch on its mother's belly. It is here that the baby red-necked wallaby's real development takes place, because at birth it is only an embryo, looking more like a worm than a kangaroo. The embryo clamps its mouth round the mother's teats, ensuring it does not fall out in transit.

Eastern Grey Kangaroo *(top left)*

The baby Eastern grey kangaroo *(Macropus giganteus)* seen here will one day be a giant among marsupials. Males of this species have a body length of up to 1 2 m; the females are smaller. However, the baby now in the pouch is going to have to munch its way through considerable quantities of grass before it can reach the impressive par size for its species.

(top right)

Under immediate threat, Eastern greys can move for short distances at a speed of 80 km per hour (50 mph), and cover up to 10 m in a single bound. Even mother kangaroos carrying young in their pouch can flee at high speed from enemies such as dingoes. However, in normal everyday activity, moving kangaroos touch the ground generally at intervals of 1.5 to 2 m.

(above right)

Eastern grey kangaroos live in quite large groups which in Australia may be referred to as 'mobs'. Inside each group or mob, a strict hierarchy is observed. The dominant beast, virtually always a male, will call the juveniles to order when necessary by kicking, cuffing or biting, and also asserts its primacy, when challenged, by the same methods.

Western Grey Kangaroo *(bottom left)*

The Western grey kangaroo *(Macropus fuliginosus)* has a tail up to a metre long which helps it keep its balance. In a newborn baby kangaroo, the tail will barely be seen — after about 30 days gestation in the womb, the tiny creature, really still only a foetus, momentarily glimpses the light of day, only to exchange it again for the warm darkness of the maternal pouch.

329

Red Kangaroo *(top left)*

Baby red kangaroos *(Macropus rufus)* already have a relatively thick fur coat. Its effect, paradoxically, is to protect these marsupials from excessive heat. Not all red kangaroos are in fact red: some have a coat that is more accurately described as grey. As a rule, the animals of this species live together in small groups.

(top right)

The world's biggest marsupial, the red kangaroo, is found only in Australia. The young do not leave their mother's pouch for the first time until they are at least six months old. And for some time even after that, they are quick to climb back in if they feel threatened. The age of sexual maturity in the young kangaroo is about 18 months.

Quokka *(centre right)*

The quokka *(Setonix brachyurus)* is one of the very smallest of all kangaroos, weighing no more than 4.3 kg. Quokkas live in pairs or in a small group. They are nocturnal, hiding during the day. Baby quokkas are not weaned off their mother's milk until they have spent about ten months in the pouch.

Kowari *(bottom right)*

The kowari *(Dasyuroides byrnei)*, also known as Byrne's crested-tailed marsupial, is one of the so-called dasyures or flesh-eating marsupials. Unlike kangaroos, these marsupials are carnivores, feeding on small mammals and insects. The females give birth to litters of about six young, which remain in the mother's pouch for about two months after they are born.

In the Forests

Eucalyptus forests are a peculiarly Australian phenomenon — and the natural habitat of the koala bear. But there are other Australian forests too, including rainforests. In all of them, baby animals are being born and are growing up, animals like the wombat, for instance, which exist nowhere else on earth.

Dingo (left)

This dingo pup (Canis lupus familiaris dingo) is one of a species of dog which has been wild for a very long time and is descended ultimately from the wolf. Dingos are most often born in a litter of five, after a gestation period of a good two months. After reaching adulthood, they live in pairs or in packs. They can interbreed with domestic dogs.

Brush-tailed Bettong (below)

A nocturnal animal, the brush-tailed bettong (Bettongia penicillata) sleeps by day in a nest made of grass stems and leaves, but like all marsupials it rears its young in its pouch. Inside, the babies spend some considerable time attached to their mother's teats. It's only when they have grown and the pouch gets too tight that they climb out and make a start on exploring the outside world.

Emu *(right)*

When one has seen the long legs of the emu chicks *(Dromaius novaehollandiae)*, it is no surprise to hear that they grow up into extremely fleet runners. Less easily predicted is that emu are also excellent long-distance swimmers — though it is true that on the Australian plains they do not often have to call on this ability. Emus feed mainly on seeds, grasses and the like, but sometimes also eat insects.

(below)

It takes about two months for a little emu chick like this to hatch. The cock bird looks after the whole business of brooding the eggs — there may be up to 25 of them, not all laid by the same female — and also minds the chicks after they hatch. The stripy-coated chick seen here will develop into a specimen of Australia's biggest bird, capable of running up to 30 mph (50 kph) an hour on its big three-toed feet.

Tammar Wallaby *(top left)*

The tammar wallaby or scrub wallaby *(Macropus eugenii)*, with a body length of up to 70 cm, is of small to middling size as kangaroos go. This particular species of marsupial lives in small troops with a fixed hierarchical order. Young female animals reach sexual maturity at about nine months old, and it will be a mere month from the date of mating that the next-generation baby is born and crawls into the mother's pouch.

Moorean Viviparous Tree Snail *(top right)*

The photograph shows two examples, an adult and a baby, of an extremely rare snail, the Moorean viviparous tree snail *(Partula tohiveana)*. It is endemic to the Polynesian island of Moorea (which means that it is found on that island and nowhere else in the world). But there are some Moorean viviparous tree snails in captivity in London Zoo — the plan is to reintroduce these snails to their native land.

Green Tree-Python *(centre left)*

Coiled tightly round the end of a branch, this young example of the green tree-python *(Chondropython viridis/Morelia viridis)* is not what one would call well camouflaged, in its brilliant red, for life in the jungles of New Guinea or Northern Australia. And in fact many juvenile pythons are taken by birds of prey. Only the adult snakes are the bright green their name suggests.

Spotted Cuscus *(bottom left)*

The spotted cuscus *(Phalanger maculatus)* occurs only in Queensland, Australia and on the island of New Guinea. With its rounded face and its prehensile paws it looks like a kind of monkey, but in fact the spotted cuscus is a climbing marsupial, in other words a pouched animal that lives in trees. This baby animal was born after a mere two weeks gestation, but there then followed a period of seven months during which it was suckled in its mother's pouch.

333

Koala Bear *(top left)*

Koala bears *(Phascolarctus cinereus)* actually deserve to be called sloths! They spend most of their time resting, if not sleeping, in the eucalyptus forests. When they do move about — and this goes for young and old alike — they move sedately, like old gentlemen. As a result, their energy requirements are fairly low. If they had a more active lifestyle, the energy they can draw from their diet of eucalyptus leaves would not be enough.

(above left)

A baby koala is born after only 35 days gestation. But of course after such a short time it is nothing like fully developed, so for a much longer period of about 35 weeks it will live in its mother's pouch to grow and mature in safety. Once finally weaned off its mother's milk, a koala lives on nothing but eucalyptus leaves.

(above right)

From its 36th week onwards, a young koala generally no longer has the option of climbing into mother's pouch. But it still very much needs (and enjoys) her close companionship, so for a while, from this point on, the mother will let it ride on her back as she clambers round in the branches. However, once the mother koala becomes pregnant again, the piggyback riding is over for good.

334

Common Ringtail Possum
(below, main picture)

The common ringtail possum *(Pseudocheirus peregrinus)* is the only opossum species in which the male is known to help in caring for and rearing the young. When the baby ringtail's mother goes off to forage for food, the father takes it on his back and generally looks after it. The common ringtail possum is native to Australia.

Herbert River Ringtail Possum
(bottom left)

Though very like a squirrel, the Herbert River ringtail possum *(Pseudocheirus herbertensis)* is another Australian marsupial. It spends the day in a hollow tree and is active at night. After the babies leave the pouch, they can still get carried on the mother's back. If left alone, they wail piercingly for her.

Short-beaked Echidna
(bottom right)

The short-beaked echidna *(Tachyglossus aculeatus)* is one of the few mammals that lay eggs. There are only two other species anywhere that lay eggs but also suckle their young. In the case of the short-beaked echidna, it takes about 10 days for the eggs to be incubated and the babies to hatch out. They are suckled by their mother for 6 months.

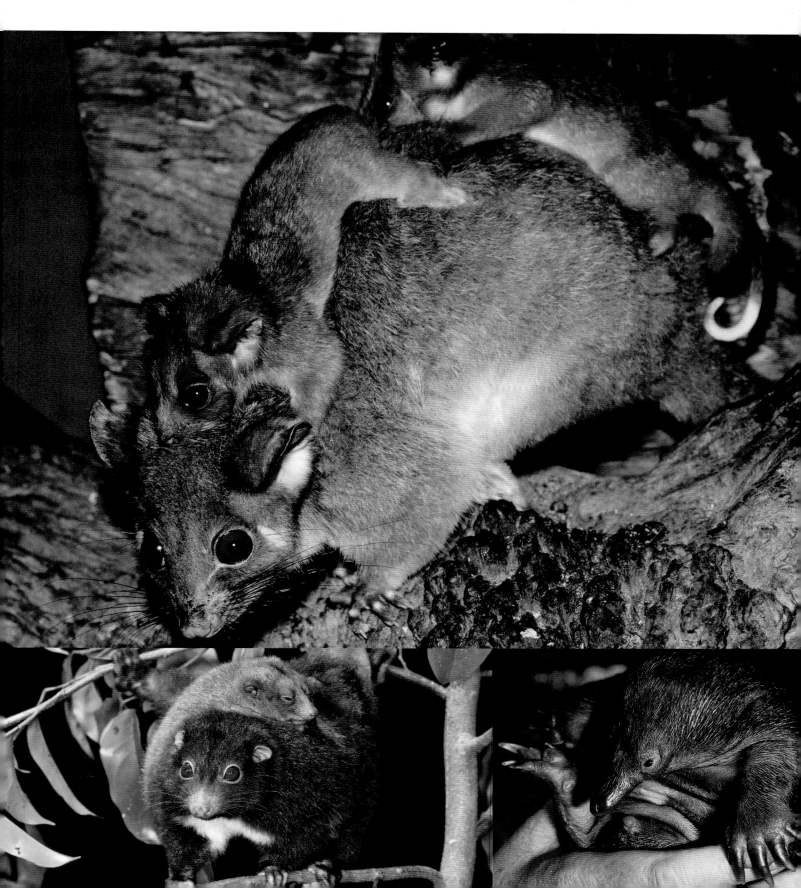

Brushtail Possum (top left)

After mating, the female brushtail possum (Trichosurus vulpecula) will have gestated her baby — always just one — for about 17 days. From this point the tiny possum will live in the mother's pouch for another four or five months, right at the fountainhead of the richly nourishing maternal milk. Then it begins the process of adapting to independent life outside, leaving the pouch for good, but getting a couple of months to view the world from the safety of its mother's back.

Swamp Wallaby (centre left)

The female swamp wallaby (Wallabia bicolor) while pregnant is capable of conceiving a second time during the 38-day gestation period for the first baby. The second embryo grows in a second uterus. When the first baby is born, slips into the pouch and locks onto the milk-giving teat, this slows down the development of the younger sibling — which in fact will not be born until Number One leaves the pouch.

Masked Lapwing (bottom left)

A precocial or 'early leaver' bird, this masked lapwing chick (Vanellus miles) has already quit the nest it was born in, but is still very vulnerable to predators or other mischance. It will be quite a long time before it has reached its full adult size of 35 cm body length, with a wing-span of 80 cm. It is also much too young for the adult masked lapwing's characteristic yellow mask to be clearly visible on its face.

Fat-tailed Dunnart (right-hand page, top)

The fat-tailed dunnart (Sminthopsis crassicaudata) becomes sexually mature at the age of six months or a little less. Following mating, a litter of up to ten young will be born — but the babies will spend the early part of their lives inside their mother's pouch, until they are more fully developed. This takes about 35 to 37 days, but then the good times in the warm rich darkness come to an end.

Common Wombat (right-hand page, bottom left)

Once out of their mother's pouch, baby common wombats (Vombatus ursinus) are like almost any other baby animals: downright inquisitive, sampling everything around them. This activity helps to prepare them for the time when they will no longer have their mother. They will have to fend entirely for themselves then, as common wombats are solitary animals, except of course when they come together to mate.

(right-hand page, bottom right)

Meeting a common wombat for the first time, one might well think one had met a cross between a badger and a raccoon. But the wombat is something entirely different, a pouched or marsupial animal which as an adult is about 1.15 m long. Even after the young have finally left their mother's pouch — at about ten months old — they are still not by any means fully grown. They do not reach sexual maturity until the age of two.

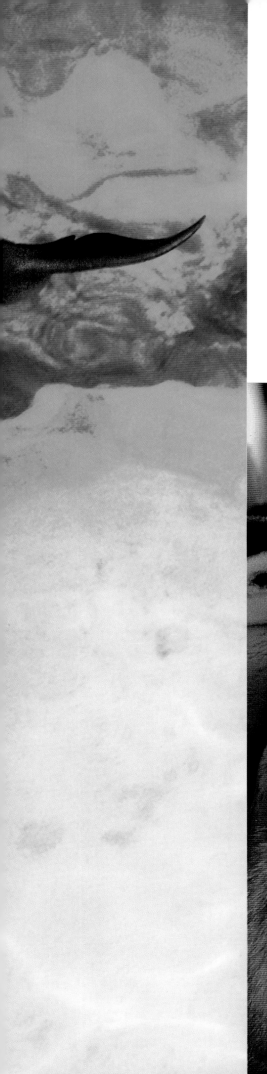

The Oceans

The Oceans, the Coasts and the Polar Regions

The salt waters of the oceans provide nourishment and living-space to fish and to many other creatures besides: they also sustain birds — both coastal and pelagic (deep-sea) birds — and a whole range of mammals, such as seals and whales. Many of the ocean-living species leave the water only in order to rear their young.

Grey Whale (top left)

Grey whales (Eschrichtius robustus) can be seen off the Californian coast between October and May. To get there, they have swum the 8800 kilometres from the Bering Sea or Chukchi Sea to the warmer waters of the Pacific, where they will mate and in due course the females will calve. These whales can often be seen rearing up vertically in the water, surveying their surroundings.

Sperm Whale (centre left)

The pattern among sperm whales (Physeter macrocephalus) is for a mother and her calf to live in a group of about 10–20 whales, all of them females and their young. Of the calves, the females will remain attached to the group for their whole lives, but the males begin to form bachelor pods once sexual maturation begins. As a bull whale gets older, it goes on progressively becoming more and more of a loner.

(bottom left)

Apart from being the biggest of all toothed whales, at 20 m long, sperm whales are unmistakable because of their square outline and their huge head, which makes up about a third of the overall length. The females can have a calf once every four years. For giving birth they prefer the warm waters of the equatorial and subtropical regions. Sperm whales can dive to depths of 3000 m, for only at such immense depths can they find their main food — giant squid.

Killer Whale (right-hand page, top)

Almost certainly the best-known — or most notorious — whale of all is the killer whale or orca (Orcinus orca). It owes its name to the skill with which it hunts. One of its techniques, for example, is to upend an ice-floe so that penguins on it are tipped into the water. Orcas are not in fact any more dangerous than other members of the dolphin family to which they belong, and they bond very closely with their young.

Humpback Whale (right-hand page, centre)

Humpback whales (Megaptera novaeangliae) cruise the oceans in groups, always forming an underwater circle round the females and their calves. They also make use of their group structure in the search for food, encircling swarms of crustaceans or tiny fish to feed on, or perhaps driving them in towards the shore. Then the huge jaws open and simply scoop their myriad prey out of the water.

(right-hand page, bottom)

As winter approaches, humpback whales migrate from the polar regions to the much warmer waters of the Caribbean. Here the females (the 'cows') give birth to their calves, which at 1.3 tons weigh only a small fraction of the 45 tons or so that they will eventually reach. Following calving, renewed mating takes place, signalled for whale-watchers by the spectacular leaps ('breaching') of the bull whales.

Southern Elephant Seal (top left)

Between mating and the birth of her pup, a female Southern elephant seal (Mirounga leonina) will be pregnant for eleven months. At three weeks old, having fed solely on the very rich, fatty milk of its mother, the seal pup will already weigh about 200 kg. After two months or a little more, it will take to the water. Now the young seal will soon be able to stay submerged for a quarter of an hour and reach a depth of 700 m; adults can make it down to a depth of 1500 m.

(top right)

The mother of a Southern elephant seal calf will suckle her baby for about three weeks after it is born. During this time, the calf gains about 8–9 kg weight every day, but correspondingly the mother loses several hundred kilos, because she is ashore the whole time and not feeding herself at all. And even before she returns to the sea to feed again, renewed mating takes place.

Southern Right Whale (centre right)

At birth, a Southern right whale calf (Eubalaena australis) is from 4.5 to 6 m long and already weighs one ton. Enormous though this may seem, it comes into perspective if one bears in mind that the adult Southern right whales weigh 30–80 tons (corresponding to body lengths of 11–18 m), or that in the bull whale the testicles alone weigh a ton.

(bottom right)

Both the Southern (Eubalaena australis) and the Northern right whale (Eubalaena glacialis) cruise very slowly, and close to the sea surface. As a result, they were the first whales to be hunted. In spite of conservation measures that have been in force for some time, the Southern right has become very rare, and the Northern so rare that at the beginning of the 21st century only 14 calves were sighted.

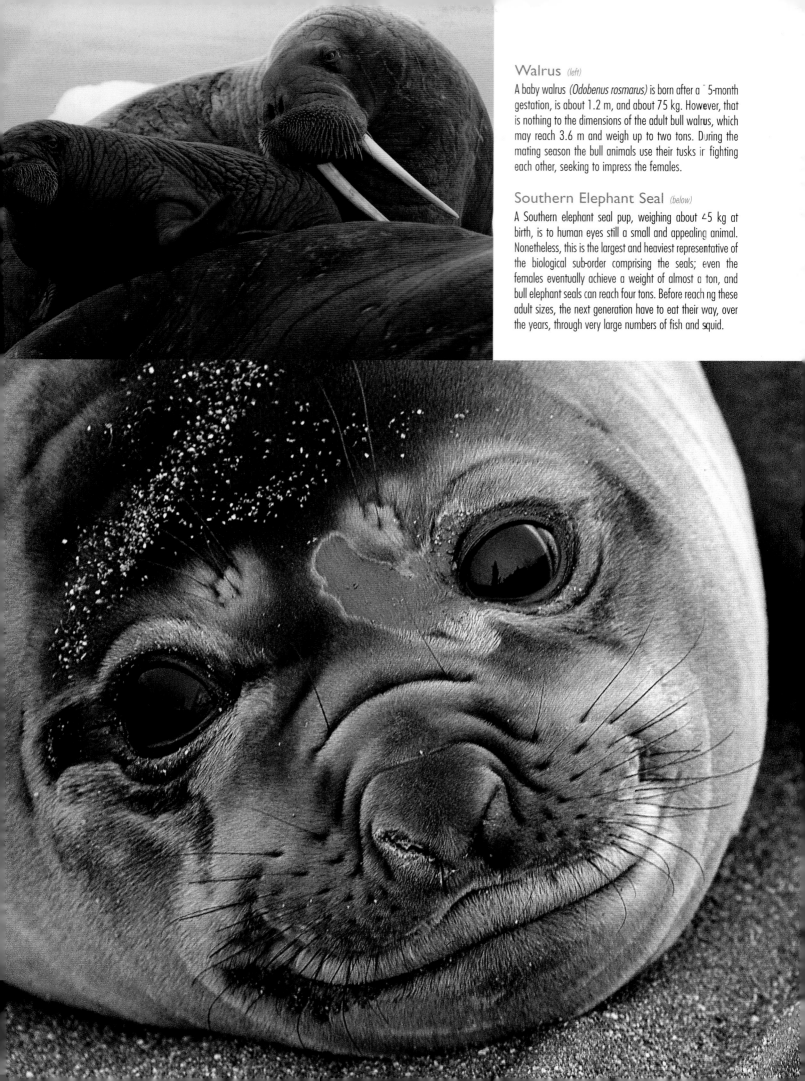

Walrus (left)

A baby walrus (*Odobenus rosmarus*) is born after a ¯5-month gestation, is about 1.2 m, and about 75 kg. However, that is nothing to the dimensions of the adult bull walrus, which may reach 3.6 m and weigh up to two tons. During the mating season the bull animals use their tusks ir fighting each other, seeking to impress the females.

Southern Elephant Seal (below)

A Southern elephant seal pup, weighing about ∠5 kg at birth, is to human eyes still a small and appealing animal. Nonetheless, this is the largest and heaviest representative of the biological sub-order comprising the seals; even the females eventually achieve a weight of almost a ton, and bull elephant seals can reach four tons. Before reach ng these adult sizes, the next generation have to eat their way, over the years, through very large numbers of fish and squid.

Black-browed Albatross *(top left)*

The Black-browed albatross or mollymauk *(Diomedea melanophris)* is one of the more abundant albatross species. It spends 90% of its time on the wing, flying over the oceans, and covers enormous distances — helped by its skilful exploitation of winds. It never spends time on land except for breeding purposes. Then, on a rocky island, it will make its nest out of dirt and pebbles, and defend it against other mollymauks.

(top right)

This black-browed albatross chick is waiting on the nest for its parents to return from, presumably, ranging far over the ocean in search of food. The young bird will reach sexual maturity at about five years old, but then will probably follow the usual pattern among young albatrosses, which is to wait a further two or three years before raising its own brood. Except during the mating season, albatrosses are solitary.

Hooded Seal *(bottom right)*

The young of the hooded seal *(Cystophora cristata)*, which belongs to the same family as the common seal, are record-holders of a quite special kind. Of all baby mammals anywhere, their species is the quickest to be weaned off mother's milk. This is done when they are only four or five days old. The 'hood' to which the name refers is found only in adults. It is a protrusion from the nose, which may inflate if the seal is alarmed or excited.

Snowy or Wandering Albatross (left)

This snowy (or wandering) albatross chick (*Diomedea exulans*), photographed in the act of calling, will one day be a real giant of the skies. Its wing-span of 3.5 m means this species has the biggest wings of any bird anywhere in the world. In body length it grows to about 1.25 m, and the typical weight is 8–10 kg. While flying, the snowy albatross uses the thermals or upcurrents in the air very much as a glider pilot does.

Light-mantled Albatross (right)

The Southern light-mantled albatross (*Phoebetria palpebrata*) has tube-like extensions on its beak. This feature has a whole order of birds named after it, the tubenoses or *Procellariiformes*, which include petrels and shearwaters as well as albatrosses. The tubes are effectively nostrils, used among other things to help the birds locate not only food but their nesting-place.

Antarctic Giant-Petrel (below)

This young Southern Antarctic giant-petrel (*Macronectes giganteus*) will eventually have a 2 m wing-span, and by then will be well able to nourish itself independently on fish and other marine animals. Birds of this species sometimes kill and eat penguin chicks. The Southern Antarctic giant-petrel breeds in great colonies on King George Island in the Antarctic, while the Northern variety prefers solitary places to nest and to incubate its eggs.

Emperor Penguin *(left-hand page)*

The male emperor penguin *(Aptenodytes forsteri)* incubates a single egg for 64 days, alone. The egg is held all this time over its feet, in an abdominal fold which protects it against the minus 40 °C cold of the Antarctic winter. The father penguin has to stand immobile while incubating and gets nothing to eat. Meantime the mother bird heads off to the sea about 90 miles away. She returns punctually for the hatching of the chick, and takes on the feeding duties which start at this point.

(top far right)

The pattern among emperor penguins — the largest penguin species — is for both parents to participate in finding food for their newly hatched chick. They have a waddling gait when moving about, but quite often they abandon the waddle and take to sliding downhill on their fronts — much simpler and much faster. At Antarctic midsummer, young penguins move off to the sea in order to catch their own fish.

(centre near right)

The emperor penguin chick's grey plumage is like a fur. In appearance it contrasts with the black head and white areas round the eyes. When about six weeks old, the chicks form groups called 'crèches'. At about five months they begin to acquire the elegant plumage of the adult bird, so reminiscent of a formal tail-coat.

(bottom right)

Emperor penguin chicks remain dependent on their parents for a long time. They can't go into the sea to hunt food until they are about five months old. Once fully grown — which means a weight of 37 kg and a body length of 1.35 m — they will be capable of diving to 500 m and staying under water for 20 minutes.

King Penguin *(top near right)*

A king penguin *(Aptenodytes patagonicus)* hatches almost bare of plumage after an incubation period of just under two months, and only gradually grows the brown coat seen here. Young king penguins belong to the altricial or 'stay-at-home' category of young, so at this stage, which lasts about six weeks, a chick will be fed by both parents. It does not have its full adult plumage until it is nearly a year old.

(centre far right)

King penguins breed on Falkland Islands beaches, in massive colonies of about 300,000 mating pairs. Each bird's 'territory' is no bigger than the radius within which the standing bird can peck any intruder effectively. When the baby penguins reach the age of about six weeks, they form so-called 'crèches' which consist of young birds only.

Rockhopper Penguin (top left)

Rockhoppers *(Eudyptes crestatus)* are the penguin species which has adults looking even more comical than the chicks. Where the fledglings only have their downy coat, white all down the front on breast and abdomen, black otherwise, and a black beak, their parents have similar-coloured plumage, but a dark red beak and a 'crest' consisting of quite prominent yellow and black quiffs of feathers sticking out from their head.

Gentoo Penguin (above left)

Gentoo penguins *(Pygoscelis papua)* make their nests along the rocky coastline of the Antarctic, building them out of vegetable matter and pieces of rock. The female lays two eggs in the nest and shares with her mate in incubating them for five or six weeks. Generally only one of the chicks survives. If both should die, the female bird will lay again.

(above right)

A gentoo penguin chick will remain with its parents for about four weeks after hatching, and then joins others of its generation in one of the young penguin 'crèches'. Unlike other penguin species, the gentoo parents still continue feeding their own chick during this phase.

Antarctic Fur Seal *(top left)*

Antarctic fur seal pups *(Arctocephalus gazella)* have an especially soft, dark pelt in their first three or four months of life, for the sake of which humans hunted this seal species almost to extinction during the 19th century. Once protection orders were made, the Antarctic fur seal populations recovered; however, numbers have now dropped again very significantly because there is no longer enough of their staple diet of krill to go round.

Humboldt Penguin *(top right)*

The Humboldt penguin *(Spheniscus humboldti)* is named after the sea area it swims in, the cold Humboldt Current flowing along the Pacific coast of South America. Along these shores, the penguin nests underground, in a burrow or cave. The parents take turns at incubating the two or three eggs that are laid, and also share in rearing the chicks after they hatch. The principal item of diet is small fish such as anchovy.

Magellanic Penguin *(bottom left)*

Magellanic penguins *(Spheniscus magellanicus)* excavate nesting holes in clayey banks or sand-dunes, and here lay and incubate their eggs, protected from bad weather and predators. However, if an invasion is threatened, the adult penguin pair are not at all afraid to defend their eggs or their chicks, and will use their bodies to bar the way into the nesting hole.

Polar Bear (top left)

When pregnant, the female polar bear *(Ursus maritimus)* digs out a cavity in the snow, reachable only through a tunnel, and there she will give birth, in most instances, to two cubs. This means that a baby polar bear almost always has a playmate of the same age to share in exploring the icy surroundings of their birthplace. A spot of rough-and-tumble between siblings is not just play, because at the same time it is early practice for the adult duties of hunting and fighting.

(top centre)

Polar bears are so well protected against the Arctic cold by their thick fur coat that they also readily swim and dive in ice-cold sea water. While swimming they are helped by stretch membranes between their toes, which enable them to paddle more effectively. To prevent the paws from getting unduly cold during the long land expeditions which polar bears often undertake, even the pads are covered with fur.

(right-hand page, top right)

Male polar bears are solitary except at mating time; however, the she-bear and offspring live as a small family. The cubs need about two and a half years to grow to adulthood, meanwhile learning all the essential survival skills from their mother. Even then they will not have reached reproductive maturity, which comes when they are about four years old.

The average weight of a polar bear cub at birth is only 500 g. Its coat will be so thin at first that without the protection given by its mother's fur and by her body warmth it would freeze to death. But even when the cubs have grown up somewhat and possess their own thick, warm coat, they are not at all averse to cuddling up to their mother and treating themselves to a drink of good milk.

Play, tussling for scraps, learning to catch fish — it's all pretty tiring, so polar bear cubs lie down and rest quite frequently. They can lie on snow or ice without feeling cold, because the protection their coat gives them is superb. In fact it lets so little body warmth escape to the outside that the animals cannot be photographed with an infrared (heat-sensitive) camera.

For the most part, polar bears live on the various kinds of seal they kill, and they will also eat carrion. But fish are very much on the menu too, and catching fish is an art that needs a lot of skill and a lot of practice. So polar bear cubs have to have regular lessons in 'angling' for fish. They show no reluctance at all, but practise assiduously and seem to enjoy it.

Polar Bear (left-hand page, top)

The polar bear cub (*Ursus maritimus*) seen enjoying a romp in this picture does not look in the least dangerous — yet. It's hard to imagine that it will soon grow into the world's largest land-based predator, with a body length of up to 2.5 m and weighing as much as 500 kg. Apart from man, polar bears have no natural foes.

(left-hand page, bottom)

Looking at this mother polar bear and her two cubs, it is difficult to conceive how people can bring themselves to shoot these wonderful animals for the sake of their pelts. Apart from its skin, the polar bear has nothing else of any value or use to human beings. Its meat should not be eaten, because it is full of trichinae (threadworms). Fortunately, polar bears are either fully protected by conservation orders or at least hunted only on a strictly limited basis.

Harp Seal (top right)

Young harp seals (*Pagophilus groenlandicus*) are sometimes called 'whitecoats' because of their pure white fur. Once a male cub has grown into a full-size, sexually mature adult weighing up to 150 kg, it will compete for a mate not by fighting with others, but by means of a special courtship display designed to impress. This includes rearing up again and again out of the water with the upper body held erect.

(centre right upper)

Harp seals have their principal habitat in Arctic waters, where they feed on a wide variety of fish. With their fully streamlined shape, these 2 m long predators are perfectly adapted to life in the water, and can dive to 300 m. Accordingly, they never stay long on land except for mating and for the birth of their young.

(centre right lower)

Harp seals are so named because of a harp-shaped dark patch on the back of an adult, which looks a bit like a saddle set on the back of an otherwise silver-grey animal. The pups look quite different: they have wonderfully soft white fur, which is so sought after by fur traders that years of protests have not succeeded in preventing the cruel slaughtering of baby seals on the ice, which still goes on today.

(bottom right)

After a gestation period of very nearly a year, harp seals give birth to their pups and suckle them for twelve days with their highly nutritious milk. The close bond between mother seal and pup loosens once the pup loses its baby fur and grows the watertight adult coat that will allow it to swim. A pup's early diet will consist of small crustaceans before it moves on to the adult diet of fish.

Common Seal (left)

The young of the common seal *(Phoca vitulina)* are generally born on sandbanks, which is why they can swim immediately after they are born. Once they are in the sea, the mother keeps a watchful eye on her new-born pup. If it tires and can no longer swim, it will hook on to her back and rest for a while. Suckling always takes place on land, as the mother's teats are concealed in a fold of skin.

(below)

It is an everyday occurrence for seal pups to be separated from their mother and then to be reared by humans. There are a number of reasons why this can happen. One is that if a mother seal has twins to look after, she can usually only swim after one of them at a time. Another is that human interference in one way or another may separate mother and pup. And then again, bad weather may be to blame.

(top left)

If a seal leaves her pup by itself for too long, the pup will begin to howl loudly for her. This is why the pups are sometimes referred to as 'howlers'. The loud call brings the mother back to her baby, provided she is not too far away or not prevented in some way from returning. She has no problem in distinguishing her own pup's call from those of others.

(top right)

For the female seal, the period of suckling her pup is extremely exhausting. She uses up a lot of energy in producing the milk — yet at the same time she has no real chance of foraging for food, as she has to keep a constant watch on the pup. Before giving birth, female seals eat as much as they can, building up a massive layer of fat, because a great deal of it will be used up again in caring for the pup.

Weddell Seal (centre left)

Baby Weddell seals *(Leptonychotes weddellii)* weigh barely 30 kg at birth, but add a further 80 kg in the course of the next six weeks. And this is achieved solely by drinking their mother's milk, which has a fat content of nearly 60%. However, these seals are not fully grown until they have reached and passed 400 kg in weight. Their adult food, as they grow, includes fish which they catch at depths of anything up to 600 m.

Grey Seal (bottom left)

The grey seal *(Halichoerus grypus)* has a fairly distinctive wedge-shaped head. In contrast to the adult animals, which have a rather dark and mottled coat, grey seal pups have white fur. But at only two to four weeks from birth, the cub sheds its juvenile coat and grows the adult one.

Cape Barren Goose (above)

Between June and August, during the Australian winter, the Cape Barren goose (Cereopsis novaehollandiae) raises its brood on the south coast of Australia, on the off-shore islands and in Tasmania. The chicks grow into dove-grey geese, better equipped for walking and running than for swimming, because the webs on their feet are relatively small.

Avocet (centre right)

This avocet chick (Recurvirostra avosetta) had hatched out two weeks earlier from a yellowish-brown, dark-speckled egg. The parents took turns to incubate it, and each time they changed over they carried out their curious ritual: the bird returning to take over the sitting from its mate would run round the nest several times, pelting the mate still on the nest with tiny pebbles and the like. And then, before sitting down over the eggs, it would turn each of them round once.

Puffin (bottom right)

The female puffin (Fratercula arctica) lays its single egg in its underground nest, which may be in a rabbit-hole or may have been specially dug out. As puffins nest in huge, jam-packed colonies near cliffs, each bird defends its nest fiercely. But to find food for their young they may fly as far as 60 miles out from it.

Shag (top left)

The shag *(Phalacrocorax aristotelis)* nests in colories along rocky coastlines by the Atlantic Ocean, the Mediterranean and the Black Sea. Usually it lays three eggs, which it incubates for a month. After the chicks hatch, the parents will spend two months or a little less in rearing them. Outside the breeding season, the shag is a solitary bird.

Herring Gull (centre left)

Like all gulls, herring gulls *(Larus argentatus)* are relatively slow developers compared to other birds. While they are fledged quickly enough, at six weeks, they need four to five years to reach sexual maturity. During all this time they retain their mottled brown juvenile plumage, then finally moulting it off and acquiring the adult plumage, grey and white with black wingtips.

(below)

It is the herring gull's exceptional adaptability that has made it the most abundant and most widely distributed of all seagulls, found even on rubbish tips well inland. Herring gulls nest on sand, in reeds, on cliffs and even on roofs, and usually lay three speckled eggs, which are then incubated for four weeks, with the parents sharing the duty between them.

Cape Fur Seal (above)

The Cape fur seal (*Arctocephalus pusillus*) belongs to the family of eared seals. Unlike the common seal, it also has two pairs of limbs, very short ones, certainly, but enough to give the fur seals reasonable mobility on land. At birth, fur seal pups are already 70 cm long; when fully grown they reach a length of up to 2.5 m.

Common White Tern (bottom left)

The common white tern (*Gygis alba*) lays a single egg — and lays it in a tree-fork, on a palm frond or on a rocky outcrop, but without making any kind of protective nest. Provided the egg makes it through the seven-week incubation period undamaged, it will hatch to reveal a fluffy, brown-and-white chick like this one. It is born with the ability to hook itself securely in place, using its powerful toes and claws, and even if it does fall it usually manages to lever its way up again.

(bottom right)

The chick of the common white tern spends the day alone, because both parents are out over the sea looking for and catching fish. During most of the day, they simply eat what they catch. But as evening approaches, they start to catch fish for their chick. When they finally return to the nest, it will be with a number of fish held side-by-side in their long, pointed beaks.

Australian Sea Lion *(above)*

After a year of gestation, the Australian sea lion females *(Neophoca cinerea)* bring forth their young in large colonies along the south coast of Australia. The males, which may reach 300 kg in weight and may grow to 2.5 metres in length, develop a thick fleshy area round the back of their neck, and a kind of mane. At 110 kg and 1.8 m in length, the females are considerably smaller.

(bottom left)

During the first two weeks of a baby Australian sea lion's life, its mother is constantly at its side. She does not leave her pup even long enough to go and search for food. But once that initial stage is over, the pup sees a good deal less of her. Her instinct is drawing her back to the sea, but she does return at regular intervals to suckle her offspring.

(bottom right)

Australian sea lions have their home in the coastal waters of Southern and South-Western Australia, where penguins provide one of the main elements in their diet. From October till December, they make their way to the beach, to find mates and reproduce — and usually it will be the same beach that they were born on. When the young arrive, only 60 cm long and 7 kg in weight, it will be in the midst of a large colony of sea lions.

Bottlenose Dolphin (above)

Bottlenose dolphin (Tursiops truncatus), the best-known species of dolphin, include the TV star 'Flipper'. After mating, the female of these 3.6 m long marine mammals gestates for twelve months, the baby dolphin is already a metre long at birth. For the first 18 months from birth, the baby dolphin feeds on its mother's milk, then moving on to crabs, fish and molluscs. It will not reach sexual maturity until it is seven years old.

(right)

Being mammals rather than fish, bottlenose dolphins have lungs and so must come to the surface regularly to breathe, as this mother and her offspring are doing. They also enjoy leaping clear of the water, and show little fear of humans on boats or on beaches. There are many instances of dolphins rescuing people who have got into difficulties at sea.

Green Sea Turtle (top left)

The most dangerous journey is the journey that the newly hatched baby green sea turtle *(Chelonia mydas)* has to make all the way to the water's edge from the 100-egg clutch high up the beach, where it was incubated with all the others for six to eight weeks by the warmth of the sand. Forward progress using the flippers is so laborious and slow that the baby turtle is easy prey for seabirds and crabs.

(top right)

This baby turtle has just extricated itself from the egg and is resting from its exertions before following its instinct to head down the beach towards the water. In spite of conservation measures now in force, some of the little turtles never get near the water. As well as being a sought-after item of diet for some animal species, they are also taken by humans. In Asia, for instance, they are widely regarded as a delicacy, and some also believe that eating the green turtles will enhance their own sexual potency.

(centre left)

Tiny though they may be when they climb out of their egg, green sea turtles are an impressive sight when fully grown. The miniature animal seen beginning its life in this photo may become a 300 kg adult. Once the turtles have reached a certain size, there are no longer any enemies or predators they need fear, except human beings. Still, humans are now increasingly making efforts to sustain the turtle population.

(bottom left)

The baby green turtles that do complete the journey from the clutch of eggs down the beach and into the warm waters of the tropical sea will initially feed mainly on small marine animals. However, older turtles — and green sea turtles often live for 50 years and more — are mainly herbivorous, grazing on the eel-grass beds in the shallows.

Manatee *(top left)*

The manatee or sea cow *(Trichecus manatus)* is a mammal that lives permanently in water. Manatees are an endangered species: factors involved include the gradual disappearance of their habitat (rivers and wetlands in coastal areas round the Caribbean), and the animals' slow rate of reproduction, with females producing only one calf every two to five years.

Small-spotted Cat Shark *(centre left)*

This 'sea purse' or egg case was deposited among the seaweed by a female small-spotted cat shark *(Scyliorhinus caniculus)*, a species also widely referred to as the lesser-spotted dogfish. It contains the embryo of a next-generation fish. It will be from five to eleven months before the embryo has developed enough for the baby fish to hatch. It will then be 10 cm long. It will go on growing until it is 60–100 cm long, but usually it is able to reproduce earlier than that.

Atlantic Spotted Dolphin *(bottom left)*

Atlantic spotted dolphin *(Stenalla frontalis)* living near the coast as a rule have more spots than others of the same species living out in the open sea. In the coastal dolphins, the spots are not confined to the abdomen, which is where they begin to form in the babies, but appear on the back as well. Sometimes it becomes difficult to see anything at all of the grey-blue colour more generally typical of dolphins. The underside of a dolphin is paler than the back.

(right-hand page, main picture)

The young of the Atlantic spotted dolphin have no spots at all at birth. The spots characteristic of this species only begin to form, starting from the belly, as the baby dolphin grows older. However, it is not possible to infer a dolphin's age reliably from the number of spots, as this is influenced also by habitat factors.

Black Swan *(right-hand page, top right)*

In a large nest which the male and female birds have shared in building, by or even in the water, the black swan *(Cygnus atratus)* lays from four to ten eggs. The hatchlings emerge in a grey downy coat and are looked after by both parents. These swans form monogamous pairs, but in contrast to other species of swan are extremely sociable.

Flightless Cormorant *(right-hand page, bottom right)*

Although a metre long in the body, the flightless cormorant *(Phalacrocorax harrisi)* has only very rudimentary little wings, not nearly big enough to fly with. Though no flier, this cormorant dives brilliantly. It is also referred to as the Galapagos cormorant, because it is found only on the islands of that name. It breeds there in small groups. Initially the two adult birds look after the chicks together, but this does not last, because very soon the female seeks out a new mate.

Blue-footed Booby (top left)

This blue-footed booby chick *(Sula nebouxii)* probably does not have any siblings, although quite often the female lays two or three eggs. The two parent birds always involve themselves in the business of raising a family, both as regards incubating eggs — which happens amid many others in large colonies — and in feeding the chicks after they hatch. To catch fish, they will often plunge straight into the water from heights of 30 m and more.

Masked Booby (top right)

Compared with its parents, the masked booby chick *(Sula dactylatra)* has all-white plumage and a black beak, whereas the adult birds have an orange beak and black flight feathers. The parents share feeding duties. Masked boobies by the thousand breed in vast colonies, each pair usually having a clutch of up to three eggs.

Loggerhead Sea Turtle (bottom right)

Length 1.5 m, average weight 150 kg: those are the vital statistics of the adult loggerhead turtle *(Caretta caretta)*. This sea turtle buries its eggs at the same spot in the beach sand where, long ago, it was born itself. This might be in Turkey, or in Costa Rica, or in Indonesia. The sex of the young turtles which will hatch about 60 days later is determined by the ambient temperature in the sand where the eggs are buried.

California Sea Lion *(top left)*

California sea lion young *(Zalophus californianus)* are light brown in colour like the adult females, while adult males are dark brown. Sea lions eventually grow to about 2.4 m in length, and when mature feed on shoaling fish such as herring. But while very young they are land-based and suckled by their mother — who, however, takes off to the sea at intervals, for a few days at a time, in order to feed and so replenish her own energy reserves.

Hooker's Sea Lion *(top right)*

With its population a mere 12,500 worldwide, Hooker's sea lion *(Neophoca hookeri)* is an endangered species. Of the world's five sea lion species, it is Hooker's that can dive deepest and longest: Hooker's sea lions have been observed diving as far down as 600 m, and staying under for 12 minutes. Young sea lions need a lot of practice before being able to match such performances.

Sea Otter *(bottom left)*

Female sea otters *(Enhydra lutis)* are attentive mothers: they carry their young on their belly for four weeks from birth, letting them float free on the surface for a few moments only for the purpose of diving for underwater food. By taking such good care of their babies, the mother sea otters help keep the infant mortality rate low. This is important for the preservation of the species. as the females generally conceive only in alternate years.

Black-footed Albatross (above)

The egg laid by a black-footed albatross (Diomedea nigripes) is about the size of a drinks can — hardly surprising, as albatrosses are very large birds with correspondingly large chicks. The most dangerous time in these birds' entire life is when they are learning to fly. Not all young birds manage a successful first flight, and if they hit the sea, as many do, they are likely to be eaten by sharks.

Grey-headed Albatross (bottom left)

The grey-headed albatross (Thalassarche chrysostoma, Diomedea chrysostoma) builds a conical nest about 80 cm high from soil, grass stalks and moss, which provides good protection for the egg and, later on, the nestling. The young albatross does not become sexually mature until about eight years old, and from then on will breed only in alternate years. However, these albatrosses reach a considerable age, living to thirty or sometimes beyond.

(bottom right)

One of the Antarctic species of albatross, the grey-headed albatross has a wing-span of up to 2.2 m and a body length of 81 cm. The female lays a single egg, from which the chick hatches out after 70 days. A young albatross like the one in the photograph is looked after by both parents — very assiduously at first, but then the attention given it gradually reduces. Their task is to keep the chick warm, protect it and feed it until it is fledged, at almost five months old.

Laysan Albatross *(bottom left)*

The chicks of the Laysan albatross *(Diomedea immutabilis)* hatch at the end of January. They are all 'only children', because the albatrosses only lay one egg each year. The nestling is fed by both parents — with fish which they have caught and swallowed. Back at the nest, the fish are regurgitated and fed to the young bird.

Juan Fernandez Fur Seal *(bottom right)*

Just why this Juan Fernandez fur seal pup *(Arctocephalus philippii)* is calling out so urgently — perhaps missing its mother? — we do not know. In fact it would have every reason to lament if it knew the truth about its species, which is that during the 19th century it was hundreds of thousands strong. Like many other seal species it was mercilessly hunted for its pelt, so that now very few are left.

(above)

The Juan Fernandez fur seal pup seen here will need quite a lot longer to grow to the adult size of 70 kg and 1.6 m long for females, or for males as much as 450 kg and 2 m in length. Because it has a soft, dense fur coat, it belongs to an endangered species. Today this seal is found virtually only in the waters of the Juan Fernandez archipelago, which is a Chilean national park.

King Shag (left-hand page, top left)

This young king shag (Phalacrocorax albiventer), alias king cormorant, alias Falkland Island blue-eyed cormorant, is begging for food from its mother. Before the king shag can breed at all, it builds a large cone-shaped nest. As shags nest in thousands on coasts and islands, these areas can be covered with nests looking for all the world like miniature volcanic cones, each within one nest's width of its nearest neighbours.

Kelp Gull (left-hand page, bottom left)

South of the Equator, the kelp gull (Larus dominicanus) is the most abundant gull species. Its chicks are reared in colonies on the southern coasts of Africa and Australia, and on the west coast of South America. They live by thieving: they steal eggs and chicks from the nests of other bird species; they steal fish out of the mouths of the seabirds that caught them; and off the Argentine coast they even rip pieces of blubber out of the bodies of Southern right whales.

Galapagos Marine Iguana (above)

The Galapagos marine iguana (Amblyrhynchus cristatus) is found only on the coasts of the Galapagos Islands off Ecuador. Where the water is shallow, the iguanas graze algae from the rocks. After this cold immersion they sun themselves to restore their body temperature. To lay their eggs, the females move some distance inland and deposit up to six eggs in a sand-hole which they will keep an eye on for a few days afterwards. The baby iguanas hatch three months later.

Anemonefish (left)

Anemonefish live in tropical reefs in the Indian Ocean and include the saddleback clownfish (Amphiprion polymnus), of which a juvenile and an adult are seen here with a sea anemone. The clownfish in the animated film 'Finding Nemo' charmed countless children into wanting one of their own. Unfortunately it is not easy to keep clownfish healthy in an aquarium.

Lesser Black-backed Gull (above)

In May/June the female lesser black-backed gull (*Larus fuscus*) lays typically three brownish, speckled eggs and then incubates them jointly with the male bird for four weeks. During the five weeks after the chicks hatch, the mother looks after them alone. She will feed them small fish including herring, and also insects and worms.

Swallow-tailed Gull (left)

Swallow-tailed gulls (*Creagrus furcatus*) live on cliffs of the Galapagos Islands and of Colombia on the South American mainland. The adult birds do their hunting at night, taking shrimp and squid. This enables them to guard their progeny by day against attack by predators such as the frigate bird. The species name of course comes from the most distinctive feature of the birds' appearance.

Great Black-backed Gull (top right)

These two young great black-backed gulls (Larus marinus) will in due course grow as big as geese: this is the biggest of all species of gull. Great black-backed gulls are thieves by nature, often nesting in colonies of other seabirds so that they can eat their neighbours' eggs and chicks. They also make a speciality of intercepting other coastal birds and robbing them in mid-air of the prey they are bringing home.

Little Gull (bottom right)

The smallest European gull, the little gull (Larus minutus) grows only as big as a pigeon. It feeds mainly on insects, which it invariably catches above water. The young are fledged about three weeks after hatching, and soon after that can feed themselves without help. But they do not reach sexual maturity until they are two to three years old.

Common Periwinkle *(left-hand page, top left)*

This photograph shows a common periwinkle *(Littorina littorea)* laying its eggs. Held together in a mass of jelly, the eggs drift around in the sea until the baby snails hatch in the form of larvae. The adult periwinkles are particularly fond of clustering on edible-mussel beds and feeding on the micro-organisms attached to the mussels.

Great Skua *(left-hand page, bottom left)*

The great skua *(Catharacta skua antarctica)* nests on the ground near the sea, using moss or tufts of grass as underlay. After four weeks their two eggs hatch. The chicks are well guarded by both parents, and have food brought to them for at least six weeks. Soon after that, the young skuas make their first flights and win mastery of the air as their principal domain.

Arctic Tern *(left)*

This Arctic tern chick *(Sterna paradisaea)* is excellently camouflaged in colour and shape as it waits among the pebbles. It belongs to a species which migrates phenomenal distances — from the coast of Greenland to the Antarctic pack-ice, sometimes even circling the Pole. In their migrations, Arctic tern may cover 30,000—60,000 kilometres in a single year!

(below)

Once hatched from the dark-spotted, brown or greenish egg in which it was incubated for three weeks, this baby Arctic tern will not be fledged and able to fend for itself until it is four weeks old. But to reach full maturity will take much longer: the Arctic tern will be three years old before it in turn can mate and reproduce its kind.

Index